The Impact of Computers on Collective Bargaining

The Impact of Computers on Collective Bargaining

Abraham J. Siegel, editor

THE M.I.T. PRESS
Cambridge, Massachusetts, and London, England

Acknowledgments

The Ford Foundation, in 1964, made a five-year grant to the Alfred P. Sloan School of Management for the support of a general research program dealing with the implications of technical change and automation for organizational behavior. The research-based conference whose proceedings are presented here was financially supported by this grant, and the views and findings of the conference participants must now be added to the already substantial results of interests stimulated and work made possible by the Foundation's generous support.

For nonfinancial but clearly essential intellectual and logistical support, I am indebted to many. Several members of the executive board of the Labor-Management Institute of the American Arbitration Association cooperated with the M.I.T. Industrial Relations Section of the Sloan School in planning and executing the conference: William G. Caples, Woodrow L. Ginsburg, James J. Healy, Wayne L. Horvitz, Donald B. Straus, and Arnold M. Zack. Mr. Straus, the president of the American Arbitration Association, has been a dedicated cosponsor throughout all stages of the project. My colleagues, Professors Douglass V. Brown, Charles A. Myers, Michael J. Piore, and David P. Taylor, were all helpful in planning the conference. Ephraim R. McLean, 3rd, an instructor in the Sloan School, was once again a mainstay at all stages of this conference as he had been for an earlier conference held in 1966 on the impact of computers on management. He reviewed conference papers, edited taped discussions, and performed these tasks with thoroughness and genuine care. My secretary, Grace Locke, negotiated many of the logistical arrangements for the conference, typed the entire manuscript with her usual built-in editorial precision, and kept an almost incredible "cool" while maneuvering these proceedings to the press in the midst of an otherwise already overfull work agenda.

Finally, I am extremely grateful for the willing help so readily proffered by the many invited participants — paper contributors and others — who "created" this conference and made it, in truly joint collaboration, a small gem of a meeting.

ABRAHAM J. SIEGEL
Professor of Industrial Relations
and Associate Dean,
Alfred P. Sloan
School of Management

Cambridge, Massachusetts
November 1968

Authors of Conference Papers

John M. Baitsell
Mobil Oil Corporation
150 East 42nd Street
New York, New York 10017
(formerly:
Associate Professor
Graduate School of Business
Administration
Harvard University
Soldiers Field
Boston, Massachusetts 02163)

Douglass V. Brown
Alfred P. Sloan Professor of
Management
Sloan School of Management
Massachusetts Institute of
Technology
Cambridge, Massachusetts 02139

William G. Caples
President
Kenyon College
Gambier, Ohio
(formerly:
Vice President
Inland Steel Company
30 West Monroe Street
Chicago 3, Illinois)

David L. Cole
Practicing Attorney and Arbitrator
Cole, Berman & Garth
45 Church Street
Paterson, New Jersey 07505

Wilbur Daniels
Director, Master Agreements
Department
The ILGWU
1710 Broadway
New York, New York 10019

John T. Dunlop
Professor of Economics
Department of Economics
226 Littauer Center
Harvard University
Cambridge, Massachusetts 02138

Woodrow Ginsburg
Director of Research, IUD
AFL–CIO
815 Sixteenth Street, N.W.
Washington, D.C. 20006

Vernon H. Jensen
Associate Dean
New York State School of Industrial
and Labor Relations
Cornell University
Ithaca, New York 14850

Gordon M. Kaufman
Associate Professor of Management
Sloan School of Management
Massachusetts Institute of
Technology
Cambridge, Massachusetts 02139

Charles Mason
Senior Vice President, Personnel
United Air Lines
P.O. Box 8800
Chicago, Illinois 60666

Roy Penchansky
Department of Medical Care
Organization
School of Public Health
The University of Michigan
Ann Arbor, Michigan 48104

Abraham J. Siegel
  Associate Dean
  Sloan School of Management
  Massachusetts Institute of
    Technology
  Cambridge, Massachusetts 02139

Christopher R. Sprague
  Assistant Professor of Management
  Sloan School of Management
  Massachusetts Institute of
    Technology
  Cambridge, Massachusetts 02139

David P. Taylor
  Associate Professor of Industrial
    Relations
  Sloan School of Management
  Massachusetts Institute of
    Technology
  Cambridge, Massachusetts 02139

George W. Taylor
  Harnwell Professor of Industry
  Wharton School of Finance and
    Commerce
  University of Pennsylvania
  Philadelphia, Pennsylvania 19104

Additional Conference Participants

Robert P. Bigelow, Esq.
Hennessy, McCluskey, Earle &
Kilburn
60 State Street
Boston, Massachusetts 02109

Donald C. Carroll
Associate Professor of Management
Sloan School of Management
Massachusetts Institute of
Technology
Cambridge, Massachusetts 02139

Robert C. Cheek
Director of Management Systems
Westinghouse Electric Corporation
Box 2278
Pittsburgh, Pennsylvania 15230

Hugh A. Craigie
Vice President
The Diebold Group, Inc.
430 Park Avenue
New York, New York 10022

Jack Ellenbogen
General Electric Company
570 Lexington Avenue
New York, New York 10022

Jay W. Forrester
Professor of Management
Sloan School of Management
Massachusetts Institute of
Technology
Cambridge, Massachusetts 02139

Mason Haire
Professor of Organization Psychology
and Management
Sloan School of Management
Massachusetts Institute of
Technology
Cambridge, Massachusetts 02139

Stanley M. Jacks
Senior Lecturer
Sloan School of Management
Massachusetts Institute of
Technology
Cambridge, Massachusetts 02139

Vernon E. Jirikowic
Director of Research
International Association of Machin-
ists and Aerospace Workers
Machinists Building
1300 Connecticut Avenue
Washington, D.C. 20036

Malcolm M. Jones
Assistant Professor of Management
Sloan School of Management
Massachusetts Institute of
Technology
Cambridge, Massachusetts 02139

Robert Lerman
Graduate Student
Department of Economics
Massachusetts Institute of
Technology
Cambridge, Massachusetts 02139

Frederick G. Lesieur
Consultant, the "Scanlon Plan," and
President, F. G. Lesieur Associates
Room 414
75 Federal Street
Boston, Massachusetts 02110

E. Robert Livernash
Professor of Business Administration
Graduate School of Business
Administration
Harvard University
Soldiers Field
Boston, Massachusetts 02163

Francis McLaughlin
Assistant Professor
Department of Economics
Boston College
Chestnut Hill, Massachusetts 02167

Ephraim R. McLean, 3rd
Assistant Professor of Information
Systems
Graduate School of Business
Administration
University of California
Los Angeles, California 90024
(formerly:
Instructor
Sloan School of Management
Massachusetts Institute of
Technology
Cambridge, Massachusetts 02139)

Frederic Meyers
Professor of Industrial Relations
Graduate School of Business
Administration
University of California
Los Angeles, California 90024

Quinn Mills
Assistant Professor of Industrial
Relations
Sloan School of Management
Massachusetts Institute of
Technology
Cambridge, Massachusetts 02139

Daniel Mitchell
Assistant Professor
Graduate School of Business
Administration
University of California
Los Angeles, California 90024

Charles A. Myers
Director
Industrial Relations Section
Sloan School of Management
Massachusetts Institute of
Technology
Cambridge, Massachusetts 02139

David N. Ness
Assistant Professor of Management
Sloan School of Management
Massachusetts Institute of
Technology
Cambridge, Massachusetts 02139

Nicholas Perna
Assistant Professor
Department of Economics
Williams College
Williamstown, Massachusetts

Michael J. Piore
Assistant Professor of Economics
Department of Economics
Massachusetts Institute of
Technology
Cambridge, Massachusetts 02139

Elbridge Puckett
Consultant, the "Scanlon Plan," and
Vice President, F. G. Lesieur
Associates
Room 414
75 Federal Street
Boston, Massachusetts 02110

John F. Rockart
Assistant Professor of Management
Sloan School of Management
Massachusetts Institute of
Technology
Cambridge, Massachusetts 02139

Morris Rosenthal
Vice President
E. F. Shelley and Company, Inc.
866 United Nations Plaza
New York, New York

Michael S. Scott Morton
Assistant Professor of Management
Sloan School of Management
Massachusetts Institute of
Technology
Cambridge, Massachusetts 02139

Donald B. Straus
  President
  American Arbitration Association
  140 West 51st Street
  New York, New York 10020

William M. Vaughn, III
  Instructor
  Graduate School of Business
  University of Chicago
  Chicago, Illinois

Donald White
  Professor of Economics
  Department of Economics
  Carney Hall
  Boston College
  Chestnut Hill, Massachusetts 02167

Arnold M. Zack
  Arbitrator
  Suite 195
  151 Tremont Street
  Boston, Massachusetts 02111

Contents

INTRODUCTION: THE IMPACT OF COMPUTERS ON
COLLECTIVE BARGAINING   1

Abraham J. Siegel

THE COMPUTER'S USES AND POTENTIAL IN
BARGAINING: A TRADE UNION VIEW   26

Woodrow L. Ginsburg

Elaboration and Discussion   52

THE COMPUTER'S USES AND POTENTIAL IN
BARGAINING: A MANAGEMENT VIEW   69

William G. Caples

Elaboration and Discussion   92

SIMULATION OF UNION HEALTH AND WELFARE FUNDS   121

G. M. Kaufman and R. Penchansky
Assisted by Byron Marshall

Elaboration and Discussion   155

THE COMPUTER IN DISPUTE SETTLEMENT: A PANEL
AND GENERAL DISCUSSION   176

George W. Taylor, David L. Cole, and John T. Dunlop

USES OF THE COMPUTER IN CONTRACT ENFORCE-
MENT: THE ILGWU EXPERIENCE   189

Wilbur Daniels

Elaboration and Discussion   199
                                                               xiii

SCHEDULING AND SENIORITY: THE UNITED AIR LINES
EXPERIENCE   203

Charles Mason

Elaboration and Discussion   217

DECASUALIZING A LABOR MARKET: THE LONGSHORE
EXPERIENCE   226

Vernon H. Jensen

Elaboration and Discussion   243

A COMPUTER-BASED NEGOTIATION: USES AND
LIMITATIONS AS A TRAINING DEVICE   260

John M. Baitsell, Christopher R. Sprague, and David P. Taylor

Elaboration and Discussion   268

COMMENTS ON THE CONFERENCE DISCUSSION   286

Douglass V. Brown

INDEX   289

The Impact of Computers on Collective Bargaining

Introduction: The Impact of Computers on Collective Bargaining

Abraham J. Siegel

Computers and information technology vitally — often vividly — touch the "neuralgic" issues relating man and his world. Within two decades of their birth, computer hardware and software have affected our organizations and our organizational behavior perhaps more than any set of preceding technical developments.

Large and small businesses, education, medicine, government, national security — all have been reshaped in the post–World War II computer and information "revolutions."

Nor is there much doubt that the computer will be a dominant factor in shaping tomorrow's world.

A blind man will direct himself by radar; a cripple will walk on automatically controlled limbs that move like human legs; robots will do domestic household chores; a turn of a knob at home will bring a complete facsimile reproduction of *The Times*.[1]

All this in the year 2000 and all easily extrapolated from today's pioneer efforts. The 2000 A.D. computer will be an object of personal ownership; transforming jobs; diagnosing diseases; checking and searching for information for lawyers and other professionals and for private managers and public administrators; monitoring air and ground traffic flows; running the housewife's shopping errands and automatically charging the family's bank account; helping to farm the seas and peruse the planets.

Dr. Robert Fano, Director of M.I.T.'s Project MAC, has put the problems and the possibilities in a nutshell: If we are "mindful at all times of the individual's feelings, his needs, and particularly

[1] *The New York Times,* December 26, 1968.

1

his pride as a human being," the opportunities to better human life are great indeed as the computer proceeds "to reshape the whole pattern of our business and private lives." [2]

The glowing projections of these opportunities are dimmed only by recursive elaborations of Fano's problematic premise to this computer-based cornucopia of the future. Cautious men — even fearful men — emphasize the legitimate challenges of remembering always to enshrine man's freedom and spirit in our technical quests and underscore the "risks and dangers" of relying too heavily on computer analysis alone for policy matters. They continue to ask, clearly rhetorically: "Have we arrived at that technocratic Utopia where judgment is a machine product?" and proceed to assert that while generally laudable, ingenious, useful, and necessary, the computer or systems analysis ". . . is no magic wand . . . it is no substitute for experience and judgment." [3]

This same coupling of references to accomplishment, opportunity, challenge, and risk mark the two days of conference discussion which is summarized here.

There was clear demonstration and recognition of past and present achievements; there was stimulating exchange on the dramatic possibilities for future breakthroughs. But there were also the cautiously optimistic overtones of the pragmatist and the contrapuntal reservations of the skeptic.

An Interdisciplinary Conference on the Uses and Potential of Computers in Collective Bargaining

The Conference Format

The papers and discussion in this volume pursue a heretofore relatively unexplored strand in the research and debate which scholars and practitioners have fashioned and elaborated on the role of computers and information systems technology. They deal with the impact of computers on collective bargaining — the organized and institutionalized relations of managers and managed in the framing of the web of rules that binds them to each other, to the

---

[2] Robert M. Fano, "The World at Our Fingertips," *The General Electric Forum*, Vol. X, No. 4, Winter 1967–68, p. 6.

[3] The quotations are from a recent memorandum prepared by the U.S. Senate Subcommittee on National Security and International Operations as cited in *The New York Times*, August 21, 1968. The memorandum was intended to set the stage for hearings to sift and audit the computer's role as a tool in foreign and national security policy making.

work process, and to the external environment of their working lives.

Papers were prepared by invitation for the third of a series of research conferences convened by the Industrial Relations Section of the Alfred P. Sloan School of Management at the Massachusetts Institute of Technology. These conferences in turn have been part of a larger set of School programs and studies on the impact of technical change on organizational behavior.

The first conference, convened in 1966 by Professor Charles A. Myers, reviewed the impact of computers on management organization and the nature of managerial work.[4] A second workshop, convened in 1967 by Mr. Frazier Kellogg, summarized and evaluated the "state of the art" in the development of computer-based man-job matching systems and the relation of these innovative private and public arrangements to a variety of prevailing and enduring labor market concerns.[5]

The third research-based conference, dealing with the uses and potential of computers in bargaining, was convened in 1968. A small seminar-style conference was planned and sponsored in cooperation with the Labor-Management Institute of the American Arbitration Association. In addition to the authors of the conference papers, a limited number of other experts from industry, labor, and universities were invited to participate in the discussion of these papers.[6] The entire set of papers was distributed to each author and participating guest in advance of the meeting. The total number of participants struck a neat balance between inclusiveness of expertise and effectiveness of conference discussion. The number of authors and other participants was large enough to include most of the experts and "frontiersmen" in both the field and in academia; it was small enough to permit personal and spirited interchange and debate of ideas. Because the authors simply "introduced" rather than read their papers at the conference, there was ample time available for discussion and evaluation by the conference participants.

---

[4] See Charles A. Myers, Editor, *The Impact of Computers on Management*, Cambridge: The M.I.T. Press, 1967, for a summary of the management conference proceedings.

[5] The proceedings of this workshop may be found in Frazier Kellogg, *Computer-Based Aids to the Placement Process*, Industrial Relations Section, Sloan School of Management, M.I.T., 1969.

[6] The names and affiliations of these additional conference guests will be found on pp. ix–xi.

There were two exceptions to this general conference format. The panel discussion on the uses of computers in dispute settlement was an impromptu badinage orchestrated at the invitation of the conference by three of the nation's most prominent mediator-arbitrators: George Taylor, David Cole, and John Dunlop. Professor Douglass V. Brown, a colleague and an eminently judicious student of the labor relations scene for almost forty years, was similarly invited at the close of the conference deliberations to outline his personal summary of the discussion.

This volume includes both the papers and the edited discussions of these papers. The resultant proceedings are a balanced and valuable first collection of "practice and potential" at an important frontier in labor-management relations.

The Conference Base

The roster of invited research papers — the substantive core of the conference — was designed to touch base with representative experts from each of the parties to the bargaining process (including those whom David Cole once described as the "nervous neutrals") as well as with representative issues relating computer technology and the bargaining process.

The first two papers are probably the most comprehensive summaries available of prevailing experience with computers in the process of collective bargaining. Woodrow L. Ginsburg, who until recently served as Research Director for the AFL-CIO's Industrial Union Department where many of the applications described were spearheaded, presents a succinct overview of the versatility with which organized labor has used the computer in its bargaining activities. William G. Caples, former Vice President for Industrial Relations of the Inland Steel Company and now President of Kenyon College, has in turn given us a comprehensive survey of current practice in management's uses of computers and information technology in collective bargaining as well as in related personnel administration uses. Both Ginsburg and Caples go beyond the "what is" to explore the "what might be" and both provide interesting personal projections of the limitations and the potentials for future applications of computer technology by unions and managers in their bargaining roles.

The paper by Professors Gordon M. Kaufman and Roy Penchansky describes and illustrates the applicability and usefulness of the computer as an aid to solution via simulation of a highly significant problem in collective negotiations — the management of health and welfare funds. The potential applicability of the kind of work done here by Kaufman and Penchansky to other substantive bargaining issues (and at reasonable cost) is clear. Since this model builds on a case where intuitive modes of reasoning would have been particularly difficult, it suggests an applicability to cases that are tough modeling problems as well as easy ones. Kaufman and Penchansky are modestly and appropriately quick to disavow an easy leap from building a reasonable model of fund financial behavior and measuring quantitatively the effects of various policy changes in fund management to the building of a more general model of an entire collective bargaining system. But what they have given us, as they point out, is an instructive example of the strategic and tactical problems faced in doing such simulation experiments and the meaningful insights into the structure of a complicated real-world system which the process of computer-based simulation permits. Kaufman and Penchansky provide in the appendixes to their paper the rigorous mathematical recapitulation of the assumptions of their model and the simulation strategy described less rigorously in the text of the paper.

The panel discussion on the computer's possible role in dispute settlement (and implicitly in dispute prevention) is a fascinating exercise involving three of the most experienced mediators and "public representatives" in the labor relations field. George Taylor, David Cole, and John Dunlop reflect on years gone by, the day at hand, and things to come in a pastiche of lore, tissue, and muscle which is always reflective, occasionally despondent, and in the end open to the prospects for new attitudes and skills which could permit, if not compel, parties to employ the new computer technology jointly in the interests of peace rather than conflict. The prerequisites for such developments are the focus of a substantial portion of the speculative probes and thrusts of these men of enormous first-hand experience.

The conference in its second day moved from the process and substance of bargaining and the dispute settlement discussion to a set of papers which provided some fascinating case studies to illustrate uses of the computer in the *administration* and *implementation* of collective agreements.

Wilbur Daniels describes the International Ladies' Garment Workers' Union's (ILGWU) experience with computer technology and speculates on the major uses to which this technology may be put. These include the enhancement of agreement enforcement and policing in an industry where opportunities for contract violations are many; coping more effectively with runaway shop problems by facilitating their early recognition; spurring the union's business agents to more vigorous implementation of both their organizing and agreement enforcement roles; permitting greater leeway in the range of feasible union proposals during the course of negotiations.

Charles M. Mason gives us an equally interesting case study of the United Air Lines's experience with the computer's uses in agreement administration and implementation. The airlines, pioneers in the use of computers for operations management, have given equally imaginative consideration to the possibilities of computer assistance in the bargaining arena. Here, too, the uses to which this technology has been put are several. They include the preparation of flight crew scheduling, seniority, and stewardess and pilot qualification lists; the distribution of overtime; and the analysis of grievances. In addition, Mason describes some fascinating management uses in preparation for and in the process of negotiation which elaborate on the possibilities noted earlier by Ginsburg and Caples in their overview pieces.

The paper by Dean Vernon H. Jensen on the application of computers to the problems of decasualizing the New York longshore labor market is a beautifully elaborated case study of what is clearly a prototype rather than a unique environment for the application of computer technology to manpower allocation problems. And the discussion following the Jensen paper brings to a head the several earlier allusions to methodology and possibilities for computers in bargaining.

The paper by John M. Baitsell, Christopher R. Sprague, and David P. Taylor describes some early fallout for the educator from the steadily expanding use of computer-assisted educational methods. The three professors — two in industrial relations, one in computer science — collaborated in devising a computer-based mock negotiations "game" which has been tested and is now being refined in one of the curricular subject packets at M.I.T. Their comments here on the uses and limitations of this training device in the teaching of labor relations courses will be instructive for others who might be interested in such teaching experiments.

Finally, Professor Douglass V. Brown offers his appraisal of the potential impact of computers in collective bargaining, and even if his extrapolations do not suggest that all our stacks are to be quickly displaced by disks and tracks, he does suggest that we have witnessed at the conference what is clearly an iceberg cap which he views, however, not as a threat to navigation but as an opportunity for more cooperative and effective cruising by computer and labor relations experts.

A Summary of Conference Themes

What findings, what forecasts, what feelings are reflected in these papers and in the deliberations of the conferees?

I group the points in this capsule summary of conference themes under the several questions which frame the bounds of the conference's attention.

1. What are the major uses of computers in the *process* of bargaining?

2. What are the *substantive issues* to which the application of electronic data processing or other computer-based or computer-aided techniques appear to be most relevant?

3. What uses of computers are presently possible in dispute settlement or prevention?

4. What is the potential impact of the uses of computers and information technology in collective bargaining?

1. The Major Uses of Computers in the Process of Bargaining

Companies and unions continue to use computers in the employment relations area primarily for the variety of "housekeeping chores" which confront all complex organizations. Even here, according to Caples's survey, computers are less intensively used than in other areas of operations management. Yet companies and unions have moved dramatically in the past five years from the keeping of "mammoth filing systems" for storing information to the development of computers as the base for management information systems which help plan strategy and make basic decisions. As Ginsburg points out, there has been a real sharpening of tools and we have witnessed a new awareness of the uses of information. Neither of the parties to the bargaining process has developed essentially new or secret data; what computers do is to make possible accurate, simplified arrangements of data; arrangements which can reveal patterns as they develop and supply details as they are needed.

It is easiest here to summarize the findings of the conference concerning the major uses of computers in the process of bargaining by moving along a time span covering prebargaining to postbargaining stages.

It is clear that even where no collective bargaining relationship prevails, unions and companies can and do use computers effectively. The major company use, of course, is for personnel administration; and in this sense it is a use independent of whether or not collective bargaining exists. Employee records of basic personal data, skill inventories, compensation records, and so on must be kept whether or not unions bargain with the company. In the case of the trade union, however, the computer has also been used antecedent to bargaining but clearly as an aid in inducing a bargaining relationship where none may exist. Trade unions have sought assistance from the computer in a variety of organizing efforts — in drives to organize entirely unorganized plants or companies; in efforts to "sign up" the still unorganized plants of partially organized conglomerate or multiplant companies; and in drives to reorganize once-organized plants.

The computer helps in the preparation of profiles of the work force composition, profiles of union election histories, and profiles of company records of unfair labor practices. The Industrial Union Department (IUD) has collected data banks of information on all of these matters. For example, the results of more than 50,000 elections conducted under the National Labor Relations Board (NLRB) in the past eight years are available to organizers who would use this information. Individual unions may, in addition, get records of their successes and failures, discover where they are being challenged by other unions, and so on. Similar records of company unfair labor practices which are available by company, union, and/or region also help the organizer in his organization efforts. These data will help an organizer identify towns, companies, and individual plants which may be ripe for unionization drives. They will help him to pick targets. By recognizing patterns in antiunion campaigns, he may be able to build more effective counter-campaigns. The lists of companies where employees recently voted a union out in decertification elections provide the organizer with targets where a base of former trade union members and sympathizers exists, and where new organizers can break in easily and quickly. Organizers find it easier to compare union plant conditions with those in target plants. In short, these data can help an organizer spot more effectively which regions to organize, which companies resist most effectively, what union campaign methods work most efficiently, and which members of the target work force are the best potential allies.

In addition to new organization efforts in a prebargaining context, trade unions have used information data banks in support of lobbying activities to effect changes in working conditions where no formal bargaining relationship may exist. Ginsburg, for example, describes how computer analysis helped make an effective case for minimum wages for the sawing and logging industry. Finally, we should mention here a point alluded to both by Ginsburg and by Daniels — the help provided unions in coping with the "runaway shop" problem. By correlating names of officers of old and new establishments gleaned from county records and corporation papers, newspapers, and so on, unions are able more easily to spot companies which seek to evade organization by relocation.

USES IN LEGALLY BUT NOT EFFECTIVELY ESTABLISHED
COLLECTIVE BARGAINING RELATIONSHIPS

Computers have proved helpful to trade unions in the stage of the resisted or unconsummated bargaining relationship as well as in the prebargaining or "organizing" stage. Ginsburg cites examples of strong cases which trade unions were able to build, during NLRB proceedings, in which they sought back wages claimed from a company which had earlier been found by the Board to have refused to bargain over a period of years, despite the fact that the trade union was lawfully recognized as the bargaining agent. One such computer-based analysis compared, for the duration of the unfair practice, the average wage increases received by workers in comparable companies in the industry with those received by the workers in the company which had failed to bargain in good faith. The analysis thus provided the documentation for the recommended remedy which sought to close this gap occasioned by the employer's unlawful evasion of bargaining.

USES IN ESTABLISHED, "GOING CONCERN" COLLECTIVE
BARGAINING RELATIONSHIPS

The most typical uses of computer-based analyses are related to prevailing bargaining relationships. Here too, however, we may distinguish among (a) uses in preparations for the negotiation of agreements, (*b*) uses during negotiation, (*c*) uses in the administration of the agreement, and (*d*) joint uses of computers by management and union in collective bargaining.

(*a*) *Uses in preparations for the negotiation of agreements.* The major activities here consist of contract analysis, analysis of company economic profiles, coding and costing of anticipated or proposed demands, and the development of mathematical models to project work force needs to help analyze the impact of probable demands on a variety of company dimensions.

CONTRACT ANALYSIS. In its national survey of key contracts, the IUD has put 22 key contract provisions of 208 major contracts (151 manufacturing companies and 57 non-manufacturing companies) covering $3\frac{1}{2}$ million workers employed in over 4,000 facilities into its computer system. These data are all easily retrievable in a variety of forms and tabulations. As new contracts in this array are negotiated, all changes are fed into the system so that the system is kept constantly updated. This information is of enormous help to the IUD and to individual unions in their efforts to compare thousands of contracts and to put price tags on complex union demands. The consequences of such effective preparation for negotiations can be telling. Comparisons of contract benefits of one company with those of its major competitors in the industry or with other comparable firms can have significant bargaining results.

These contract analyses are provided in two basic forms. First, there are general and routine reports distributed by the IUD or by a national union's research division. Second, there are special-purpose reports which can arm the trade union negotiator with data and strong arguments for his specific negotiations of the moment. The technical features of the IUD system permit "custom tailoring" of reports which will help negotiators detect weak and strong points of prevailing agreements and encourage them to suggest new frontiers for their own bargaining domain.[7]

ANALYSIS OF COMPANY ECONOMIC PROFILES FOR COALITION BARGAINING IN CONGLOMERATE AND MULTIPLANT COMPANIES. The IUD, in addi-

---

[7] In Canada, the Industrial Relations Centre at McGill University has just set up an equivalent of the IUD data center in its new collective bargaining information retrieval system. This is a service which the Centre is willing to provide to any potential user and it has been operative since September 1968. Any subscriber to the labor agreement information retrieval system can obtain within twenty-four hours facts and answers which formerly may have taken weeks of research. The service affords negotiators of Canadian agreements the same sort of comparative contract analysis as just described for the United States.

tion to its national survey of key contracts, also coordinates the activities of seventy-seven corporate or industrywide committees to help unions cope with new problems posed by widely diversified corporations that cut across the jurisdictions of many unions. By means of this coordinated bargaining, various unions dealing with the same company seek to hammer out together the basic demands they will make of the conglomerate or multiplant company. As an aid toward this objective, the IUD has developed a number of company files used by these company committees. These are economic profiles of about two hundred major companies built up from a variety of sources — government records, union files, private financial reporting services, and so on. They provide detailed records of finances, product lines, plant locations, key officers of the companies and their interlocking relationships with other companies, records of divisions of the company which are profitable and those which are not, a history of mergers and acquisitions, and so on. There are files that provide, for each of the company's agreements, records with respect to the agreement expiration date, vacation provisions, and plantwide wage information — in short, all of the relevant information which negotiators would need in their efforts at coordinated negotiation. The patterning of these company economic profiles permits union negotiators not only to use the information they have more effectively but to spot gaps in that information and to remedy these gaps by doing additional research. Ginsburg's detailed description of the problems in one such conglomerate multiplant company is illustrative of what is an increasingly typical bargaining relationship, i.e., one in which a single company is involved with multiple unions and multiple agreements. Caples's survey bears out the fact that this pattern is one which is likely to expand rather than diminish in the near future.

CODING AND COSTING OF ANTICIPATED OR PROPOSED DEMANDS. It is not necessary to elaborate on the obvious role which computers and information technology can serve in helping unions and companies get more accurate estimates of the anticipated or projected costs of demands which they expect to find put to them or which they themselves propose to make. Several of the conference participants referred to this particular use as an important one prior to negotiations.

DEVELOPMENT OF MATHEMATICAL MODELS. Here, too, there is little need to go beyond the listing of what is as yet a relatively infrequent usage of information technology both by unions and by companies. A number of Caples's respondents, however, referred to this particular use of computer-based information technology; and, relatively rare though it may be at the moment, the likelihood is that such modeling will increasingly come to be recognized as a useful tool for the parties.

It is clear from the conference discussion that for trade unions the linking of specific files — NLRB election results, NLRB unfair practice charges, contract analyses, corporate economic profiles — provides a broad view of the industrial relations picture of the firms with which they deal. It is clear that for companies the capacity to anticipate the impact of probable demands permits framing a series of alternatives (which may indeed be more favorable to both parties), and it is equally clear that the capacity to use this technology as a way of foraging unilaterally in a variety of contract areas may be an extremely helpful exercise in thinking through the company's plans for the renegotiation of an agreement.

(*b*) *Uses during negotiation.* Conference participants generally agreed with Caples's assertion that uses of the computer and of computer technology in preparations for negotiations and in the administration of the agreement once it had been negotiated were much more prevalent than uses during the actual course of the negotiations. There were some allusions to the costing of alternative contract proposals in real-time comparison analyses, and there were references during negotiations to the IUD contract-clause "text" bank in situations where relevant texts were considered either unusual or especially favorable. Caples also refers to some routine and special report preparations which then required further hand method analyses to yield meaningful information, but only half of Caples's companies used this sort of computer assistance during collective bargaining negotiations.

(*c*) *Uses in the administration of the agreement.* As in the case of the preparatory stages for negotiation, the postnegotiation stages involve substantial use of computer technology to aid the parties in the administration of the agreement. These uses consist primarily in assisting grievance analysis, arbitration analysis, contract clause references, enforcement and policing of contracts, and in the estimation of the effectiveness of specific programs negotiated.

Mason, for example, describes the aid rendered by computers in the indexing and reporting of grievances — functions especially important in his company since grievances arise and are handled at so many locations. Effective grievance analysis under such geographically dispersed industrial structures is vital if equitable treatment for all employees is to be achieved. Such analysis can also help check out union claims that people are disturbed about one or another particular clause in a contract. The grievance index will give the frequency of employees' complaints with respect to any and every particular contract provision. Similarly, arbitration analysis can help in spotting uniform or divergent interpretations of specific contract provisions.

Wilbur Daniels devotes a good portion of his paper to the discussion of the ILGWU's concern with the enforcement and policing of contracts in an industry where the opportunities for contract violations are many. The sources of the enforcement problem in this instance lie clearly in the industry structure. The industry is one with many small employers and a high rate of company mortality (20 to 30 percent). There is, in addition, a predominantly female labor force (with an equally high turnover rate), complex piecework incentives, and increasingly dispersed geographical location of establishments. All lead to elusive, inadequate, or inaccurate records. The ILGWU has, therefore, perennially sought to enforce and police earnings provisions, piece rate provisions, contributions to benefit funds, contracting out, dealing with nonunion work provisions, and so on. The computer has proved enormously helpful in these efforts. The union can check on earnings provisions by auditing payrolls provided on tape. It can police the payment of minimum guarantees to the individual (craft and progression minima) and the minimum guarantees accorded each craft and each craft section. The computer is especially helpful in discerning whether or not the group is "making out." The union can easily check contributions to benefit funds by cross-referencing and matching contributions to payrolls (contract and in-shop) against company sales. Daniels makes the interesting point that the role of the business agent is still vital in contract enforcement but notes that this computer tool not only helps the union representative but it also prods him toward more effective enforcement. Daniels suggests that some of the union's business agents may feel that Big Brother may be watching them as well as the employer; "that thing at 1710 Broadway" is thus occasionally seen as checking on the business agent as well as the boss. Daniels feels that the trade union must educate the agent to the uses and potential of "the thing" before such fears fully disappear.

Mason describes computer-aided techniques which help him go

beyond grievance analysis to estimate the effectiveness of specific programs. He refers, for example, to company interest in reviewing the effectiveness of certain salary policies or of policies relating marriage and turnover reduction. And it is clear that a good portion of the technology is devoted to many cost-benefit analyses of company policies that go beyond the industrial relations questions specifically examined here.

In using this technology for the administration of the agreement, Mason stresses the need to build and reinforce the confidence people have in the total information system. He does not feel that this necessarily involves (as an earlier discussant had suggested) the use of a "neutral computer" but feels rather that the trust of the company's employees will be won through ongoing exposure to the accuracy and fairness of the system. Mason underscores the need for such accuracy and fairness in building and implementing the system as a basic operating principle if we seek to avoid situations like the Renault experience where workers (uninformed about the basic rationale of management's information system) struck because they protested the use of computers in the selection of people for layoffs. People, he feels, should have the right to discuss what they feel are errors in the system at any time and should be involved from the beginning in the implementation of computer applications. Flying people, Mason points out, are generally "machine- and change-oriented" and never have objected to new technology per se. They have been concerned only with how the technology affects working conditions. He suggests implicitly that this can be transferable as an operating principle to other situations, although perhaps with some greater measure of effort.

(*d*) *Joint uses of computers in collective bargaining.* All of the conference participants seemed to agree that it would be useful to have computer-assisted "fact generation," employing joint study groups, agreed to by all bargaining parties. The need to agree on what would be considered relevant data for analysis and discussion of issues being bargained was, however, equally stressed. Caples found, and the others conceded, that only few parties actually share data or share bargaining analyses or cooperate in planning formal bargaining analyses. Jensen's discussion of such joint use for the decasualization of the labor markets in longshoring seems to be an exception to the rule and Mason's point made in the course of his presentation seems to explain quite easily why such reticence in

joint use may prevail. Mason felt (with Donald Straus a frequent dissenter) that joint use and joint queries by trade union and management may not prevail simply because they may not be advisable in the light of basic strategy in bargaining. "Many times," he says, "you want to know an answer but you don't want the other party to know you are even interested in the question. You discard more than you adopt but you have to educate yourself with respect to the options without publicity or without sharing these views at too early a point in the bargaining process." The explanation is a sensible one and suggests that truly joint uses of computers in a kind of simultaneous interrogation of a data bank may not be a stage towards which unions and companies will readily or quickly move.

2. The Substantive Issues to Which the Application of Electronic Data Processing or Other Computer-based Techniques Appear to be Most Relevant

The preceding discussion on the uses of computers in the process of bargaining has alluded in passing to the variety of substantive issues to which computer-aided techniques may be usefully applied.

It is clear from this discussion that virtually every contract proposal and provision may eventually be included in the world of computer-assisted bargaining if only to the extent that computers may replace hand methods in costing these proposals. It is clear from present practice, however, that computers have been most relevant in several generic instances.

First, it is apparent from the Kaufman-Penchansky paper that a number of complex substantive bargaining issues which lend themselves to simulated modeling will be explored in a much more sophisticated fashion in the future than they have been in the past. Simulation, as Kaufman and Penchansky point out, is the process of building a model of a real-world system, taking care to verify that the components of the model match components of the real-world system and that the relationships among these components in the abstract model accurately mirror the components in the real world. The model builder strives to ascertain that the data originally used to build a model fit the attributes of the parameters which are contained in the model. Then this model is used to generate data which can be interpreted as if they were occurrences in the real world. In other words, what is involved is the use of an abstract symbolic model to generate hypothetical experience which may be far more useful than pure intuition in gauging the behavior of complex systems. The case of the behavior of union health and welfare funds described by the Kaufman-Penchansky paper is illustrative of the simulation and modeling applications that are conceivable with the new information-systems technologies.

Second, it is evident from the papers and the discussion at the conference that manpower issues, where large masses of data are involved, may be more systematically and efficiently handled through computer-assisted applications (as in the case of manpower requirement projections or mobility of manpower studies in industries like longshoring or construction). Jensen's case study shows how these applications help reduce the casualness of the labor market by facilitating the mechanics of hiring and by increasing mobility in the employment of men through speeding the linkages between men and available jobs. It illustrates as well how effectively the system could be structured around the extremely complex seniority system which regulated and affected entry and movement within the longshore labor market.

Mason's array of uses noted in the airline case is a similar illustration of the applicability of these techniques to manpower problems. Flight crew scheduling, the preparation of seniority lists, the distribution of overtime, the distribution of flying to each pilot and stewardess domicile — all previously done by committee — are now done by computer.

These applications in the instances cited in the conference papers involve anything from simple punched card sorters, readers, and printers, to fairly complex and extensive program hardware and software. In each application, however, the author or conference discussant has stressed the greater accuracy and the lesser number of costly errors entailed in the achievement of the task involved. And Daniels's example of the computer's effect on the greater measure of precision possible in the formulation of substantive requests implies the extension of such accuracy to the realm of implementation and enforcement of collective agreements. A 10.444 percent increase is, as he points out, just as easy to compute and police as is a 10.4 percent increase or even a mere 10 percent increase.

Most important, perhaps, is the extension of the realm of the possible through which man may roam in his interaction with these computer and information systems. Mason's emphasis on the use of the computer to get many ideas concerning the "possible" in mulling substantive proposals or reactions to substantive demands may in the long run prove to be the most fascinating implication of computer technology for substance in collective bargaining.

3. *The Uses of Computers in Dispute Settlement or Prevention*

In mediation and arbitration the use of the computer as an information retrieval device may be helpful in bringing forth prior decisions and settlements. In providing easier access to "stored facts" or in providing alternative combinatorial packages and possibilities (either prior examples or present possibilities), computers and their associated data banks can be useful in many situations. George Taylor, in his discussion on this point, emphasizes the need to keep in mind the uniqueness of the special or the small situation and cautions against relying on overall comparisons yielded by such computer-based surveys. Indeed, he feels these may be more trouble than help if the mediator or arbitrator fails to understand that there may be reasons for differences between situations. Taylor thus feels that instant availability and retrievability of data could help mediate a dispute, but only if the data base can be used as a special-purpose tool to zero in on a particular situation, not with a view toward providing readymade answers, but as a tool for trying to achieve a meeting of the minds.

Cole agrees on the need for new tools and feels this need particularly at this point which he describes as "a period of irrationality in labor relations." In commenting on some of the failures in his recent mediation activities, Cole asserts that in each of these procedures there had been ample opportunity for fact-finding but feels also that the access and resort to this process were limited by the fact that everyone seemed to be after "that last lousy nickel." In principle, then, Cole appears to agree with Taylor concerning the usefulness in mediation of availability and quick retrievability of facts from a data bank; but in fact he seems to feel that this is useful only if both parties want it, develop it jointly, and shun exercising "muscle" to the hilt.

Ginsburg reasserts the usefulness of facts for small bargainers who generally do not have as easy access to all the facts as do larger bargainers or have only small research staffs which cannot stay on top of recent developments, and it is here that he hopes that development of these tools can be very helpful both to negotiators and to mediators and conciliators.

Straus, in urging the use of computers as a tool in achieving agreement, points to the possible situation where the computer has been programmed to print out the total impact of settlement for the union membership. Cole agrees that such computer-based "merchandising" of a settlement may be effective and points to the Kaiser Steel package which was clearly and effectively merchandised and probably could not have been sold otherwise. He elaborates further on this point by stressing the fact that a great deal of information is disseminated to Kaiser employees from month to month and that this elaborately broken down information is computer-generated. Dunlop, too, underscores the usefulness of quick accessibility of facts in dispute prevention and settlement by references to illustrations from the Armour case. Here agreement was reached first by a set of experts on pensions and health and welfare funds and then, as a consequence of their agreement on cost estimates of alternative packages, these experts could provide the basis for a general settlement. Dunlop, however, adds the interesting point that, while negotiators must be certain and explicit about facts during negotiations, they should have some measure of "chest-thumping" leeway with the facts for public face-saving in selling agreements to respective constituencies. How proposed settlements are explained may make a difference in whether or not proposed agreements are acceptable.

Zack stresses the point that in the field of public employment, where one often begins with no prior experience, data banks could be especially helpful to the parties. Setting things on the right track by providing recourse to useful and accurate information seems to him to provide great promise in mediation and conciliation of disputes in these sectors.

Finally, Cole reiterates in this context the earlier view expressed by Mason concerning the joint use of computers by the parties. Mason, it will be recalled, suggested that such joint use could get in the way of uninhibited "free association" exploration by each of the negotiators interacting separately with his machine. Cole points out with respect to joint mediation uses that a mediator might not want anyone to know what he was thinking at a particular moment in time or with respect to a particular issue, and therefore feels less optimistic than Straus does about the potential joint use of computer analyses in dispute settlement efforts.

4. The Potential Impact of the Uses of Computers and Information Technology in Collective Bargaining

In the course of the conference discussion there were several occasions to note the extent to which computers and information systems technology are currently used in bargaining and to comment on the prospects for the future uses of computers in labor relations. A number of the conference papers sought as well to project the major consequences of such uses for the process and substance of bargaining, for the internal organizational structure of unions and companies, for other parties less directly related to the bargaining process, and for the "public interest." Many of these points and themes have already been referred to in the preceding sections of this summary chapter. This final section outlines some of those not heretofore noted.

THE EXTENT AND GROWTH OF COMPUTER USES IN BARGAINING

At present it seems clear that the uses of computers and computer technology in collective bargaining are in their infancy. But they are growing rapidly, and prospects for the steady expansion of electronic data processing into most aspects of collective bargaining are excellent.

On the union side it is evident that the IUD has been the major spearhead in the application of information systems to decision making and strategy in bargaining. Many individual unions, of course, use computers for straightforward housekeeping chores — recording dues payments; updating membership rolls; maintaining pension data, voter lists, or mailing lists; and for a variety of other internal personnel or administrative functions. Few international unions, however, have moved from pure information storage and filing to the new awareness of the potential uses of information for bargaining strategy. At present, it is unlikely that more than a dozen large unions have developed their own computer-based information systems for bargaining. Among the unions which have developed such uses are the Machinists, the Automobile Workers, the Communications Workers, the Laborers, the Maritime Union, the Newspaper Guild, the Federation of State, County and Municipal Employees, the Steel Workers, and the Ladies' Garment Workers. Many more unions, of course, have availed themselves of the services of the IUD.

On management's side too, computer-based data processing has yet to be used by the majority of companies for strategic decision making in collective bargaining. In Caples's sample, for example, 46 percent of respondent companies have begun using computers for preparation in collective bargaining. Most companies have a basic employee record, machine records for current payroll, records for premiums paid for employee benefit packages, and machine records of pension data. But less than half maintain historical wage-salary data and the maximum retention period for those that do is five years. Only a little over a third of Caples's respondents maintain records on time not worked where significant costs may be incurred, e.g., absenteeism, vacations, sick leave, and so on. In his discussion, Mason points out that these operations are now mostly batch process. We find inputs of data, processing of data, and the generation of reports from central computer facilities.

In sum, although there have been, within a reasonably short period of years, substantial advances in the uses of computers in bargaining and other behavioral areas, it is apparent that such uses have lagged the uses in the physical sciences; and within the employment relations area it is clear that uses for collective bargaining tend to lag those in general personnel administration.

What factors have accounted for this moderate pace? Caples and others identify the following basic reasons. The data base available for use by the trade union or the company is often less than adequate. As has been noted, only limited data are currently available in machine records for use in electronic data processing. Second, programming takes too long and time is not always available. Third, hand methods are often adequate. Fourth, difficulties with hardware, software, modeling, and gaming situations have been too frequent. And fifth, trade union leaders, often not familiar with, and hence fearful of, the new technology and language, have too often been reluctant to move ahead. In short, cost and time limitations have been the basic reasons accounting for the record of expansion to date.

Caples stresses a second basic consideration which turns on the distinction between well-structured and poorly-structured problems. In personnel administration, as distinguished from collective bargaining, we find that the problems involve the counting and identifying of people, the recording and analysis of personnel actions, and the collection and payments of money. Each of these phenomena is easily translated into symbolic language and hence lends itself more readily to electronic data processing. Collective bargaining problems, on the other hand, are more poorly structured; and Caples asserts that it is this greater complexity which has tended to hold back the evolution of current management practice with regard to computer usage for bargaining purposes. He states, "The use of computers presupposes considerable advance understanding of the problem scope, availability of accurate input, reliable factoral weighting, and logical resolution of problems; somehow these elements still are rarities in the bargaining process."

What of future trends in the usage of computers for bargaining? Here there seems to be general agreement that we will see rapidly ascending trajectories. In Caples's survey, two-thirds of the respondents indicate that they intend to develop or improve applications for bargaining at some future point in time; and a substantial proportion indicate that they have definite plans for such applications already on hand. Caples himself views the future of electronic data processing applications to collective bargaining with "cautious optimism" and sees these extensions primarily in the preparation for negotiations and in the uses for the interpretation and administration of contracts. In actual bargaining, Caples feels that what gets discussed are the assumptions underlying the particular sets of facts presented to support a bargaining position or objective of the parties. The critical factor thus becomes the gaining of acceptance of the assumptions on which the data are based, and it is for these reasons that Caples feels confident that the applications in the preparation and implementation phases will be the growth areas for computer applications in collective bargaining. Mason, too, feels that we are on the verge of a period holding great promise for future applications; and he stresses, in addition, the fact that the future may lie more with real-time random access systems than with batch process operations. He feels that such real-time random access systems are more rewarding and may be used more in future input and output of data to and from many locations; he points to a variety of such potential uses in his own industry.[8]

What reasons are offered to account for this projected extension of use? Mason's references to his own industry provide a first clue.

[8] Crew schedulers can check qualifications immediately instead of maintaining records at each location for all 10,000 stewardesses. Current flight crew information will permit accurate assignments, insure legality of trips, and so on. Bid and transfer requests for 38,000 employees will be more easily handled with the availability of immediate information with respect to seniority and other qualifications. In short, the projected growth to 75,000 employees by 1975 will make necessary such more efficient uses of the computer.

To begin with, it is clear that the initial uses for internal record and housekeeping chores tend to push and lead the trade unions and companies both to seek other applications and other uses. It is clear that for both parties there exists a need for more efficient ways of maintaining and retrieving information with respect to each employee and for the consolidation of the masses of raw data which each now possesses. Vast amounts of information are also required of both parties for government reports. The Labor-Management Reporting and Disclosure Act and the Pension Fund Disclosure Act are but two illustrations of this increased call for consolidated data. Mounting tasks face the research staffs of both trade unions and companies, and in each instance we find limited personnel available to perform these tasks. In addition, it is clear from the discussion throughout the conference that increased information is needed for more complex issues in collective bargaining. Health and welfare issues, retirement fund management — these are illustrative of the questions which cry out for computer-based data processing techniques. There are also new areas for collective bargaining which require more sophisticated information systems. As hardware and software developments provide increased sophistication, the parties will tend to find some of the impediments to growth referred to earlier diminishing. Also, cost sharing by employers may help eliminate economic constraints; the development of a computer "utility service" would propel management to increased uses of computer technology in collective bargaining as well as in other policy areas. Parties also react to each other. The use by a company will tend to spur a union to explore electronic data processing in bargaining and vice versa.

All parties agree to the basic structural reasons propelling both unions and companies toward such extended usage. As Caples has pointed out, many companies find themselves bargaining many agreements with many unions. It is natural for them to have, or to seek, coordination of data for such bargaining through electronic data processing. It is also characteristic to find frequent bargaining (and in many cases almost continuous bargaining) in these multiple bargaining units and multiple trade union/multiple locals/multiple agreement cases. On the union side, in turn, we have seen that such corporate conglomerate structures may spur the formation of company committees for coordinated or coalition bargaining which is, in turn, abetted by computer information systems but which, in its turn, also sparks the further evolution of such usages into bargaining decision making. In sum, there is much to give significant impetus to the growth of computer-based electronic data processing in bargaining in the near future.

INTERNAL EFFECTS ON THE PARTIES

Little reference was made in the conference discussion to any significant intramural changes on the management side of the bargaining table. There were, however, some references to some possible effects on the trade unions. It is evident that in those instances where computers and information technology have been used in the development of bargaining strategy, such extended usage has been accompanied by an expanded role for the research department of the union. It is clear, too, that published contract reports and summaries can serve, and have been used effectively, as training and educational tools for both new and old staff members of the trade unions. The International Association of Machinists, for example, periodically calls industry conferences in which these reports serve as the basic training tool for the union representatives. One union leader during our discussion noted the possibility for insuring better communications within the union by assuring accurate delivery of union publications through computer-processed mailing and distribution. Finally, it is apparent that there may be an ultimate, vital linkage between improved information on which organization tactics and strategy may be based and the accelerated growth of trade union organizations.

The conference discussion also pointed to some possible changes for parties other than the parties involved directly in bargaining. It is clear, for example, that the American Arbitration Association, perhaps the most prominent private dispute settlement agency in the world, is searching for more effective uses of the new technology in the performance of old functions of dispute settlement by arbitration, conflict prevention, mediation, and so on. It is clear, too, that in the field of education, computer technology has provided a new base for exercises to help students gain a better feel for the bargaining process and for face-to-face negotiations. It is clear that the Baitsell-Sprague-Taylor discussion views these computer-based exercises as merely facilitating the process of gaining experience with such exchanges and not as a substitute for them. The educators are, however, enabled to make their gaming issues a bit more complicated and hence a bit more real; but they see the new educational technology as in no way replacing the human side of negotiations

— a conclusion quite similar to that reached by all of the conference participants with respect to these functional roles in the real world.

SOME PUBLIC INTEREST IMPLICATIONS

The earlier discussion on dispute settlement also summarizes the conference conclusions on this particular theme, to which the community has traditionally given substantial attention. "Cautious optimism" would seem to be the key word with respect to the potential for the diminution of industrial conflict as a consequence of the extension of computer-based technology in bargaining. It should be noted that the conferees clearly felt that the greatest potential for such moderation lay in the area of disputes over rights reflected in grievances over contract interpretation, rather than in the potential for the diminution of conflict arising over the negotiation of new terms or interests.

With respect to the inflationary pressures of bargaining under coalition or coordinated structures, the conferees noted merely that uniformity of wage demands made possible by better-researched and better-coordinated bargaining strategy could be offset by the equal possibility, implicit in such coordinated strategies, for the facilitation of intramural mediating efforts on the part of union representatives who seek to moderate unreasonable union demands by referring to a "more reasonable" prevailing pattern. A third policy area discussed at the meetings dealt with the range of conceivable freedom with respect to negotiated work rules. Mason, for example, was not too optimistic about the beneficial use of computers in devising optional benefit plans for different groups in the work force. The "cafeteria approach" to benefits is an experiment attempted at General Electric and other companies, but tax laws seem to be more of a problem here than administrative feasibility. This view was confirmed by Ellenbogen, who asserted that the notion that individuals or small groups could choose their own "benefit tray" from a whole panoply of possible combinations did not seem at this point to be very manageable.

SOME GENERAL OBSERVATIONS

Professor Brown's summary of the discussion artfully captures the flavor of some of the conference highlights. In industrial relations, he asserts that judgment and hunch will continue to play a major role; however, so will computers, which will be used both by firms and by unions. These conclusions are complementary and reinforcing and not antagonistic. It is clear that computers will increasingly be used as storehouses of information and facts and as retrieval devices for such information with respect to the personnel function, including the administration and policing of collective agreements. It is clear, too, that computers will be increasingly used as a tool in the preparation for negotiations in all sizes of firms, with utility services developed for smaller firms. With respect to actual negotiations, the discussion of the conference may have underestimated the role of computers. Even in the simplest use of computers, as an information storehouse, facts are important to have; and the availability of information may avoid many problems and impasses due to misinformation or misconception of the facts. Aside from facts, computers can be helpful during negotiations as "costing out" devices, and as generators and evaluators of new arrangements and potentialities. Mediators may have their efforts blunted by the increased sophistication of professional bargainers who, with these new tools, have many more facts and see more possible new solutions — the basic services which mediators had earlier provided. With respect to uniformity in agreements, Professor Brown argues that the computer is neutral and that only policy can decide this issue. The computer's usefulness in model building and simulation is enormous; this use as a tool in simulating and evaluating alternate consequences of different policy choices may prove to be one of the most powerful of all possible uses. Finally, Professor Brown concludes with the caveat that suggests simply that we consider the costs of computer uses as well as its benefits. But he ends on an "upbeat" note. Both groups, computer specialists and industrial relations experts, he suggests, will, in consequence of the extended use of computer technology over time, be required to learn more about each other's area of respective expertise. Here, indeed, is the last intriguing challenge implied in the extended uses of computers and information technology in bargaining in future years.

The Computer's Uses and Potential in Bargaining: A Trade Union View

Woodrow L. Ginsburg

Introduction

The use of electronic data processing equipment by unions for collective bargaining and related purposes has steadily expanded. This growth must be viewed against the background of evolving union and industrial internal organization and of their bargaining interrelationships during the postwar period.

Among the factors which must be considered in assessing the potential value of computers for unions are the mounting tasks facing research staffs in many of the AFL-CIO (American Federation of Labor and Congress of Industrial Organizations) affiliates and the concomitantly limited capacity of these staffs to carry out their many assignments with present personnel. Nor can we overlook the important matter of how management goes about preparing for negotiations.

Anyone with even the briefest contacts with union-management relationships since 1947 will be aware of a whole series of changes in the collective bargaining arena. Reaching agreement on contract language after lengthy periods of negotiations has become ever more complex and technical. The information which each side brings to the bargaining table grows geometrically as coverage of wages and working conditions is constantly being extended into new areas. Part of this trend also results from unions bargaining to win greater protection for their memberships on a myriad of issues related to the work place and job security. An equally significant element has been the opening up of new fringe benefit areas such as protection against loss of income from illness, accident, and temporary layoff. Another group of fringe benefits covering other forms of insurance

26

and pensions has contributed to the increasingly technical and complex nature of the bargaining situation. Basic agreements between unions and management which consisted of perhaps five to ten pages covering the essentials of union recognition, grievance procedures, and some brief sections on seniority and wages were typical twenty years ago. Today that relatively simple contract has been replaced by a series of documents that run to hundreds of pages. It is not at all unusual for the basic agreement — that is, the agreement that covers wages, working conditions, and fringe benefits, but does not cover the insurance, pension, and other welfare provisions — to run over a hundred pages. Pension and insurance agreements supplementing the main contract are sometimes of almost equal length. A number of unions also add special supplements relating to protection against loss of income during layoffs. And this list of agreements may be expanded in many major collective bargaining situations by specialized contractual arrangements dealing with the rights of workers in case of plant shutdowns due to automation, apprenticeship standards for skilled workers, joint union-management wage committees, and so on.

Various estimates ranging upward of 150,000 have been made for the total number of labor-management agreements in effect today throughout the country. The number seems quite reasonable in light of the fact that there are about 50,000 local unions affiliated with 129 AFL-CIO international unions, plus more than 50 other national and international unions not part of the central labor body.

The mushrooming of the number of agreements and supplemental agreements and the multiplication of their length results from the technical nature of the subjects covered as well as the extension of contracts into so many new areas of wage, welfare, and working condition issues. In turn, the scope of bargaining has been broadened by unions' responses to the varied and numerous changes which have occurred on the industrial scene.

All the data point to an acceleration in the speed of change. Individual plants are constantly diversifying their output and modernizing through the introduction of new machines and new processes. The corporate structure itself is undergoing dynamic and radical shifts. Mergers which join companies in widely separate fields of endeavor have become the rule rather than the exception. And the emerging corporate structures pose new challenges for union leaders trying to represent their workers more effectively.

Research staffs trying to keep pace with the economic developments affecting the industries with which their unions bargain are more than fully occupied. Providing an endless stream of facts and figures for specific collective bargaining is another essential task. The largest negotiating encounters — those with the "Big Three," "Big Four," "Big Two," or some other small number of giant firms which dominate so many basic industries — get most of the public attention. Most of the research departments of the industrial unions devote major portions of their time and energies to preparation for such key negotiations. But, besides these front-page situations, there are countless bargaining sessions for which basic facts and figures about wages; settlements in the industry, the area, and in similar-sized plants; past trends of economic gains; and so on must also be supplied.

The job of organizing contract data for literally hundreds — and, in many cases, thousands — of separate agreements has placed a persistent and heavy burden on many union research technicians. They have carried the load by means of inventing many techniques to code, summarize, and otherwise boil down to manageable size the hundreds of pages of agreement texts. Different systems of summary cards, sheets, or tables, using essentially manual procedures, have been adopted. In some cases the pressures have led to performing the analysis for only a representative sample of the contracts in smaller units, while trying to stay current with those in larger firms.

The task shows no signs of becoming lighter and has sparked discussion and, in a number of unions, action to utilize electronic data processing to cope with the problem.

On the management side, industrial relations staffs are confronted with similar tasks. A recent book, *Management Preparation for Collective Bargaining*,[1] reviews in some detail how industry readies itself for negotiations with unions. (The sample on which the authors based their book was relatively small. Some one hundred representatives involved in forty separate industrial relations situations were interviewed. However, they did represent a rather good cross-section in terms of industry, size, and type of organization.)

Management spokesmen are keenly aware of the new complexities of bargaining, particularly in multiplant firms' situations, where negotiating with more than one union is common. They

[1] M. S. Ryder, C. M. Rehmus, and S. Cohen, *Management Preparation for Collective Bargaining*, Homewood, Illinois: Dow Jones-Irwin, 1966.

have strengthened their industrial relations operation, given it greater responsibility, and generally feel they are now far better prepared at the bargaining table.

Two key phases of bargaining preparation are discussed in the book: the first involves the collection, analysis, and interpretation of data; the second, based on this material, deals with the setting of bargaining policy.

But what kinds of information does management gather? Experienced negotiators will be familiar with the listing contained in the book. Its authors point to "information such as area wage rates for comparable skills, wage and fringe benefits paid by competitors, and local union and plant employee desires. . . ." [2]

In multiplant corporations, much of this information is gathered locally, forwarded to corporate headquarters, and coordinated into a unified management position.

There are many references to how the company negotiators draw up their bargaining postures. The size of their economic package is based upon many "comparisons of wage levels and recently bargained amounts in the industry country-wide and, for skilled crafts, by wage rates in the locality." [3] While area practices for certain units of the company are of particular importance for wage rates and certain working conditions, frequently "the fringe benefit structure . . . may follow the company's overall benefit policy as negotiated in its master agreement." [4]

In short, in the postwar period we have seen an enormous jump in the kind and amount of economic and contract information and trends which both union and management representatives need for effective bargaining. For unions, this explosion of knowledge has spurred the search for techniques which will facilitate furnishing their officers with the appropriate tools to carry out their collective bargaining responsibilities. The one which gives real promise is a modern electronic data processing system.

The Use of Computers in Contract Analysis

There are three main areas of contract analysis research utilizing computer technology. The first two involve the operations which the Industrial Union Department (IUD) directed: the establishment

[2] *Ibid.*, p. 20.
[3] *Ibid.*, p. 30.
[4] *Ibid.*, p. 24.

of a national survey of provisions from major agreements and the use of the computer capability for our coordinated collective bargaining activities. The third covers the work done by a number of international unions which use electronic data processing (EDP) for their own contracts. Special attention is given to the International Association of Machinists (IAM), the union which has developed the most elaborate system.

One approach seemed most promising as we at the IUD began to investigate setting up a computerized agreement research operation to cover leading or pattern-setting agreements. That was to pool the combined experience of many of the research staffs which for years had been carrying out various programs of contract analysis work. For the system to be of optimum value, we knew it had to be capable of producing results which would have the widest possible use among our affiliated unions.

National Survey of Key Contract Provisions

In close cooperation, then, with research technicians from about fifteen of our IUD–affiliated unions, we developed a list of twenty-one key contract provisions. These provisions, the consulting group agreed, formed a basic body of agreement clauses which would be of special significance for negotiation purposes.

Many research departments, in their contract analysis work, were already making surveys and tabulations of most, if not all, of these provisions from the contracts of their unions. To be sure, the twenty-one categories and their details (which in the aggregate total more than five hundred individual items), while covering the key wage, fringe benefits, and working conditions clauses, did not include each and every provision of the contract. However, the agreement information that has been collected — and its volume continues to grow — has proved extremely useful in a variety of negotiation situations.

First, just what do the data cover?

In our initial research task, we analyzed the key provisions in 151 large manufacturing and 57 large nonmanufacturing agreements. These cut across the entire industrial spectrum. After coding and other processing steps were completed, we transferred the information to magnetic tape. The speedy retrieval of selective material in a virtually unlimited variety of forms and arrangements was now possible.

As time has gone on, the number and kinds of requests we receive continue to grow and diversify. Many of the presentations we have developed on collective bargaining data have in turn sparked requests for a different comparison, a revised tabulation, or a modified survey.

Let me give a number of specific illustrations which reveal the kind of bargaining assistance the computerized data are providing.

To begin with, in June 1967, we prepared a national tabulation of the key provisions in the major agreements; we published separate reports for manufacturing and nonmanufacturing industries. Within each of these two broad industrial sectors, we arranged the contracts by large subgroups — food-meat products, clay-structural products, basic steel products, general building contractors, and construction-electric. We did not merely summarize the coverages of the provisions in terms of the number of agreements and/or workers with certain benefits. So often in negotiations it is important to be able to identify by name and size the bargaining unit where a particular wage increase was won or a specific fringe benefit prevailed. This need led us to present the full array of clauses, with their eligibility rules and other features, for each contract in the survey.

While doing this for a number of provisions, such as vacations and holidays, we tabulated the extent of coverage for a range of benefits for all the contracts. Our June 1967 tables are a benchmark from which we can readily measure progress in making contract improvements, and we are now in a position to document and analyze industrial relations trends.

Just as varied arrangements of groups of contracts and/or provisions can be prepared through the electronic data procedures, so statistical summaries are being programmed for computer handling for an expanding number of basic clauses and their many facets.

In extracting from each of the major, and lengthy, contracts the salient points on each of their twenty-one provisions, we were aided by the cooperation of technical staff from a number of unions. In a sense, the contract form from which the data are then processed represents an important first step toward a common language of agreement analysis. It can greatly facilitate the exchange of information and the preparation of comparisons of prevailing contract provisions.

Many trade union researchers currently review, analyze, and summarize the contracts of their own international. For a large number of them, with little added effort — or, in the EDP jargon, with little

added input — they can provide the details of the twenty-one provisions on the standardized analysis form which they jointly created.
Such a process could vastly expand the size, comprehensiveness, and
potential of the survey.

As it is, the IUD has been enlarging the scope and usefulness of
the survey by adding the agreements covering plants in the coordinated collective bargaining work of the department. The national
survey, with its 208 agreements, includes more than 3 million workers employed at about 3,000 different facilities. We have added the
same kind of contract facts and figures for an additional 500 agreements for individual plants of some 17 companies where coordinated
collective bargaining efforts have been undertaken. This latter group
is steadily increasing, as contracts for other coordinated bargaining
committees are periodically being converted to the computerized
program. (This activity is explored further in the next section.)

Some Applications of the Survey

What the national survey, along with its potential for different
combinations of its content, has done is to offer to many unions a
new and valuable tool in the area of contract analysis. Through
the IUD, union research staffs can obtain the kind of specialized,
detailed contract information and comparisons which they need but
are unable to prepare because of lack of time and resources.

As one attorney, who over the years has worked with several
smaller unions and seen how such material could be useful, said,
"The IUD's contract survey operation puts on the desk of officials
in dozens of smaller unions a ready-made research capability — a
capability which, on an individual basis, those unions would not
support."

But requests for reports have by no means come exclusively from
medium-sized or small unions. The capability of the system has been
tapped by a number of the larger union staffs as well.

A major union, which bargains for a majority of the employees
at one of the nation's leading electronics manufacturers, wanted a
special report made of the basic contract provisions in effect at
twenty major firms. Most of the companies were in the same or a
closely related branch of industry. Some were from other important
industrial groups. Settlements on wages and working conditions at
these twenty firms had played an important role in negotiating
sessions between the union and the firm during the past, often

establishing the general dimensions of the final economic package and the broad framework for other collective bargaining issues.

In this particular case, the tabulations gave strong support to the union's demand for a cost-of-living clause — a demand of growing importance in this period of sharply increasing prices, for many of the key competitor firms had such a contract clause. Similarly, on a number of other significant provisions, the tabulations of prevailing conditions gave added force to the union's arguments.

To be sure, the union staff could have prepared the same kind of bargaining brief without the aid of the EDP contract analysis system. But the time required to have done so on a manual basis was substantial, and adding that job to other work of the department would have involved real strain.

Updating the Survey

Another aspect of these specially tailored tabulations is worth noting for it has proved to be of value to other unions. As key contracts are signed, their terms become important to many other sets of negotiations. During the past year, for example, an entirely new group of benchmarks for new economic and fringe levels has been developed in a series of major agreements. In manufacturing, for example, these innovations occurred in the meat-packing contracts at Armour and Wilson; the rubber union's settlements with the largest producers in the industry; and in the auto, the agricultural implement, and the can industry settlements.

Many of the industrial union research technicians keep a close tab on such settlements. Typically, they analyze them for overall gains and improvements in clauses of particular concern to their own union negotiators. What we are beginning to modify with our national contract survey is the duplicative efforts of summarizing and comparing such new agreements. Each of our affiliated unions will obtain periodically a report on recently negotiated agreements. The arrangement of such contract information can be tailored to any single union's needs. For example, in the formatting, the tabulation for one union was headed by some of the union's largest contracts and the sequence of new agreements was essentially on an industry grouping; for another union, going into negotiations with a particular company, the provisions from that company's contract headed the list.

In such a case, whether the firm is one of the giants with which the union deals or one of the hundreds of smaller firms, the material is presented in the sequence which the research technician sees as being most useful. Many times, we know, our present provision coverage, either in scope or detail, may not furnish the precise bit of information a union thinks it needs at the bargaining table. But we are able to, and do, provide a convenient, broad-ranging view of collective bargaining changes — a view that constitutes a building block for negotiation material.

The many changes which occur on the industrial relations scene are reflected in a look at our first group of 208 major contracts. They had typically been negotiated in the period from mid-1964 to early 1967, and, with a few exceptions, were still in effect at the time of our survey. Since then, more than a hundred of those contracts have passed their expiration date; and we, again with important cooperation from a number of unions, have entered the new, revised provisions into our system.

Details on each of these one hundred contracts are not needed or useful for every union's bargaining. But the number gives a feel for the size of the job confronting individual unions in seeking to stay current on pattern-setting contracts in other industries.

As many of the contracts were of three years' duration, both the expired and the new, we now have as a by-product of our work a chronology of gains in wages, key fringes, and other contract provisions. The word "by-product" is the essential one for underlining the increment derived from the computer processing. For we are now able to track, typically for a six-year period, the wage increases won in major settlements. (As our system picks up renewals and additional contracts, the same important chronological information will be available for a far larger number of contracts.) And this enlargement of our reporting capacity is an integral element of the machine-processed portion of our contract analysis.

Text Entries

Several other features of the system have proved worthwhile. One such feature relates to the text entries we have made on unusual clauses, or clauses which do not fit our prestructured analysis form. With the individuality of bargaining relationships, and the complexity of the process, we were aware that many times a particular feature of a benefit or working condition would not fit neatly into one of the designated slots under each category. Rather than restrict our analysis through an artificial forcing of unusual contract conditions into an inappropriate slot, we have provided for text entries. An explanatory note which summarizes the main features of the contract item is entered on the survey report at the end of the tabular presentation for the provision category. Such information supplements the other data in our tables and, here again, has led to a useful by-product: a file of all the agreements in our major survey, along with the new contracts that replace them. Upon request from a union, we are now able to amplify the information on any of the items which appears in our printed materials with the actual agreement language.

An Index of Contracts

As we have noted, we have been able to determine the location of some 3,000 plant and other facilities of the total covered by the 208 major agreements. In a large number of these, we have also been able to identify the product manufactured, the number of employees, the type of bargaining unit, and other relevant characteristics. Such information enables us now, virtually entirely through machine processing, to present contract data by industry, by region, by type of unit, by size, or by various combinations of such factors.

To a union which is concerned with the level of benefits and the existence of particular contract provisions in a local or a regional area, our file can provide substantial amounts of data. Again, as we increase the number of contracts in the system — and this is an ongoing activity — we increase our capacity to provide area, industry, and other tabulations.

Without the speed of selection and printing which the system provides, it would be far too lengthy and expensive to compile the many separate tabulations — each, in effect, tailored for the special needs of the union requesting it.

Coordinated Collective Bargaining

Let us turn from the broad application of computerized collective bargaining data to some of its specific uses in the activities of coordinated collective bargaining at particular firms. Here we will begin with how the IUD has been employing electronic data processing techniques, particularly, for the informational exchange and comparative contract analyses involving its over eighty "company committees." These are committees established to develop a cooperative, integrated approach where more than one union, generally three, four, or more, bargains with a single employer. In addition to the bargaining aspects of such committees' work, some potential new approaches to organizing nonunion facilities of the firm are being explored or developed. As an illustration of these latter procedures, we have included a brief description of how a second major file of data — National Labor Relations Board (NLRB) election histories — proved useful in the case of the General Electric Company.

The Problem of Conglomerates

As we have noted, the postwar period has been characterized by an ever more complex industrial relations scene. Playing a significant role in this trend is the rapid increase of mergers involving corporations making completely different and unrelated products, as well as mergers which cut across broad industry lines.

For example, when the Federal Trade Commission reviewed the merger activities of companies with $10 million or more in assets, it found that between 1960 and 1965 over 70 percent of all such larger mergers and acquisitions involved conglomerates. Only 13 percent of the major mergers which took place during that period joined companies making the same or similar products.

In the process, the situation where one union had jurisdiction over most, if not all, of the plants of a company whose output centered on a particular product has become a rarity. Replacing such circumstances are the cases where ten, fifteen, twenty, or more different unions, as a result of conglomerate mergers, now face the same employer at separate places and separate times when bargaining begins.

There are many examples which can illustrate this point. Among the most graphic is the development of the firm of Ling-Temco-Vought. That corporation, some ten years ago, employed less than a thousand workers in five plants throughout the United States. Over the years it continued to expand and acquired new holdings in aerospace, electronics, communications, and power cable industries. By 1967, it had grown to a firm employing some twenty-one thousand, and at that time dealt with eight separate major AFL-CIO international unions. In 1967, LTV merged with Wilson and Company, a firm which also had diversified into many different product lines. At the time of the merger, Wilson was in three major fields — food and meat processing, sports and athletic equipment, and chemicals — and itself employed some twenty-two thousand workers.

These workers were represented by seven international unions, none of which was among the eight international unions dealing with LTV. With the completion of the merger, there were fifteen separate major international unions dealing with one giant, highly diversified, multiplant conglomerate corporation.

The Food Machinery and Chemical Corporation (FMC) has also shown a spectacular growth in the past decade. This multiplant, multiproduct corporation is involved in the manufacture of such diverse products as film and fibers, industrial chemicals, machinery and equipment, and defense items.

In 1956, FMC had approximately sixteen thousand employees with sales approaching $300 million. By 1966, the number of employees had more than doubled to forty-three thousand, and sales had passed the $1 billion mark. About twenty-five thousand of FMC's forty-three thousand workers, employed at some sixty-four of over a hundred plants controlled by the corporation, were covered by agreements with fifteen unions.

In 1967, FMC acquired the firm of Link-Belt. At the time of the merger, Link-Belt had more than thirty-five plants and warehouses, and about eleven thousand employees. About five thousand of these additional FMC employees at fifteen of the Link-Belt facilities were represented by six of the fifteen unions with which FMC had previously bargained.

Coordinating the bargaining efforts of fifteen different unions with agreements at seventy-nine different plants controlled by a single corporation like FMC involves a major effort.

The Benefits of Central Files

Clearly, if local negotiators are to be successful in obtaining uniform wage rates and fringe benefits within a single corporation, they first must have the knowledge of what contractual provisions are in effect at all other plants of the corporation. This knowledge depends upon the primary fact of having contracts from all the plants where unions have bargaining rights. And to secure such contracts, of course, in turn depends upon knowing which union or unions do, in fact, have such rights at each facility and in securing copies of the contracts in effect between that union or unions and the management at that facility. But there is no central file of the over 150,000 union agreements. Nor is there a central file or directory which identifies every facility where a union or unions have collective bargaining agent status.

To create such a file would be an enormous task and to keep it current in light of the thousands of changes which take place each year, in terms of new plants, mergers, acquisitions, and business failures, would likewise be a massive undertaking. Any attempt to grapple with such a tabulation using manual methods alone could not be considered feasible.

Each year about eight thousand separate elections are conducted by the National Labor Relations Board to determine whether or not employees at a particular establishment wish to have a union represent them as their bargaining agent. Since mid-1961 — and we have used this date, for that was the time the NLRB began publishing regular monthly information on individual elections — over fifty thousand representation elections have been conducted. In approximately thirty thousand of such elections, a majority of the workers cast their ballots for the union which was petitioning to represent them. Stated in another way, each year about five thousand new union bargaining units are created.

But, up to recently, if anyone wanted to know the organizational status at any particular plant of any particular company, he would have had to engage in the cumbersome job of contacting perhaps a dozen or more international unions, any one of whose jurisdiction might well have included the facility in question. Or, as another technique, he might have contacted state or local central labor bodies in the community and requested the information from them. But while cooperation in exchanging information is generally high among different union groups, in all too many cases the requested information was not provided.

The trend towards the conglomerate structure in so many corporations has only added new complex dimensions to the negotiators' need for getting a comprehensive picture of the organizational status at all plants. For, if the bargaining effort by a particular union or a group of unions is to be strengthened, it requires as broad a base as possible of organized union strength within the company.

To begin to cope with the complex and detailed dimensions of a central union status file, we at the IUD have put on magnetic tapes the records of all the NLRB representational elections held since the July 1961 date mentioned above. These approximately fifty thousand-plus elections have been arranged for the first time in an alphabetical listing. From it, the IUD has been able to get ready access to the organizational status of individual plants. It has enabled us to shortcut enormously the determination of who holds bargaining rights at many of the plants of corporations at which coordinated bargaining efforts are under way.

At the same time, it has been of immeasurable assistance in answering requests from individual unions seeking organizational status information. Countless times, a particular union dealing with a corporation wants to know whether other plants of that corporation — whose location the union may not even be aware of — are, in fact, covered by a union contract.

Such inquiries are of exactly the same nature that we referred to above when union representatives at a particular plant of a multiplant corporation began the job of assembling the information on what contract provisions prevailed at other of the corporation's plants.

Let us return to the illustration of the coordinated bargaining at FMC and some of the problems involved.

FMC — An Illustration

As we noted, at FMC there are agreements in effect with fifteen different unions covering sixty-four plants. Our IUD staff members were able to obtain the agreements covering fifty-three of the seventy-nine plants where, after much research of the kind I have referred to earlier, it was learned that unions held bargaining rights. The staff utilized the same kind of contract analysis summary form which we have been using for our surveys of major union agreements throughout manufacturing and nonmanufacturing industries. On the basis of this computer-based analysis, the IUD developed a series of tables covering contract provisions and plant information.

Following are examples of some of the reports which we were able to generate in very short order after the basic analysis had been completed.

The first example (Figure 1) is a portion of the listing of the expiration dates in the contracts, arranged chronologically. At the outset, such a listing demonstrates some of the complexities of bargaining with a conglomerate.

As a check of the expiration dates of the thirty-seven contracts listed on this sample page will show, there are twenty-eight different expiration dates, ranging over the period beginning with October 1, 1967 and extending through June 1, 1969.

The comparison of contract provisions in effect at different plants of the corporation has also been greatly facilitated by the use of

COMPANY	UNION	EFFECTIVE DATE	EXPIRATION DATE		COMPANY	UNION	EFFECTIVE DATE	EXPIRATION DATE
COLUMBUS, OHIO	USA	10/01/64	10/01/67		PORTLAND, ORE	IAM	07/01/65	07/01/65
HOUSTON, TEXAS	USA	10/16/64	10/15/67		CHICAGO, ILL	USA	08/01/65	07/31/68
MONTEBELLO, CAL	TCWH	00/00/65	10/30/67		S FRANCISCO, CAL	IAM	04/01/65	03/31/68
VANCOUVER, WASH	ICW	11/01/65	10/31/67		MODESTO, CAL	ICW	09/01/66	09/01/68
CARTERET, N.J.	ICW	11/08/65	11/08/67		EUGENE, OREGON	IAM	09/01/65	09/01/68
LYNDHURST, N.J.	ICW	11/22/65	11/22/67		PT WASHNGTN, WIS	IAM	09/01/66	09/01/68
LANSING, MICH	UAW	12/01/64	12/01/67		GREEN BAY, WIS	USA	09/16/65	09/15/68
MINNEAPLS, MINN	UAW	12/18/64	12/17/67		LAWRENCE, KAN	ICW	10/01/66	10/01/68
STONEYCREEK, ONT	USA	02/06/66	02/06/68		ATLANTA, GA	USA	11/01/65	10/31/68
DON—POCATELLO	ICU	00/00/00	04/01/68		AM. VISCOSE DIV	TWUA	12/01/65	12/01/68
HOLLISTER, CAL	TCWH	04/01/67	04/01/68		MIDDLEPORT, NY	IAM	12/03/66	12/03/68
PORTLAND, ORE	IAM	04/01/65	04/01/68		FRESNO, CAL	IAM	05/11/66	12/31/68
TIPTON, IND	USA	04/01/66	04/01/68		HOUSTON, TEXAS	OCAW	04/01/67	01/01/69
CEDAR RAPIDS, IA	UAW	04/01/66	04/01/68		FRESNO, CAL	TCWH	05/12/66	01/07/69
SEATTLE, WASH	IAM	04/01/65	04/01/69		NEWPORT, IND	OCAW	01/17/66	01/17/69
RIVERSIDE, CAL	IAM	05/08/65	05/01/68		SAN JOSE, CAL	IAM	05/09/66	03/31/69
AM. VISCOSE DIV	TWUA	06/01/65	06/01/68		SEATTLE, WASH	TCWH	05/01/65	05/01/69
DETROIT, MICH	UAW	07/01/65	06/30/68		KETCHICAN, ALAS	IWA	06/01/66	06/01/69
					SO EASTERN, ALAS	IWA	06/01/66	06/01/69

Figure 1   Agreement dates — FMC Corporation.

COMPANY	UNION	1/2 YR	1 YR	2 YRS	3 YRS	5 YRS	10 YRS	12 YRS	15 YRS	20 YRS	25 YRS	30 YRS
				AMOUNT OF VACATION PROVIDED FOR THE LISTED YEARS OF SERVICE								
BUFFALO, N.Y.	ICW		1 WK	2 WK			3 WK			4 WK		
CARTERET, N.J.	ICW		1 WK	2 WK			3 WK			4 WK		
LYNDHURST, N.J.	ICW		1 WK	2 WK			3 WK			4 WK		
DON—POCATELLO	ICW		1 WK	2 WK			3 WK					
FRESNO, CAL.	TCWH		1 WK	2 WK			3 WK?			4 WK		
HOLLISTER, CAL.	TCWH		1 WK	2 WK			3 WK			4 WK		
HOUSTON, TEXAS	OCAW			2 WK		3 WK	4 WK			5 WK		
LAWRENCE, KAN.	ICW		1 WK	2 WK			3 WK			4 WK		
MIDDLEPORT, N.Y.	IAM		1 WK		2 WK		3 WK			4 WK		
MIDDLEPORT N.Y.	OEIU	1 WK	2 WK				3 WK			4 WK		
MODESTO, CAL.	ICW		1 WK	2 WK			3 WK			4 WK		
NITRO, W. VA.	UMW50		1 WK 40HR	2 WK 80HR			3 WK 120HR			4 WK 160HR	5 WK 200HR	
RICHMOND, CAL.	IAM		1 WK	2 WK			3 WK			4 WK		
VANCOUVER, WASH	ICW		1 WK	2 WK			3 WK					
CHICAGO, ILL.	USA	1 WK 20HR	1 WK 40HR		1 WK 60HR	2 WK 80HR	2 WK 100HR		3 WK 120HR		4 WK 160HR	
COLUMBUS, OHIO	USA		1 WK 40HR			2 WK 80HR			3 WK 120HR			
EUGENE, OREGON	IAM		1 WK	2 WK								

Figure 2 Vacation schedules and pay—FMC Corporation.

the computer. Figure 2 shows one of the techniques the IUD has utilized to provide a quick tabulation of prevailing conditions, in this case, the amount of vacation after specific years of service. The variations are not great; but clearly from the array, each local union can spot where its vacation clause lags behind those of other plants of FMC.

And on the single sample page we have reproduced here, all the locals are made quickly aware of the fact that, of the seventeen separate plant locations listed on the sample sheet, in only two were the workers covered by a clause which allows five weeks of vacation with pay.

Depending upon the collective bargaining needs at this particular company, a great many more comparisons are possible. Again, many are similar to those discussed in the overall contract comparison section involving regional tabulations or tabulations by industry, size of plant, and so on.

Company-Plant Information File

Almost a prerequisite to determining organizational status at the many plants of the new diversified corporations so common on the American industrial scene was the need to develop a listing identifying each plant and its location. The need for such a listing has prompted another kind of computerized program, one focusing on plant information, including product, size, type of bargaining unit, and union involved. Providing such a listing to members of a co-ordinated bargaining conference group serves several purposes. One, it provides an overview of the corporation, its bargaining relationships, its industrial mix, and so on; and two, it identifies those locations for which bargaining agent information is not available and thereby acts as an aid in the research effort to get a complete picture of the organizational status at each and every facility of the company. A sample from the file on American Standard, Inc. is shown in Figure 3.

We are also linking a number of our other files, such as NLRB election results, NLRB unfair labor practice charges, and contract analysis, to the corporation plant survey material. The new file can provide a broad union-status, industrial relations picture of the firm.

NLRB Election History — The Case of General Electric

The availability of NLRB information on election history has been put to good use in numerous individual company situations.

PLANT NAME AND LOCATION	UNION NAME	LOCAL	SIZE OF UNIT	TYPE OF UNIT	SIC NUMBERS
AMERICAN STANDARD INC BALTIMORE MD — PLUMBING & HEATING	UAW IAW TCWH	344 186 311	565 75	P&M MAINT	34310
AMERICAN STANDARD INC BUFFALO NY — INDUSTRIAL DIV	USA	897	200	P&M	34431
AMERICAN STANDARD INC BUFFALO NY — PLUMBING & HEATING	USA USA	4537 1199	135 790	GUARDS TECH P&M	33214 34331
AMERICAN STANDARD INC AERO RESEARCH — ADVANCED TECHNOLOGY CHICAGO ILL					36430 36740
AMERICAN STANDARD INC COLUMBUS OHIO — INDUSTRIAL DIV	UAW	667	437	P&M	34336 35641 35851
AMERICAN STANDARD INC DEARBORN MICH — INDUSTRIAL DIV	UAW UAW	254 254	550 85	P&M TECH OTHER	35641 35642 35854
AMERICAN STANDARD INC DETROIT MICH — CONTROLS DIV	UAW	174	620	P&M OFFICE	36220 36216
AMERICAN STANDARD INC ELYRIA OHIO — AIR CONDITIONING	IMAW OPEIU	268 177		P&M OFFICE	34332 34336 35857
AMERICAN STANDARD INC HUNTLAND TENN — PLUMBING & HEATING					
AMERICAN STANDARD INC KEWANEE ILL — INDUSTRIAL DIV	BBF IMAW	195 134	350 16	P&M ENCRS MAINT	34335 34336 6392
AMERICAN STANDARD INC KOKOMO INDIANA — **IBOP MASTER CONTRACT 1 PLUMBING & HEATING	IBOP	26		P&M	32610
AMERICAN STANDARD INC LOUISVILLE KY — PLUMBING & HEATING	ATC BMP IMAW	1 8	168 PLO12 PLO12	ATC ATC	34310 34320

Figure 3　IUD data center major corporation survey — plants and organizational status.

In many of these, one or more unions have contracts covering a group of plants, or divisions of plants, within the corporation.

Take General Electric, for example. In the course of the coordinated bargaining effort of 1966, it became clear that, despite long years of negotiations with the corporation and the assembling of great quantities of material by many of the unions, there were gaps in the knowledge of the status of union representation at a number of the plants.

Typical of the bargaining relations at many highly diversified companies manufacturing a wide variety of products, there were dozens of different unions within General Electric's vast operations. Those unions which had organized certain plants obviously knew the extent of their bargaining jurisdictions. But a complete picture of the union status at every other plant of General Electric was unavailable.

More than that, it was exceptional for any one union to know of all the drives then being conducted at unorganized plants of the corporation, and which unions were carrying out such organizing efforts. With expansions, construction of new units, and acquisitions of other facilities all occurring at a rapid pace, the lack of comprehensive, complete, detailed information was understandable.

Also, the history of the organizational drives at any plant might be well known to the union or unions which had attempted to win an election there; but, again, the overall, full picture of union organizational activities at each and every facility of the corporation was not available to many of the unions which now have representation rights in some units of the corporation.

To be sure, if over the years the records of each organizing drive and each election at a General Electric plant had been sent by the union involved to a central office, it would have been possible to construct the detailed, comprehensive organizing history mentioned above. Through such a cooperative centralizing activity, the data on each plant's location, size, products manufactured, time of the election, and the petitioning union could have been reviewed and analyzed, and would have provided the basis for developing future organizing plans.

Even on a current basis, to keep track of all union organizing activities at the widely dispersed facilities of General Electric would entail excessive and lengthy communications. For it was not unusual in recent years to find eight, ten, or more international unions attempting to win representation rights at GE plants. But, as a matter of fact, most of the unions are not equipped with large enough research staffs and other facilities to have undertaken such analyses on their own.

Through the election history which the IUD developed from the NLRB records, it was possible to develop quickly and completely a report on more than six years of organizing activities at the GE Corporation. With the eleven key international unions and the information each of them had on the plants where each held bargaining rights, we were able to develop the most comprehensive overview of organizational status and election history.

For a recent twelve-month period, for example, we found that there were thirty-one separate elections held involving eight different international unions, covering over seven thousand employees of the corporation, in sixteen states. The specific details on each of the thirty-one elections which we have been able to present to the unions can help shape future organizing strategies and efforts.

This most recent history is supplemented by a longer range look at what has been happening in organizing drives in the corporation. As examples, we show in Tables 1 and 2 the historical election data at one plant, and then a portion of the one-year election survey covering the three states of Florida, Illinois, and Indiana.

The Shelbyville, Indiana, example outlines the successive efforts made by three different international unions to win bargaining rights among the production and maintenance workers at that factory. The details reveal the votes each union got, the change in the size of the bargaining unit, and the trend of pro-union sentiment over the years.

Since, under NLRB regulations, representation elections can be held only once every twelve months, the dates on the table of recent elections provide a timetable reference of when next a union could seek an election at each plant which remains unorganized.

Use of EDP by Individual Unions for Collective Bargaining

The IAM's Experience

Not long ago a Sunday newspaper magazine supplement ran a rather amusing story of how a computer reviewed and evaluated the essays of a group of high school students. The computer reported on each essay, pointing out its weak and strong points. In a number of respects, the International Association of Machinists' EDP program can indeed perform a similar function in reviewing

Table 1　NLRB Election History — General Electric, Shelbyville (Indiana) Plant. Cases closed July 1961 through June 1967.

Product	Date	Eligible Employees	Unit	Union	Votes For	Votes Against
Heating equipment and plumbing fixtures	2/63	473	P&M	IUE	155	288
	11/64	442	P&M	IAM	179	224
	12/65	491	P&M	IAM	207	250
	5/67	653	P&M	SMW	235	334

Table 2　NLRB Election History — General Electric. Cases closed July 1966 through June 1967.

State and City	SIC No.	Mo/Year	Bargaining Unit		Won or Lost	Union	Votes	
			Type	Eligible to Vote			For	Against
Florida								
Daytona Beach	367	6/67	P&M	404	L	IBEW	110	162
Jacksonville	361	8/66	P&M	26	W	IUE	18	4
Largo	381	6/67	P&M	547	L	IAM	139	363
Miami	363	7/66	OTHER	3	W	IUE	3	0
Miami	363	7/66	OTHER	28	W	IUE	19	6
Illinois								
Morrison	361	11/66	P&M	1594	L	IUE	415	1040
Indiana								
Shelbyville	343	5/67	P&M	653	L	SMW	235	334

contracts. The IAM has had long experience with contract analysis operation involving the use of EDP equipment.

The IAM contract staff summarizes agreements which are received at its international headquarters. Details are presented through a computerized system on a standard preprinted form covering a wide range of contract provisions with many of their main features. The forms and their wealth of contract facts enable the union to answer quickly and effectively questions about individual contracts and their specific clauses. As part of an elaborate EDP system, the agreement material can be arranged and presented in innumerable ways, similar to the description of the techniques used by the IUD program.

For example, when an IAM representative wishes to know about the contracts for breweries, since he is about to bargain at a brewery plant, he is sent a selection of contract forms which enables him to see exactly what is in effect at some of the key competitive breweries in the same and/or other areas of the country.

Besides this kind of contract information furnished upon request, having a computer memory bank of the details of contracts enables the IAM to publish regularly a wide variety of contract reports and summaries. In many ways these publications provide an important educational and training function. New staff members assigned to a particular region or industry or company can get a comprehensive view of agreements for the units they will be serving. For example, a representative for the New England area might receive from the IAM Research Department a listing of the companies under contract to the IAM in the state where he will be headquartered. If his duties carry him to adjoining states, similar information for those areas is available. He might well receive some summary tables showing the industry mix in the area, the prevailing contract provisions for a large number of separate, individual contract items, key wage rates, wage increases, and similar information.

The union holds many different industry meetings each year — brewery, atomic energy, aerospace, electronics, and so on. And in conferences such as these, the union officials typically receive, among other materials, extended reports on collective bargaining in their industries.

For example, at a recent electronics session, the industry was divided into major subgroups. Contracts were then grouped by electrical machinery, radio and TV, communications equipment, and by electronic components. Included in contract information were the following: one, the average wage increases for the current year, as well as for the two previous calendar years, grouped into nine categories — under 3 cents an hour, 3 cents to 5 cents an hour, and so forth up to 20 cents an hour and over; two, the number and percentage of agreements in each category; and three, the number and percentage of employees in each category. For each industrial grouping, the average wage increase was shown in either cents per hour or in percentage terms.

As for contract provisions themselves, here are some provisions which are printed out on the computer-prepared sheets: union security; minimum report pay and call-in pay; hours of work in the standard work week; overtime pay; Saturday, sixth day, and holiday pay; shift differentials; vacations; duration of agreement; travel time; and worker rights in case of automation and technological changes.

There are many other bargaining situations where the IAM's system is efficient and effective. Take the case of the approximately two thousand contracts the union holds with auto repair shops. Information about working conditions and wages in these shops is selected by the criteria of area, size, or other factors which either the negotiator and/or technical staff deems most pertinent.

Or take the case of International Harvester. This corporation's major manufacturing plants are organized by the United Automobile Workers (UAW). But throughout the country, in about ninety service stations carrying on maintenance and repair work, are mechanics for whom the IAM bargains. What the computerized contract survey system allows the IAM to do is to pull together these ninety separate agreements, each a relatively small unit, and list the key contract provisions for each. The EDP operation then summarizes the material which enables the negotiator to compare readily the provisions at the particular location where he is bargaining with other company service stations.

The surveys for individual companies in many ways are similar to the coordinating collective bargaining contract analysis of the IUD, though the latter always involves the additional complication of covering multiple union situations.

Intercity differentials which are exposed by this kind of analysis are readily identified; and, as a result, union negotiators are in a stronger bargaining position. It would be unrealistic to expect an IAM representative in a Missouri facility of a firm to know precisely the terms of employment in the New York plants of that same company. However, with the computerized system, this information is on tape and can be readily produced and made available to him.

While a manual analysis operation is still the first essential step in handling the more than eight thousand separate IAM agreements, all subsequent processing is done electronically. The volume of individual requests answered and the number of regular and special reports produced would all have to be sharply reduced if the EDP system were stopped. Less sophisticated techniques to retrieve, sort, and tabulate contract data would take such an enormous amount of time that it would clearly not be feasible to do as much of this work as is currently the case. Pressures to comply with special requests, which so frequently arise, would virtually foreclose the kind of regular publication of company, industry, area, and other types of bargaining reports.

Just what are the time differences involved? A good illustration is furnished by a railroad survey which it was essential to compile several years ago. At that time, the report on the contracts in the industry, with their wage and other clauses carefully tabulated in various forms, took several months to compile. And this was after the agreements had already been processed by the IAM contract staff and handwritten summary sheets were available. A similar study handled recently through the computer processing procedure took only minutes!

Experience of Other Unions

Some of the illustrations from the IAM experience have counterparts in the work being done by a number of other industrial unions. So far, these other unions have not progressed as far in developing computerized contract analysis service. They do, however, have in operation a number of programs of contract analysis research that are at various stages in the overall range of research methods possible — from completely manual systems at one end to fully computerized analysis at the other.

While we at the IUD have been seeking new ways to expand the effectiveness and capability of our own EDP system, these unions are taking similar steps. The United Steelworkers' Union, for example, which has been using mostly a punch card technique for analyzing its over 3,500 agreements, has now introduced new computer equipment with high speed capability. Such equipment promises to make it possible for the union to furnish contract information on a far more comprehensive and frequent basis.

The International Brotherhood of Electrical Workers (IBEW), as another example, has a computer installation for various union financial and administrative functions, and is delving into the potentials of applying the technology to collective bargaining purposes. The Communications Workers of America are actively planning and programming for conversion of their current methods of handling all records and reports to the most modern high speed computer.

But the IUD affiliates do not have to wait for that day when each will have at its own headquarters equipment capable of preparing the kinds of reports now being generated through the IUD's EDP system. We have been using our equipment to help any union which wishes to prepare contract analysis reports for its own locals, like those of the IAM, by area, industry, and other relevant characteristics.

Here is an example of this service. The Textile Workers Union of America (TWUA) was holding a conference for the officers of its locals in some sixty-five plants in the weaving industry. For those sessions, a comparative contract analysis tabulation was desired. The TWUA research staff made the analysis of the contracts tailored to requirements selected by the union. The handwritten entries made on the IUD's forms were then transferred to magnetic tape; and, utilizing a computer program, a special report was run in minutes. That kind of service is available to each of the IUD-affiliated unions, both small and large.

We have been experimenting with other types of programs as well. Some are now fairly well developed and involve assisting an individual union in carrying out internal record-keeping and related chores.

One IUD affiliate for some time had hoped to create a careful inventory of its 1,200 local bargaining units by such factors as region, type of operation, and hiring rate for administrative and policy purposes. This is obviously not a complex venture, but for a small union with limited resources it proved more than its staff could attempt. After some investigation, we were able to develop a program utilizing our EDP equipment which more than met the original needs of the union.

That program illustrates well how the capability of computer technology greatly expanded the usefulness of some basic raw data; and, in this case, also performed at very low cost a function that otherwise could not feasibly be handled. A whole series of listings of the products of the company plant at which the local holds bargaining rights, the minimum rate paid, the expiration dates of the contracts, and so forth, have been made for the local union. The various lists, summaries, and other tabulations are being carefully reviewed and analyzed for internal union and bargaining functions. Some of these reports, unavailable heretofore, may also have a special impact on fair labor standards legislation, particularly since the exemptions under that act have special importance for this union.

As was true for our contract analysis programs, other unions can capitalize on the programming done for these reports. They, too, can obtain the same kind of detailed tabulations in combinations geared to their internal administration and needs.

Some Other Computer Applications

A number of additional applications of computer technology should be mentioned, even briefly, to indicate some of the potentials.

One of the current key issues which unions have been pressing before the NLRB involves remedies for workers whose employers have been found guilty of failure to bargain in good faith, thereby delaying consummation of the first contract. A search of the computerized NLRB election history data provided speedily a careful selection of situations, in terms of pertinent time periods and unions involved, which then could be checked for material supporting the union arguments.

A similar aid was provided some union organizers who wanted a listing of election wins in two southern states during a past two-year period. Here, the list generated was in the form of a card file, with each card containing the data from the memory bank, plus a questionnaire design to be used for supplementary checking.

Another use of our election history file has been to furnish regular reports to each of the sixty IUD unions of their own representation elections. They represent only the first steps of a far more intensive look into election results which we feel can now be feasibly undertaken. A complementary tool in this research is a newly developed file of seventy thousand unfair labor practice charges filed before the NLRB over the past six years.

Our discussion here of the union contract pertained essentially to the content of its provisions. We also recognize, however, that the manner in which these provisions are administered, particularly for certain clauses, deserves equal attention. How grievances and arbitration cases are resolved influences significantly the industrial relations environment. Libraries of laws and legal decisions, on a computer basis, are multiplying. Perhaps the computer capability offers some promise in the administration of contract areas also.

A completely different venture, one which the IAM is exploring, involves the profile of a union. The IAM membership card contains the worker's age, time he joined the union, skill category, residence, local union, and so on. Computerizing such facts will give the officers, promptly, a real insight into trends in the composition of the organization's membership.

Clearly, much more is possible. Without going into the more advanced telecommunication systems which would enable each union to have instantaneous access to the "bank" of contract data, there is much that can be done to broaden the use of computer technology for bargaining purposes. As more of our affiliated unions either install their own EDP equipment or work cooperatively with our systems, the opportunity for greater and more effective interchange of data will expand. Similarly, as the number of contracts and the scope of provision coverage increases, the system should create an ever stronger base of information.

Elaboration and Discussion

Ginsburg The topic "The Computer's Uses and Potential in Bargaining" is a rather broad one; and I want to start right off by saying, and this is in consonance with many of the remarks in the other papers, that we do not see the computer as any substitute, particularly in the direct collective bargaining confrontation, for the judgments which the parties themselves are eminently qualified to make and which are determined by many factors other than the facts alone.

Seeing that I have had a little hand in the development of the whole system, I wish I could say that since we began disseminating information through the use of electronic data processing procedures that wage settlements and fringe settlements have been appreciably higher than they were before. As a matter of fact, this is the case; but anyone who rushes to attach a cause and relation to this would, I think, be a little premature.

The 1966 General Electric negotiation was really one of the first in which we began to see whether or not we at the Industrial Union

Department, which is the central body for some sixty separate international unions, could provide some assistance in a coordinated way to assist the bargainers in their negotiations. One of the first tasks we undertook was to try to get data quickly, centering on the main features of the outstanding provisions in those key contracts which had bearing on the General Electric negotiations.

Now this isn't anything different from what the research staff of the IUD, or the research staffs of many of the other international unions, normally does. But after looking at the whole question of providing information for our sixty affiliates, we did think that we could improve the techniques we were using in the trade union movement for disseminating information, for gathering more information, for analyzing that information more effectively, and hopefully for providing more insights for use in collective bargaining.

Our first major effort was to see whether or not we could employ this new magical tool to further our potential in the whole collective bargaining arena. We tried in a very simple way, and I think here we had a very great advantage because we did start simply, to see if we could develop a technique that would be both inexpensive and yet at the same time further the needs of our affiliates. When I say a simple way, I mean we did not commit ourselves to buying any expensive equipment which would have immediately given us the onus of justifying that those people working on that equipment were producing a job that was worth keeping, that the investment had been worthwhile, and so on. Instead, we began almost entirely with software. Morris Rosenthal, one of our computer consultants, was our chief piece worker; and many of the international unions helped in trying to develop a format through which the unions could improve their exchange of information.

To a group as sophisticated as this conference, I don't think I have to say that collective bargaining agreements have become far more complex and cover a far wider area than ever before and that keeping track of what is going on everywhere is an ever-increasing burden on many international union research staffs. Not only do they have to keep track of what is going on, but they are constantly being asked for all kinds of specific information which might assist the collective bargaining efforts of a small union in a small plant in Illinois or a large international bargaining association dealing with several hundred thousand employees. While the major negotiations are the ones which get the focus of public attention and are on the front page, the day-to-day work in any research department in most international unions is perforce concerned with those many smaller local unions which are, in a sense, trying to follow the industry pattern or develop their own bargaining relationships with their employers. So we have tried to expand the large key negotiations, while at the same time developing material which would be helpful to the smaller individual union situation.

As you know, there are some 150,000 separate contracts written throughout the United States and these encompass about 130 international unions affiliated with the AFL-CIO. There are also about fifty or sixty independent unions. As these contracts get longer, and as more are written each year, the task of keeping track of them and finding out what is happening — and where — is obviously more complex.

I must say that in my twenty years of experience in the trade union movement, we have had excellent cooperation. When, for example, the Rubber Workers sent out a letter requesting assistance on strike information to twenty or thirty other key unions, they were able to get a fair amount of response to the key questions they were interested in. But you can't constantly be doing ad hoc research and accumulating information for a specific set of negotiations; in effect, having many, many people retread or retill the same ground. So what we tried to do, having explored some of the potential, was to get some twenty of the key international unions, the largest of those affiliated with the IUD, to come to several planning sessions and see if we could not get together among ourselves and decide — subject to change at any time — what were the key items of information we were interested in having from the contracts which were in effect in these key international unions.

As you might expect, what we found as we developed this was that each international had its particular problems. We got a reiteration of the fact, so well known, that collective bargaining is peculiar to a particular kind of industry, peculiar to a particular area, and so on. While some of the researchers at the meeting kept saying, "Let's not ask each other for too much because it will make the job more onerous," others said in response to a particular item, "Let's add the details on this one."

For example, in the chemical and oil unions, they were tremendously interested in rotating shifts, tremendously interested in what happens on continuous operations. Although they wanted other sections of the contract analysis shortened, they wanted those sections expanded. In the Telephone Workers Union, the researchers from that union felt there were specific conditions that applied only to utilities, and to the telephone industry in particular, and that these weren't applicable to the rest of industry. Naturally they wanted that section of the analysis which dealt with their unique problems expanded. Quite understandably, each person wanted those issues that most pertained to his bargaining to be expanded.

Through this give-and-take process, we boiled the list down to some twenty-one major issues; and on each of these major issues, maybe ten or fifteen separate items. I guess we came up with about five hundred to a thousand separate features in a collective bargaining agreement. We are still in the process of revising this list because, after we had made our first survey, everybody saw places where we had asked too much and other places where we had asked too little. So we are still reworking, remolding, and reshaping and we know that this will take some time.

There were several major goals which we had in mind that we accomplished. First, we are getting even greater cooperation among our own union research people. This is only an internal administrative matter, but we think it is helpful. We are now getting a better exchange of information through the centralization of some of the kinds of things I have been talking about.

The second thing we are doing, particularly for the moderate and middle-sized international unions, is to help them to revise their own systems. In the past, each international union has done this on an ad hoc basis in terms of its own needs, and many of the systems they have devised have contained numerous shortcuts. The attempt to systematize and obtain information quickly has been going on in many of the international unions and many of them have devised a variety of ingenious ways for handling the enormous amount of detail in the collective bargaining agreements they have. We were at the American Amalgamated Clothing Union last week and the researcher said to us, "I have been here a long time and we are faced with so many requests that I now have eighty-six form letters which I use. I try to fit the requests we get into one of these form letters, so that we don't have to go through the laborious process of looking up things, checking things, and then formulating new correspondence. If a request comes in of a certain type, we immediately scan to see if it fits one of these eighty-six form letters. Of course, unfortunately, a great number do not."

For our contract analysis, we started out with what we considered to be 200 key contracts; and of these, 150 are in the manufacturing area and 50 in nonmanufacturing. Obviously, this reflects our own particular bias. Being the Industrial Union Department, virtually all of our membership is in manufacturing and related activities; but we did try to get a sense of what was happening in the rest of the country, and so fifty of the contracts are from the nonmanufacturing segment of industry.

We now have in our magnetic tape file over two hundred major contracts, each of which covers over five thousand workers. This means that over three million workers and their conditions of employment, at least as far as the main features are concerned, are now on tape. We have been able to go from the concept of very large-scale bargaining, whether it be GE or United Rubber, to being able to retrieve information very quickly and perform special kinds of studies and analysis for particular groups. One of the things that we feel makes this system worthwhile is the kind of requests that we are getting for information. These requests are for information which people indicate was not available before; or, if available, it was not being gathered together and worked on because of manpower, time, or financial considerations.

The Textile Workers, for example, ran a special conference for a group of their cotton plants in certain states. With their assistance on some of the input and on some of the analysis, we were able to develop a special comparative contract analysis program for them for sixty-five local unions. For plants in Illinois, where there was some special organizing activity, we were able to extract from our very large sample of these two hundred major contracts the plans for those companies that were located in Illinois. If need be, we could identify and focus on the plants of the two largest companies in the Chicago area, and, within these plants, on any of the twenty-one basic provisions. In effect, we have established a library of data, a data bank; and, with the programs that have been developed, we can extract any number of specific items, be they in terms of the size of the plant, the union involved, the area involved, or the fringe benefit involved, for anyone who faces a collective bargaining issue related to that item.

Of course, this is a two-way street. The person doing the bargaining frequently may not be aware that other data are available which might buttress his case, so we still are in the process of a lot of two-way communication about what is needed. As each of the new studies which we issue gets out into the field — and we are issuing major studies at least every six months — the requests we get back in the IUD start showing that people want new ways for arrangement of the information, new ways of seeing how certain items compare, and new ways for seeing how what they have compares with what others have.

Besides this bank of two hundred major contracts, one of the other major fields in the collective bargaining area is the work the IUD has been doing in coordinating bargaining. As you all know, the very rapid rise of corporate diversification and the rapid rise in the number of conglomerates, with the crossing of product lines and industry lines, has been characteristic of this postwar era. We are attempting to pull together the many unions who face a particular employer and see if we can't put some sense in the various contract provisions, which in many cases vary considerably from plant to plant and from division to division. We presently have some eighty of these company committees working through the IUD.

I am not saying that we are seeking uniformity per se; but we are at least trying on certain key issues, particularly on such things as pension and welfare benefits which apply quite broadly to a whole company, to achieve some uniformity. We are starting with some of these broad issues and seeing if we can't get at least some greater uniformity here.

When you bargain with corporations that have been growing at the tremendous pace that many of them have been in this postwar period, it is difficult to keep up with such things as who has a contract with this company at Plant X, how many unions are involved in the various different contracts, how many plants are organized, and so on. Just keeping track of one major company, like Ling-Temco-Vought which I referred to in my paper, is quite a burdensome job; and with fifteen different research departments all working independently, there are bound to be duplications. What we have tried to do is pull all of these efforts together and coordinate them. We now have at least five hundred separate agreements with these large conglomerates and the number goes up by at least a hundred a month. We are getting the specific details on the contracts which each of the unions has with the company in question — in the case of LTV there are five separate international unions involved — and are trying to organize them.

We have also found that there are many other side benefits that we are getting from our research work which have proved useful. One of these things has been the development of something which will help to attain uniform expiration dates. In my paper I used the example of FMC. Of the thirty-seven contracts which I took as a sample, there were twenty-eight different expiration dates which unions had to face and take into consideration when they dealt with FMC. Being able to put this information together quickly and rapidly and in the order that we wanted, and being able to present it to the so-called company committees or their bargaining committees, has proved to be extremely useful. I think it has given the people in the bargaining committees not only an appreciation of this new research tool, but it also gives them for the first time a better feeling on what is happening in coordinated bargaining as far as knowing what is going on throughout the company. Before, we used to do this by hand and we have cut the time it takes to prepare these kinds of reports down to a third; and as each report is developed, we see even greater opportunities in broadening our coverage and getting even more analysis and interpretation accomplished.

One of the strangest uses to which we put some of our material, strange in a sense that it may sound negative from the union's standpoint, was in a very important strike held a year ago. We were able to demonstrate to the union bargaining committee that one of their demands didn't really make sense in terms of the total overall package. The leadership had achieved a substantial package and were willing to settle, but some of the key personnel felt that a contract of short duration still had to be a part of the package. It was the stumbling block. Now short duration contracts are an ingrained part of this industry's collective bargaining relationship and in a sense there is no mechanistic way you can change it. But we were able to take the two hundred large contracts we had and make a simple run on the average duration of these contracts, showing all those of less than two years' duration, all those of two to three years', and all those of over three years'. And this took us no more than a day or two to do. This simple tabulation, added to a lot of other facts, to be sure, was instrumental in bringing the bargaining committee around to the point that, even though the package did contain this somewhat unseemly element, it wasn't out of line with other contracts. The committee could go back to their representatives in the plants, and to the stewards and the rank and file, and explain, "Yes, this is a departure; but here is the basis for it and here is how it is done elsewhere."

It is important, of course, for collective bargaining committees to be fortified with the facts necessary to support their point of view. But they should also be informed when some of their views and some of their demands at certain points are beyond what has normally been done before, and when they are beyond typical industry or comparable industrial group patterns. I am not saying I want to be a damper on new ideas or retard the pushing forward and breaking of new ground; but at least such information gives the key negotiators the facts and figures to bolster their position when they feel they are behind and possibly to modify their demands when it appears they are pressing too far ahead.

Another thing I would like to emphasize is, while those of you from the companies may feel that we in the trade union movement know every single thing about every single plant in the United States, this assumption is just a little bit amiss. I remember having lunch not long ago with somone who just assumed that we had a kind of wall map in our office with little pins indicating every unorganized plant along with information on the size of it, the organization to which that unorganized plant belonged, who had attempted to organize it, and what was their success in trying to sign up members. He just couldn't conceive that a trade union organization the size of what we have in the United States isn't able to do this.

Well, maybe someday we will, but right now there are very few unions which are in a position to identify those plants within their jurisdiction that are not organized and to determine what has been the history of organizational efforts within those companies. We have our turnover in the trade union movement just as anyone else does, and a representative who well may have known the situation in a plant two or three years ago is not always the representative conducting the current organizing campaign.

I use these remarks as an introduction to an additional major phase of what we are trying to do in our computer work at the IUD; that is, to develop a comprehensive file on the union status and industrial relations activities of companies on a plant-by-plant basis. As our source, we have been working with the NLRB records which, since July of 1961, have come out as monthly reports of representation elections. The elections which have been held since July 1961 now number over seventy thousand; and in this same period, thirty-five to forty-five thousand new bargaining units have been established as a result of those elections. Unfortunately, these reports were in a form where it was very difficult for anyone to work with them in a comprehensive way or to cut through them to get at specifics. The NLRB itself was very happy to cooperate with us because we were able to give them their first alphabetical listing of these elections. For us, we were able to organize the information not only by company but also by industry. And again, in each of these things you will notice I am talking about the many different arrangements we were able to make with the data to increase their usefulness — something which could have been done before but which would have taken so much hand labor that it wouldn't have been done.

Strangely enough, requests for information from this file have become one of the biggest demands we have at the IUD. Such questions as, has there ever been an election at a certain plant, who won, what unions were involved, and so on, are typical. In the past, answering such things was very laborious and time consuming. A representative would usually drop a note to the research department of his own international who would in turn drop notes to fifteen or twenty other unions who might have organizations in that industry. Or he could go in and collar somebody at the door as he came out and ask, "Is there a union here? Do you know if there have ever been other unions in this plant? Do you know if the company has other plants around the country with unions?" We are trying to pool the great amount of information which is in file drawers and research offices around the country and centralize it conjointly with such things as the NLRB information.

The NLRB, besides conducting some eight to nine thousand elections each year, also gets involved in some fifteen thousand unfair labor practices each year. We have tried to add this element to the file. In effect, what we are trying to do is build a body of information which will give us a complete profile on a particular plant: which union is there; the size of the plant; the products of the plant; other divisions of that same company which are organized; key contract provisions at each of these plants; how these stack up against other key contract provisions in the area or in the industry nationwide; how this company has behaved in terms of its basic industrial relations; what kinds of unfair practices have been filed; what the effect of the unfair practices has been on arriving at an agreement; and, if there is no bargaining unit right now, what the history of organizing attempts in the past has been and which unions have been involved in such organizing attempts.

As before, there are secondary benefits we get from such data. Take the case of elections won. In the South, as you probably are aware, one of the biggest problems the union has to face after winning an election is the problem of gaining the first contract. We have had greater success in winning elections in the South than ever before; but even after the elections are won, this does not mean that we can negotiate a contract. The employers have utilized the many procedures of the NLRB to delay, delay, delay the final consummation of that first contract. Now we are able to focus on a particular state or a particular company and track where elections were won and then subsequently where contracts were negotiated and where contracts were not negotiated.

For example, in the case of the Ex-Cello plant, we were able to develop a measure of the wage gains at other plants in that industry during the period that Ex-Cello was not negotiating with the union and trying to reach a contract agreement, even though the UAW had won bargaining rights. Since that span was a year and a half, we were trying to find what the workers at that particular plant were theoretically denied in the absence of having a contract. We were able to take all the elections which the UAW had won in the same period that the Ex-Cello election was won and go back to those contracts that were negotiated and see what the wage gains were in those first contracts. We came up with some figures which were presented to the NLRB which was, in effect, the equity that the workers in this particular plant had been denied as a result of no contract having been consummated during this protracted period. I think we were able to make a significant contribution in being able to quantify, at least to some extent, the losses that these people sustained.

In another example, as we have alerted different researchers to the capabilities of the IUD programs we have, we also tried to give them a few notions of how they can organize some of their own internal administrative material which concerns each of their local unions. One example in particular involved the Woodworkers Union, where there are some 1,200 separate unions. Here is a union which operates with just one research director and two staff personnel to assist him; he tries to keep track of what is happening in all of these 1,200 locals. The director had planned to spend about a year and a half of clerical time to get the data he wanted, organized in the form he wanted. By systematizing, we were able to cut the cost to something like one-fifth of what he had planned to spend and yet provide him with a series of listings which he finds particularly useful.

In sawing and logging, saw mills of less than a certain size are not covered by the minimum wage law. We were able to prepare for presentation to Congress a ready-made wage scale analysis in support of changes in the law when it comes up for review. Both the SLAA and we at the IUD think it is very powerful and convincing. This had nothing to do with trade union bargaining as such, but it again shows one of the new facets we have been exploring and developing and one which is proving to be useful in helping the researchers carry on their day-to-day work.

I think we see that a heightened interest is developing now in the whole EDP operation, as more unions are looking into its potential and more unions are seeking ways to computerize their data as well as some of their administrative tasks. Since we have developed a kind of standard format, we feel we are getting a far greater body of data which are quickly retrievable, usable, and interchangeable, making them available when you want them and in the form you want them.

Straus Maybe this is an overgeneralization, but if I hear you correctly, other than helping you to run your department and in getting data together as preparation for negotiations, you haven't really used the computers in the sense of sitting down at the bargaining table and using computers for data retrieval and in trying to see what the other fellow is up to, have you?

Ginsburg No, they have only been used in presenting evidence in support of demands in the bargaining situation. Some unions have built models of their Supplemental Unemployment Benefits plans or pension costs, but we haven't yet tried to cost out complete packages. We are only at the stages which involve the preparation and development of data for the bargainers' use.

Straus Have you ever presented information from your computers that was used at the bargaining table and had it challenged by the computer of the enemy?

Ginsburg Frankly, no, but the IBEW's bargaining committee has found its computerized presentation particularly effective. In one case they took out their sheets and said, "Here are the data on the twenty key firms competing with you (the company they were facing at the bargaining table)." The company challenged the presence of a cost-of-living clause in a particular plant. The union bargainer responded, "Just a minute," — and, with a bit of glamour and showmanship no doubt — he opened up a computer printout and said, "This is what our computer run showed." The company went back and checked it; and, in this case, our computer happened to be right.

Myers   In reading your paper and in listening to your comments, I get the feeling that information retrieval of this sort makes for more effective bargaining by the committee. There is a certain parallel on the management's side to the extent that with better data — data which are more available and more systematic — management is relieved of some of its routine, structured work. It would seem that your bargaining committees would be more effective if they have better and more inclusive data.

Ginsburg   I would agree with that completely. I think anyone who has looked at research activities within the trade union movement knows that it is an enormous task just to keep pace with what management is doing. When you have a small research department in a small union, it becomes an overwhelming task just to be able to prepare a brief financial report or a brief wage comparison report for bargaining. When I was with the UAW, there were twenty persons there; and we dealt with 3,300 separate concerns with 3,300 separate contracts. Any one company can make these analyses for itself, and when the chief company bargainer comes in, he knows what is being done at General Motors or Chrysler or Firestone or Uniroyal or General Electric or Westinghouse; but what about the union bargainer? It is an enormous task to keep track of all the different locals and provide the union with the same kind of information that the company has.

Penchansky   Isn't it quite possible that over time the basis for reaching decisions is going to change? If we start to look at a broader range of contracts, for instance your example of the multi-industry companies and the striving for uniformity, we find we have one corporation but twelve different industries and we must start looking at the wage setting and job decisions for all twelve of these industries. This should really begin to change the factors that are considered in the bargaining of contracts and may change the basis for reaching decisions.

Ginsburg There is an assumption in your question and comment. It is that we have been able to develop this so-called coordinated bargaining with one representative bargaining for some twelve or fifteen internationals. We still have not reached this stage yet. We have never been able to get a company to sit down and meet with one bargaining committee representing all of the unions involved. We are trying to get uniformity in major welfare benefits as a start and then uniformity in other key fringe benefits as the next step. Also, when you look at my FMC example and see twenty-eight different contract expiration dates within the company's thirty-seven plants, you know that it is very difficult, even within one division of the company, to muster any muscle against the company because even if you close down two or three plants, there are still six or seven in the same division making the same item.

George Taylor On expiration dates, you know the Chase Copper and Brass employees did not want the uniform expiration date as proposed by the rest of those in the industry. This was also true in a couple of other cases. In the end, this proved to be the clincher in objecting to such uniformity.

I feel somewhat like the fellow who sold horsewhips up in Lancaster, Pennsylvania. A fellow from Philadelphia came in and found this Pennsylvania Dutch place full of horsewhips. He said, "You must sell a lot of horsewhips." The fellow answered, "The fact of the matter is, I don't; but the fellow who sells horsewhips to me sure sells a lot."

Over the years you get various criteria being emphasized. At one time, cost of living had a big play. Then in a tight labor market on the downswing, the ability to pay, whether or not you are able to, becomes a factor. Now uniformity has become the factor. You have to watch this focusing of the spotlight on one particular item, which is what your activities tend to do. Such approaches tend to solidify positions; and what people don't realize is that this too, like all of the rest of the things in bargaining, is a tool of persuasion. And unless it is used as a tool of persuasion, it can make the actual agreement-making process all the more difficult. All of these items are but one of the series of factors, and maybe these matters should be considered before either side makes its position firm.

I think this thing called collective bargaining can be broken down into three steps. One, before you start to hammer out your differences, you should reach agreement on the facts which are applicable in this situation. This is especially important, I think, and it should be done before positions are taken, before feet get set into concrete. The second step is, of course, the actual bargaining itself. The third step is perhaps not pertinent to this discussion, but I would like to mention it anyway. This is, if the parties can't solve the substantive issues after a direct analysis of the data, perhaps there should be a third phase of collective bargaining in which there would be some mutually agreed upon procedure, other than a strike, which would serve as basis for settlement.

Ginsburg   I certainly would subscribe to your first notion, Professor Taylor. But this has been rather hard to get, these long committee meetings before negotiations, these so-called study groups. I did serve on one with American Motors, where we went over all the age distributions and looked at the vacation allowances that were actually being paid, and who did and who did not work during their vacation, and so on. It helped all of us get some notion of how legitimate was the demand on vacation allowance. I think that this kind of thinking is very valuable. I agree with you that it serves a useful purpose.

Jirikowic   Insofar as our aerospace negotiations which come up this year are concerned, many of our committees are now working with the companies getting basic data on pensions, welfare, wage distributions, and so forth. There is no question this will serve to make for more intelligent proposals and gain a better understanding among our people. Whether or not these data will contribute to a peaceful settlement, no one knows; but it makes our committees much more knowledgeable.

Straus   Then why don't we speak out? If collective bargaining is not to be a hit or miss affair, if this is a desirable thing, why not say so and make the best use of the data available?

Ginsburg   Of course, you point out one thing that is very important; the lack of data that either side gets. This is especially true for foreign data and for domestic data on companies that are not organized or that have independent unions. If you ever want to go through a futile exercise sometime, try to find out wage cost data from somebody who is not organized.

George Taylor   Would you agree with the pre-position taking?

Ginsburg   If this were not an emotional process, yes; but I wouldn't at this stage because I don't think we have reached the point where people are that objective in their approach to it.

Cole   Wasn't the Human Relations Committee part of this fact-finding approach?

Ginsburg   Yes, and we are coming back to this idea to a degree. There is another name for it now; but, yes, it was what I am talking about and it was very successful.

Anonymous   A point has been raised that I think we ought to question. Let's assume we have reached the computer millennium and we have *all* of the relevant data. I think we have to ask ourselves how many times do you settle agreements on the basis of data or facts? It seems to me that logic has very little to do with this business. Even if we get all this information and know everything that exists in the world, I am not at all sure that this will necessarily advance the process.

Ginsburg   I think you are talking about a different level of industrial relations. You are talking about the day-to-day relations on the floor between the foreman and the shop steward.

Anonymous   No, I am talking about agreements at the bargaining table.

Caples   Where you have political factors such as the president of the union who wishes to keep his job.

Union Representative   Very frequently, facts are very useful for after-the-fact rationalization. After the agreement is made, you still have to get it approved by the membership in some way or another. I suppose, Charlie [Mason], that even with your exalted status, it helps you if you have some data to get across to your Board of Directors that the contract just negotiated is a pretty good agreement.

Mason   Are you talking of the airline situation in 1966, where we had lots of facts but didn't get a settlement? Are you talking of data used in reaching an agreement or data used to support the position you had when you started?

Union Representative   I am talking about its rationalizing use in getting the agreement accepted after the negotiating table — a very important part of the process.

Mason I agree.

Anonymous But the data don't get you the solution. It is the artfulness of the bargainer.

Ginsburg Just as it was the artfulness of the man who was able to swing his bargaining committee behind the demands for the longer contract.

Lesieur I wonder if this development of EDP has changed the role and function of the research departments in the IUD or in the individual international unions in any significant way. It seems to me that there are several possible things that may have happened, and they might well lead to different conclusions about where the significant decisions are now made in the trade union movement.

One view is that the researcher merely assumes the staff function as it was originally conceived, that of simply organizing and providing information to negotiators. If this is the case, perhaps there will now be fewer research people at the bargaining table than there used to be because you simply need to send the bargainers a tab run rather than to be there yourself with a file cabinet full of stuff. I remember the research director for the Locomotive Firemen who had a trunk he took with him to negotiations. He had to be there personally. Consequently, he had a far greater influence on the bargaining process than he might have had if he had merely stayed at international headquarters.

On the other hand, it may be that being able to organize the data the way you choose will have a more significant influence on the bargaining policies of the trade unions than may have been the case when your techniques were elementary and your information was scanty. You already have the machines and are developing highly detailed computer systems.

My own comment, let me quickly add, would be that we are not nearly at this stage of transforming the department or the way we operate. We are in the process of helping a number of negotiators do what they think is a more effective job.

Jirikowic As far as we're concerned, our purpose hasn't changed; but our use of the Univac has certainly changed the servicing of our field staff. We have approximately 9,000 different agreements with 15,000 employers in 200 industries. We have approximately 2,100 locals and 8,150 full-time staff people. We receive on the average of thirty to forty requests a week for data from our staff. If we used our former system, which was a key sort card, it would take days. We now use the computer for just two hours on Mondays, Wednesdays, and Fridays. As requests come in, an order is placed with our Univac and we receive the complete printout in short order. These printouts are a summary of the agreement, with about 200 to 220 different items checked, along with a complete wage schedule. This goes out to the representative and he can use them to buttress his demands or any other way he chooses.

It is because we are such a diversified union that this has particularly helped us. I would agree that these data play a much greater role in negotiations for a small union in, say, Boise, Idaho, servicing a shop of thirty or forty people than they do when we sit down to bargain with the airlines. This has served to make our representatives aware of what is available for their particular industry.

Going further, within a year or so, we will be providing our representatives with a complete profile of our membership within a particular city or within a particular shop. Our representatives move around a bit, and they want to know what our membership is like. So first, we will give them a summary of the agreements we have, by industry; then we intend to provide a profile of our membership, with such things as how old they are, how many children they have, and how long they have been in the union. Thus when a representative walks into an area, he will have a lot of good basic data rather than having to spend two or three months doing his own research.

Ginsburg   I find this profile idea fascinating. Not all unions — just a handful — have a membership card and other information from their membership which enables them to do this. Most unions are on a checkoff and that is their only contact with the international union. The IAM, for a variety of programs, especially their welfare programs, does get tremendously great amounts of data; and I daresay they know more about their membership, and the geographic nature of it, than anyone in the country.

The Computer's Uses and Potential in Bargaining: A Management View

William G. Caples

Introduction

The technological response to demands of physical systems and scientific-engineering applications in both the public and the private sector has been phenomenal in the past decade. A concomitant of this development has been the growth and refinement of information technology essential to the manipulation and communication of factual data. The precision of treatment and predictability of data in the physical sciences provided logical fields for computer applications in the past two decades.

The quantification, manipulation, and communication of data reflecting human action and interaction present a somewhat more difficult problem. Perhaps this accounts for the lag in computer utilization in the industrial relations field.

There can be no question of the fact that the computer has increasingly come to play a significant role in the management of American business. At the same time, it should be noted that its use has been uneven when viewed against the wide variety of possible applications. Only limited use has been made of EDP in industrial relations; and, as Charles Myers observed at the winter meeting of the Industrial Relations Research Association in 1966, ". . . the use of computers in preparing for collective bargaining is even newer. Possibly some firms have used computerized employee records to calculate costs of alternative management proposals or union demands, but I am not aware that any have access to data banks

69

containing information on what other firms have done in collective bargaining." [1]

Since we are at the threshold of possible expansion of information technology into the field of collective bargaining, it seemed to me that it would be most helpful to explore two principal areas: one, the current practice or state of the art in management's use of EDP in collective bargaining; and two, suggestions regarding current limitations and the prospects for future applications.

A search of the literature and a variety of personal contacts revealed that considerable attention has been given to the application of EDP to the general field of personnel administration.[2] There is no need on this occasion to review this material in depth, but I would like to call attention to two surveys in which reference was made — or significantly omitted — to applications to collective bargaining.

Bueschel,[3] for example, surveyed eighty-nine industrial firms, government agencies, and nonprofit institutions to determine actual and potential applications of data processing in the personnel department (broadly defined). Bueschel's primary interest was in the impact of real-time systems on the personnel function, but some of his findings are pertinent to our discussion.

Of the eighty-nine companies surveyed, about two-thirds had been using data processing for an average of three years. This fact may be somewhat misleading in terms of computer applications since about a third of this number were still using electric accounting machines (EAM). Data processing was being used extensively in the personnel function by about 25 percent of the companies surveyed. Of those not using data processing, fully two-thirds had plans to

[1] C. A. Myers, "Some Implications of Computers for Management," *Proceedings of the Nineteenth Annual Winter Meeting, Industrial Relations Research Association*, San Francisco, December 28–29, 1966, Madison, Wisconsin: The Association, 1967, p. 200.

[2] Barrie Austin, "The Role of EDP in Personnel," *Management of Personnel Quarterly*, Vol. 3, No. 4, Winter 1965, pp. 24–30; R. T. Bueschel, "How EDP Is Improving the Personnel Function," *Personnel*, September/October 1964, pp. 59–64; R. T. Bueschel, *Management Bulletin 86: EDP and Personnel*, American Management Association, 1966; R. T. Bueschel, "Real-time Data Processing for Industrial Relations," *Management of Personnel Quarterly*, Spring 1966, pp. 24–30; E. Lanham, "EDP in the Personnel Department," *Personnel*, March/April 1967, pp. 16–22; Julius Rezler, "Automation and the Personnel Manager," *Advanced Management Journal*, Vol. 32, No. 1, January 1967, pp. 76–81; University of California, Institute of Industrial Relations, *Electronic Data Processing and Personnel Management*, Los Angeles, California: The Institute, 1967.

[3] Bueschel, *supra*.

implement a program within a year. On the other hand, one in ten companies had no intention of using data processing.

Pertinent to the present inquiry is the frequency of use in these eighty-nine companies of EDP for labor relations. Seventeen companies, or 27 percent of the sample, reported using computers for "labor relations and seniority." This is substantially below the 82 percent who reported EDP applications for employee records and the 78 percent reporting uses for compensation purposes. In terms of other functional applications, 36 percent of the companies surveyed used EDP for skills inventory, 26 percent for employment, 18 percent for testing, 8 percent for attendance, 6 percent for personnel research, 4 percent for medical, and 3 percent for safety.

Elizabeth Lanham[4] surveyed 333 companies in a wide variety of industries to determine the impact of EDP on the personnel function. Of these firms, 254 utilized EDP in one or more phases of their operation. When it came to EDP applications in the personnel field, however, applications were much less frequent. Only 142 of the 254 EDP users were using it for personnel records and reports; 97 companies were planning to extend EDP to include personnel uses; and 94 of the 333 companies reported no EDP planning for personnel records and reports. Lanham's report referred to bargaining-related usage (e.g., grievance records, payroll analysis) but it did not reveal any specific applications to collective bargaining.

The Survey

In the absence of any systematic collection of data dealing with the applications of EDP to collective bargaining, we decided to conduct a questionnaire survey in an attempt to identify the state of the art in this specific field. The questionnaire was designed to obtain information regarding:

1. The availability of data for EDP processing.
2. Computer usage in preparation for bargaining.
3. Computer usage during bargaining.
4. Problems and limitations in the use of computers for bargaining and preparation for bargaining.
5. The use being made of computers by unions with which respondents were negotiating.
6. Their viewpoints regarding limitations and the prospects for use of computers in collective bargaining.

The survey sample was drawn from the firms listed in the 1967

---

[4] Lanham, "EDP in the Personnel Department."

Table 1   Distribution of Respondents by Company Size and Major Industrial Classification.

Industry Group	Number of Companies Solicited	Respondents with No Bargaining Unit Employees	Respondents by Letter: Do Not Use Computers in Bargaining	Respondents by Questionnaire: Number of Bargaining Unit Employees (in Thousands)						Total Respondents
				Under 10	10–24	25–49	50–99	100– Over	Sub- Total	
Manufacturing	100	3	16	15	17	12	8	3	55	74
Transportation	25		1	0	2	3	1	0	6	7
Finance	25	5		0	0	0	0	0	0	5
Utilities	25			2	3	1	0	0	6	6
Merchandising	25			0	0	0	0	1	1	1
Insurance	25	2	1	0	0	0	0	0	0	3
Totals	225	10	18	17	22	16	9	4	68	96

Fortune Directory; and it included the one hundred largest manu-facturing corporations, twenty-five transportation companies, twenty-five life insurance companies, twenty-five commercial banks, twenty-five merchandising organizations, and twenty-five utilities.

The Respondents

Replies were received from 96 of the 225 organizations included in the survey. As might be expected, the heaviest response came from industrial and manufacturing organizations. A detailed analysis of respondents by industry group in relation to company size meas-ured by number of bargaining unit employees can be found in Table 1.

You will also note that ten of the ninety-six reporting companies indicated that they had no collective bargaining agreements. An additional eighteen companies replied by letter stating that although labor agreements were negotiated, they made no use or only very limited use of computers in their bargaining. Three of these eighteen companies reported that they were exploring the use of computers for bargaining. Four others replied that bargaining was done locally at many different locations involving small numbers of employees. It was their feeling that the circumstances did not seem conducive to computer usage. It was not possible to include these companies in the cross-tabulations, but they will be considered later in the analysis.

Completed questionnaires were received from sixty-eight organiza-tions including fifty-five manufacturing corporations, six transporta-tion companies, six utilities, and one merchandising organization. The number of bargaining unit employees in these companies ranged from 2,500 to just over 400,000 employees. The median bargaining unit employment was approximately 22,000 employees.

Number of Unions

Presumably one of the important variables in determining com-puter usage in collective bargaining would be the number of unions involved in negotiations with a particular company. A simple tabu-lation (Table 2) indicates that responding companies negotiate with as few as one union in a single location to as many as eighty-five independent unions at as many locations.

Between these two extremes, however, the data are not as clear-cut. Some respondents reported only the names of international unions with whom they negotiated. Others reported in terms of local

Table 2   Number of Unions Dealt With, by Company Size (Number of Bargaining Unit Employees).

| Number of Unions | Number of Bargaining Unit Employees (in Thousands) | | | | | |
	Under 10	10–24	25–49	50–99	100– Over	Total
1	3	2	2	0	0	7
2–5	6	12	8	4	4	34
6–10	4	3	2	2	0	11
11–20	2	0	1	0	0	3
21–50	0	4	3	3	0	10
Over 50	1	1	0	0	0	2
Unreported	1	0	0	0	0	1
Total Number of Companies	17	22	16	9	4	68

unions, and some companies reported both the internationals and the number of locals in each with which bargaining agreements were made.

An examination of the data shows no clearly discernible pattern of relationship between the number of bargaining unit employees and the number of unions involved in negotiations. One company dealing with 85 independent unions had 7,700 employees in bargaining units ranging from 6 to 2,150 employees. Another company reported 150 individual plant agreements with 27 international unions covering a total work force of 22,000 people. At the other extreme, a steel company reported one union agreement covering a 25,000 employee bargaining unit.

However, for the sample of responding companies, multiple unions are the rule. The median number of independents or international unions bargained with is probably about four per company, while the median number of locals is on the order of eight per company. Because of reporting variations, there is a distinct possibility that these estimates are understated. A complete enumeration of the number of separate agreements per company would, I suspect, double these median figures.

A further examination of the data reveals that where multiple union representation is found, there is no simple pattern of distribution of employees among bargaining units. There is a range from a concentration of employees in one union with only small numbers in all others to a fairly even distribution among all unions represented. For example, one manufacturer reported as follows: International Association of Machinists and Aerospace Workers (IAMAW) — 22,341 members; International Brotherhood of Electrical Workers (IBEW) — 309; International Brotherhood of Firemen and Oilers (IBFO) — 39; International Brotherhood of Teamsters, Chauffeurs, Warehousemen, and Helpers of America (TCWH) — 76; UPGWA — 211. This pattern was more or less typical in steel, auto manufacture, aircraft manufacture, and the farm equipment industries. In chemical, oil, and other industries the number of workers per union tended to be more equally distributed. For example, in one such company, the distribution was: International Chemical Workers Union (ICWU) — 2,480 members; Oil, Chemical, and Atomic Workers International Union (OCAWIU) — 2,320; International Union of Operating Engineers (IUOE) — 930; United Steelworkers of America (USWA) — 830; United Mine Workers of America (UMW) — 240; International Brotherhood of Electrical Workers (IBEW) — 240; and 17 other unions with less than 200 members each.

The existence of multiple unions in a company is important, I believe, with regard to the use of computers in bargaining for two reasons: first, the presence of multiple unions and many agreements suggests the desirability of a system of contract comparison which might be computer based; and second, one pattern of distribution may be more conducive to the adoption of EDP for bargaining purposes than other patterns of distribution.

Frequency of Contract Negotiations

Another factor to consider in terms of preparation for bargaining is the frequency with which contracts are renegotiated. At one extreme is the possibility of continuous bargaining such as exists under the railroad agreements. Although such conditions may involve only a limited number of issues, preparation for bargaining may be pursued on a continuing basis. At the other end of the continuum, a contract reopened as infrequently as every five years tends to result in a burst of preparatory activity beginning a few months before the reopening date. In companies with multiple agreements, it is characteristic to find that contract termination dates are spread out in time so that collective bargaining at some location is almost a constant occurrence (Table 3).

In the sample of companies for which data were available, the modal frequency of contract negotiations was every three years. Almost half (thirty-one) of the companies reported that their agree-

Table 3   Average Frequency of Contract Negotiations, by Company
Size (Number of Bargaining Unit Employees).

Negotiation Frequency	Number of Bargaining Unit Employees (in Thousands)					
	Under 10	10–24	25–49	50–99	100– Over	Total
Every 1–3 Years	2	1	0	0	0	3
1–4 Years	0	1	1	0	0	2
Every 2 Years	3	7	2	0	0	12
2–3 Years	6	2	4	1	0	13
Every 3 Years	5	10	8	6	2	31
3–5 Years	0	0	0	1	0	1
Continuously	0	0	0	0	1	1
Unreported	1	1	1	1	1	5
Total Number of Companies	17	22	16	9	4	68

ments covered this span of time. Only two companies reported longer
term agreements.

The Data Base

In terms of current practice, the spread of union agreements and
the frequency of contract negotiations are only two of many significant variables to consider in evaluating computer usage for contract
negotiations. A highly significant factor is the data base available
for use in this regard.

In an attempt to assess this important variable, thirteen items
were listed in the questionnaire for respondents to check if they
were maintaining data on machine records and had them available
for electronic data processing. The items selected included a sample
of those which seem most relevant to preparation for collective bargaining. For any one company, the median number of items reported in this sample was six. There were no significant differences
found in the availability of data on the basis of comparisons by company size (Table 4).

On the basis of this information it must be concluded that only
limited data are currently available on machine records. Most companies — at least seven out of ten — have a basic employee record,
a machine records current payroll system, a record of premiums paid
for the employee benefits package, and a machine records pension
system. However, less than half of the companies maintain historical

Table 4 Frequency of Inclusion of Items in the Data Base, by Company Size (Number of Bargaining Unit Employees).

Data Base Items	Number of Bargaining Unit Employees (in Thousands)					Total	
	Under 10	10–24	25–49	50–99	100–Over	Number	Percentage
Basic Personnel Data[a]	17	17	15	8	3	60	88
Wage and Salary Data							
Current	17	15	16	9	3	60	88
Historical	7	6	9	5	2	29	43
Absenteeism	7	9	4	2	3	25	37
Sick Leave	10	10	3	5	2	30	44
Vacation Time Off	10	8	5	3	2	28	41
Grievances and Arbitrations	0	2	1	1	1	5	7
Employee Benefits							
Part. & prem. paid	13	15	11	7	3	49	72
Charges & ben. paid out	7	11	6	5	4	33	49
Case data[b]	1	5	2	3	1	12	18
Pensions	11	14	13	9	3	50	74
Contract Clauses							
For company contracts	0	1	0	0	1	2	3
For other-company cont.	0	0	0	0	0	0	0
Total Number of Companies	17	22	16	9	4	68	100

[a] Age, sex, length of service, marital status, etc.
[b] History of each hospital claim.

wage and salary data. Of those that do retain historical data in this
area, the most frequent retention time is five years. A number of reporting companies maintained records for one or two years while a
few have data for ten or more years. It was interesting to note that
companies with the longest historical payroll records were not necessarily those companies with extensive data bases in other areas.
Just over a third of the respondents maintain machine records on
time not worked where significant costs might be incurred (i.e.,
absenteeism, vacation time off, sick leave, and so forth).

Looking at the employee benefit area, we find that two-thirds
of our reporting companies have machine records showing data on
plan participation and premiums paid. Almost half of them have
information available on charges and benefits paid out. On the
other hand, only eighteen percent had case data available to analyze
such factors as length of hospital stay, surgical procedures, nature
of illness, and so forth. This type of information is of real significance in terms of negotiations for benefit packages. Most companies
find it necessary to go to the jacket files, pull a large sample of
cases, and tabulate case history data in order to tailor coverages to
areas of greatest need. Studies of this type are required prior to most
negotiations. In our own case (i.e., Inland Steel), we have not maintained this type of information on machine records largely because
of the cost. Apparently other companies have also concluded that
the need does not warrant the cost.

Finally, the data base of reporting companies is almost nonexistent
in areas of crucial interest. Five companies indicated that they have
information about grievances and arbitrations in their data base
and only two have used computers for recording and analyzing company labor contract clauses. No companies reported computer usage
in connection with contract clauses in other company contracts.

Overall, one is forced to the conclusion that the data base on
which bargaining judgments must be made is limited. For most
companies, available data involve a few standard items which are
in the personnel records for other purposes including employee
identification, payroll administration, and work force reporting.

Use of Computers in Preparation for Bargaining

With this as background information, let us take a look at the
way in which computers are currently being used to prepare for
bargaining (Table 5).

The most common usage is to have routine reports produced by

Table 5   Uses Made of the Computer in Preparation for Bargaining, by Company Size (Number of Bargaining Unit Employees).

| Use Made | Number of Bargaining Unit Employees (in Thousands) | | | | | |
	Under 10	10–24	25–49	50–99	100–Over	Total
Little or None	7	6	3	1	0	17
Routine EDP Reports Reviewed and Hand Analyzed	12	14	14	5	2	47
Special Runs Obtained for Hand Analysis	10	15	9	6	3	43
Anticipated Demands Run on Specially Devised Programs	0	3	0	3	0	6
Mathematical Models Developed	0	1ᵃ	0	0	0	1
Total Number of Companies	17	22	16	9	4	68

ᵃ Such models are being developed, and have not yet been used.

EDP and then have them reviewed and analyzed by hand methods with regard to bargaining issues. Another frequent application is to have special runs made to obtain computations and estimations through machine methods.

Only seven companies reported that anticipated demands are coded and entered into the computer with specially designed programs to obtain cost estimates directly from the computer. One company reported the development of mathematical models to project such factors as work force composition and enable them to use such projections in estimating the impact of probable or known bargaining demands.

Little or no use of computers in preparation for bargaining was reported by seventeen of the sixty-eight companies replying to the questionnaire. To get a more realistic picture in this area, we should include in this analysis the fact that eighteen companies replied by letter to the effect that they did not use computers in their bargaining. This results in a finding that just over forty percent of our respondents are not using computers for this purpose. Again, we must conclude that the use of computers to prepare for bargaining is in its infancy — or possibly it is still in the foetal stage.

Anticipating this result, we asked these same companies to help us identify the problems which they encountered in attempting to develop computer applications. We have already noted the fact that the data base is quite inadequate at most companies. As you can see in Table 6, this is confirmed through the report of thirty-eight of the sixty-eight companies that necessary basic data are not available in a usable form for computer applications.

Table 6   Problems Encountered in Using Computer, by Company Size (Number of Bargaining Unit Employees).

Problem	Number of Bargaining Unit Employees (in Thousands)					
	Under 10	10–24	25–49	50–99	100–Over	Total
Data Not Available	9	9	13	5	2	38
Difficult to Get Computer Time	5	6	5	3	1	20
Programming Takes Too Long	7	9	10	3	2	31
Hand Methods as Fast	10	7	6	2	2	27
Other[a]	2	4	1	2	1	10
Total Number of Companies	17	22	16	9	4	68

[a] Comments listed in Appendix, Note 1.

Another very common problem relates to programming. Almost half of the companies indicated that programming for special reports takes too long or they are faced with the fact that programmer time is not available. In reviewing this with our programmers, they felt this could have other causes, such as requests for special report programming failing to be clearly and simply stated or failure to ask for reservation of programmer time sufficiently in advance of need. Difficulty in obtaining time on the computer was cited as a problem by twenty of the sixty-eight companies. In the opinion of twenty-seven companies, the type of analysis they required could be done just as quickly by hand methods.

The basic problems in using computers in preparation for bargaining can be summarized under the headings of utility, programming, and the high cost of both computers and programming time.

Use During Bargaining

Another dimension of the topic under discussion involves the use of computers during bargaining (Table 7), as opposed to their use in preparing for negotiations. As might be expected, companies reported even less usage of computers during bargaining than in their preparatory work.

Table 7   Use Made of Computers During the Bargaining, by Company Size (Number of Bargaining Unit Employees).

Uses	Number of Bargaining Unit Employees (in Thousands)					
	Under 10	10–24	25–49	50–99	100–Over	Total
Practically None	12	9	6	1	0	28
Routine Reports Analyzed by Hand	6	5	5	2	2	20
Special Reports Analyzed by Hand	7	11	11	7	3	39
Demands Analyzed on Real-Time Bases	0	1	1	1	0	3
Simulations and Math Models Used	0	0	0	0	0	0
Describe[a]	0	4	3	2	2	11
Total Number of Companies	17	22	16	9	4	68

[a] Comments listed in Appendix, Note 2.

We received no indication of any company having developed mathematical models or simulations in order to test and keep current an analysis of the effects of alternate demand packages and company offers. Three companies reported that bargaining demands are fed into the computer for cost estimates and similar analyses on a real-time basis.

The most common usage was in the preparation of routine or special reports that required further analysis by hand methods in order to obtain meaningful information. Over one-half of the companies reported that they made little or no use of computers during bargaining, if we include our letter responses along with those obtained from the questionnaire.

The same kinds of problems were noted with regard to using computers during bargaining as those identified in the area of preparing for negotiations. In addition, there were a number of comments which might best be summarized in the words of one respondent who wrote: "The use of computers presupposes considerable advance understanding of the problem scope, availability of accurate input, reliable factor weighting, and logical resolution of problems; somehow those elements still are rarities in the bargaining process."

Union Relationships

With this rather dismal view of current management practice with regard to computer usage for bargaining purposes, we can turn briefly to an examination of the subject in relation to unions. We asked for a response to two general questions:

1. How does your use of computers enter into your relationship with the union(s) with which you negotiate?

2. To what extent do you judge the *principal* union with which you negotiate makes use of computers in preparing for your negotiations?

The pattern of replies is very similar to both of these inquiries (see Tables 8 and 9). Over fifty percent of the companies indicate that

Table 8   Use of Computers and Relationship with Union, by Company Size (Number of Bargaining Unit Employees).

Use	Number of Bargaining Unit Employees (in Thousands)					
	Under 10	10–24	25–49	50–99	100– Over	Total
Make Little Use	14	12	8	2	0	36
Use Results Insofar as Necessary	3	6	7	6	4	26
Share Data and Analyses	0	0	3	1	0	4
Cooperate with Union in Planning Special Analyses	1	3	1	1	0	6
Other[a]	0	4	1	2	1	8
Total Number of Companies	17	22	16	9	4	68

[a] Comments listed in Appendix, Note 3.

Table 9   Estimated Union Use of Computer, by Company Size
(Number of Bargaining Unit Employees).

Estimated Uses of Computer	Number of Bargaining Unit Employees (in Thousands)					
	Under 10	10–24	25–49	50–99	100– Over	Total
Little or None	14	12	9	2	1	38
May Use, but Lack Data for Effective Job	4	7	7	5	2	25
Makes Sophisticated Use of Computers	0	0	1	1	1	3
Describe[a]	2	2	2	2	1	9
Total Number of Companies	17	22	16	9	4	68

[a] Comments listed in Appendix, Note 4.

there is little or no use of computers in their union-management relationships. In the opinion of fifty-six percent of our respondents, the principal union with which they negotiate is not making use of computers in preparing for bargaining.

A number of companies indicate that they use the results of their analyses in discussions with the union if relevant issues arise. Only four companies indicated that they share their data and analyses with union representatives. There were six companies who stated that they do cooperate with the union in planning special analyses of data pertaining to bargaining issues. A few comments were received indicating that, in some instances, reports in tabular form are given to the union in such matters as seniority listings, work force additions, dues deductions, and the like.

In terms of union usage of computer applications, over one-third of the respondents indicated that while unions may use computers to analyze some data, they lack the data sources to do a very effective job. Three companies reported that the principal union with which they negotiated was making sophisticated use of the computer in developing, analyzing, and defending contract demands.

Since Mr. Ginsburg has prepared a paper on the unions' use of computers in bargaining, there is no need for me to devote any further time to this matter except to note that the state of the art appears to be about the same for both parties.

Plans and Limitations

I think it is fair to state further that we are probably at the same stage of the game in terms of future applications (Table 10). Two-thirds of our reporting companies stated that they did not have any plans formulated for computer applications in this area, but that they intended to develop applications at some future point in time. Thirteen of our companies stated that they had definite plans for such applications, while ten acknowledged that they had no plans for future applications at this time.

Table 10   Future Plans for Use of EDP in Bargaining, by Company Size (Number of Bargaining Unit Employees).

	Number of Bargaining Unit Employees (in Thousands)					
Plans	Under 10	10–24	25–49	50–99	100– Over	Total
None	5	4	1	0	0	10
None Formulated, but Intend to Develop Uses	9	14	9	7	3	42
Plans Made[a]	3	4	4	1	1	13
Total Number of Companies	17	22	16	9	4	68

[a] Comments listed in Appendix, Note 5.

The kind of planning which is being done suggests that most attention is being given to the refinement of basic personnel data along with more sophisticated treatment of wage and benefit data. The other significant area of attention involves plans to develop internal catalogues of grievances, arbitrations, and contract clause references for use by the company.

We have already referred to some of the limitations expressed by our respondents. Cost factors, along with time considerations, were frequently mentioned. The function of the computer is viewed as being limited primarily to economic matters. In the view of many managers, contract issues do not lend themselves to mathematical treatment. Whether, or how, good models of complex gaming or strategy situations can be developed will be discussed elsewhere in this symposium.

It was pointed out by some companies that frequent bargaining in decentralized situations poses some difficult problems in special applications of computer technology. Others feel that computer hardware and software simply have not yet reached the level of sophistication required for use in collective bargaining. One of my colleagues in reading this disagreed, saying, "Not so; it is the human ability to make the logic explicit that is lacking." This issue, I am sure, will also be debated.

This does not mean, however, that the outlook for future usage is dim or discouraging. The utilization of coalition bargaining is seen as a force in the direction of greater application of information technology. Several companies indicated that while costs might be prohibitive to develop a computer application for their company, there is a real possibility of such a development if groups of employers can pool their resources or share a computer at a central location. Another force in the direction of computer applications is the acknowledged increase in the complexity of wage items, benefit packages, and other economic factors.

All in all, there is good evidence that most management people believe that there will be an increased use of computers in collective bargaining; but they aren't quite sure how or when this will come about.

The Problems and Potential for Computers in Collective Bargaining

In concluding this paper, I thought you might be interested in my own views on the matter. In order to present an informed viewpoint, I think we must examine the needs of collective bargaining, the problems which arise, and then ask ourselves how computer capabilities can serve these needs. We need to examine these relationships within the context of time, cost, and trends.

The Information Needs

As I see it, there are three phases of bargaining activities that need to be examined with regard to potential computer applications.

Phase I encompasses all of those activities which relate to preparation for actual negotiations. The range of activities moves from statistical studies through problem areas under the existing agreement to an analysis of the social, economic, and political climate within which negotiations will be carried out.

Phase II might be defined to include activities carried out during the period of actual negotiations. Such activities involve face-to-face discussions across the bargaining table and the exchange of information, demands, and positions leading to discussions which culminate in a final agreement.

Phase III involves activities associated with the interpretation and administration of the contract provisions agreed upon at the bargaining table. Such activities would range from the processing of grievances and arbitration cases to recording and analyzing the impact of an economic package.

Information for effective decision making is vital during all three phases of the bargaining process. However, there are meaningful differences with regard to the type of information which may be required, the time factors involved, and the significance of the data in resolving issues.

As one of our respondents pointed out, "Contract issues are not of a mathematical nature." Furthermore, I am occasionally reminded of a printed admonition that reads, "My mind is made up — don't confuse me with facts." For a number of reasons such as these, I would predict that the development of computer applications in connection with Phase II activities will be the last to come on the scene.

We have already observed that applications in the human relations field have lagged behind computer usage for the manipulation and control of physical processes and interactions. Within the industrial relations area, we find the greatest use being made of computers in the field of personnel administration for purposes of counting and identifying people, recording and analyzing personnel actions, and the collection or payment of money. For these purposes, definitions can be precise and the process can be easily translated into symbolic language.

The same cannot be said with regard to most activities in the field of labor relations and collective bargaining. In this field, initial efforts have been associated with the manipulation of financial data reflecting cost per manhour, cost of insurance claims, and the cost of other benefit programs. Activities of this nature are primarily associated with Phase I, Preparation for Bargaining, or Phase III, Administration of the Agreement. This is not to say that information of this nature is not pertinent to the ongoing collective bargaining activities in Phase II. It is to say that computer applications with regard to manipulation of quantifiable data for use during negotiations have encountered some real problems. The treatment of data in Phase I and Phase III is based upon existing and known conditions. Basically, it is a recording of what has happened, not a projection of what will happen.

Projection of future events, even in the realm of economic data, rests on a set of assumptions. In many respects, such assumptions with regard to human behavior are founded on belief rather than experience. The importance of assumptions with regard to problem resolution in the mathematical and physical science fields is well known. They are equally important in dealing with problems of human behavior, but all too often assumptions relative to anticipated human behavior have proved to be erroneous when tested against actual experience. Rapid calculations, speedy transmission of data, and impressive printouts are of little value if the data rest on a set of assumptions that are open to question. It is true that you can set up a variety of hypotheses and assumptions to reflect various alternatives. When this is done, however, you run into some real problems in terms of time and cost pressures.

The critical factor is the problem of gaining acceptance of the assumptions upon which the data are based. The use of computers for the generation of data utilized at the bargaining table offers no greater assurance that the results of the analysis will be any more acceptable to the opposing party than data laboriously developed by hand methods. It is reasonable to assume that data which do not support a bargaining position or objective of one of the parties will be rejected by that party regardless of how it was developed.

For these and other reasons, I find it difficult to believe that computer applications will be a positive force in resolving bargaining issues at the bargaining table. Their greatest value will be in helping to arrive at positions prior to bargaining and identifying the results of agreed-upon contract provisions reflected in experience after the agreement has been reached.

The second application in the labor relations field involves attempts to compare contract clauses, provisions, and language in agreements with different unions or agreements with the same union in different geographical locations. The possibility of such action has already been demonstrated, and it would appear knowledge gained from the use of computers to retrieve case law, locate patents, and similar types of library activities would be helpful here. In many instances, such comparisons are already being made by hand methods. Machine methods would certainly be helpful as the number of contracts to be compared increases and the provisions of the agreements become more complex. Again, the value of such analysis relates to Phase I and Phase III of the negotiations. Results may lend support or weaken positions at the bargaining table, but they are not likely to be significant in resolving the issues.

As I see it at the present time, then, the growth area for computer applications relative to collective bargaining will be in preparing for negotiations and analyzing the impact of collective bargaining agreements in company operations. The use of computers during actual negotiations is apt to lag behind both of these areas.

Problems in Using EDP

Within this conceptual framework, it might be well to note that there are some very real problems to be overcome in expanding the use of EDP for collective bargaining purposes. As indicated earlier, we need to examine the informational requirements of collective bargaining which might be served by machine methods within the context of time, cost, and trends in collective bargaining.

Computer applications in terms of machine capabilities can be divided into two general categories: one, applications involving the solution of programmed or well-structured problems; and two, those calling for the solution of nonspecifically programmed or poorly structured problems.

Examples of the former can be drawn from clerical and other routine jobs such as pricing orders by catalogue and working out payroll deductions, plus a long list of somewhat less repetitive jobs such as planning production and employment schedules or determining the product mix for an oil refinery. Examples of poorly structured problems are generally drawn from areas of decision making for which there is no exact precedent; i.e., a general's decision to attack or a company's decision to launch a particular sales campaign.

While it is true that the machine is developing many more capabilities than we dreamed of a few years ago, most of the "profitable" applications are still confined to such routine jobs as payroll functions, processing insurance data, making out accounts payable and receivable, and other ordinary business tasks.

Few people have speculated more boldly about the role of the computer in management than Herbert Simon. In his view, heuristically programmed computers (discovery of solutions to loosely structured problems) will be a long time surpassing men on jobs where they exercise their senses and muscles as well as their brains; i.e., examining a piece of tissue in medical diagnosis or the performance of work in face-to-face service jobs. Relative costs, Simon goes on, will decide who does the job.

Collective bargaining applications, by and large, fall into the area of poorly or loosely structured problem solving. As yet, computers put to heuristic problem solving do not have anything remotely like the advantage they have over man in arithmetic and scientific computing. There is still a substantial area of research and development required in this area. Hardware and software costs are, and will be, substantial. Yet, these are only a portion of the total cost considerations. For the moment, let us confine our discussion to applications involving existing equipment and techniques.

In many instances, the information required for collective bargaining is not collected in a routine fashion. In other cases, data available from routine reports designed for other purposes must be differentially treated. This means that something unusual or different has to be performed in order to obtain the desired results. Lacking the data base, time and money must be expended to secure the necessary information.

Furthermore, establishing data collection procedures to be carried out on a continuous basis where the use is limited to collective bargaining purposes is a costly matter. As we have seen, negotiating a contract is a sporadic and infrequent occurrence for any one company. Continuous bargaining is the exception rather than the rule. Issues change and information requirements vary in relation to the issues. The alternative to providing for continuous data collection is to develop specific programs and procedures for the collection of data to be used in each negotiation. Adopting this alternative poses time and cost problems that are equally serious although of a different type.

The problems of special programming and batch operations are not unique to computer applications in the field of collective bargaining. Frequent reference was made in our survey to difficulties in getting time on the computer. Others indicated that programmer time was not available. Computer personnel and equipment must be fully utilized in the day-to-day operation of the business if the cost of such an operation is to be supported. Intermittent demands for special applications are difficult to accommodate. Similarly, special programming skills required to service collective bargaining requirements may not be available within the company.

I feel sure that in many instances a cost-benefit analysis would reveal that hand methods of analyzing and interpreting data for collective bargaining purposes would be less costly from the standpoint of both time and money than machine methods. It is highly unlikely that small, single plant operations would either need or could afford the use of computers for their negotiations. As a company increases in size and scope of operation, communication requirements become more voluminous and complex. More machine applications become possible. Under some forms of coalition bargaining, computer applications may become almost mandatory. Clearly, the potential for EDP application is greater under conditions of industrywide bargaining than it is for negotiations involving one company and one bargaining unit.

To put it another way, the greatest impetus to the use of EDP for collective bargaining will come from trends toward increasing centralization of negotiations and the growing complexity of economic issues. In terms of present requirements and the state of the art, it seems to me that we would have to view the future of EDP applications in collective bargaining with cautious optimism.

The Future for Computers

We need to be alert to the progress and expanding technical capabilities of both hardware and software in the computer field. Advances in time-sharing and on-line capabilities should increase the feasibility of utilizing electronic data processing for collective bargaining purposes. We need to explore the possibility of computer applications in a number of areas. Some of the areas which might lend themselves to such applications are:

1. The analysis of actual costs of past contracts and their relation to the costs estimated at the time of the agreement.

2. Determination of relative costs of various package proposals.

3. Computation of costs to individual companies involved in industry or areawide bargaining.

4. Analysis of the impact of compensation changes upon rate structures or price and profit levels.

5. The possibility of using the computer as a retrieval device for ascertaining comparable contract clauses during negotiations.

6. Analyzing the impact of contract clauses on workers and groups of workers depending upon different profiles, geographic areas, and production methods.

Such a listing is limited only by the imagination of people and a knowledge of machine capabilities. Perhaps we should examine the implications of computers for mediation and arbitration with programs and data available for analysis of prior agreements. It is certainly within the realm of possibility to consider the computer as a retrieval device for prior decisions and settlements. The day may even come when it is possible to resolve disputes through an essentially unbiased evaluation of facts. This, however, is easier to speculate upon than to achieve.

Taking a cold, hard look at the future of computer applications for collective bargaining from a management standpoint, it seems to me that much will depend upon four considerations:

1. A determining factor will be the extent to which we can develop a data base for collective bargaining so that it fits into other current and continuous uses.

2. The expansion of industrywide or coalition bargaining would be a strong positive force in the development of future applications.

3. The degree of attention, time, and money devoted to the development of software for use in bargaining will be a factor.

4. The progress which can be made in the development of computer utility service will influence the possibility of future applications.

Man-computer communication is increasing rapidly. Computers can provide management with an extension of time, personnel, and knowledge. Early computer applications were made possible by fitting a problem to a solution which could be programmed. Today, the types of problems which can be solved are restricted to those which fit certain closely defined rules. Eventually we can anticipate that computers will be available to people for use in problem solving and information processing, and the users will find that they have increasing power to structure and carry out solutions tailored to their problems.

Regardless of these developments, we will still be faced with the question, "To what extent can union-management negotiating issues be resolved on the basis of fact?" And, we are still faced with economic realities. The economics of the situation is well summarized in the remark of an airline pilot who, when asked if he worried over being replaced by an electronic guidance system, replied, "No. Where can you get a nonlinear servomechanism control device which can be produced by unskilled labor for $2,000 a month?"

An examination of current uses of the computer in business suggests that its key role might well be described as "artificial intelligence" *within well-defined business systems.* Research on computer methodology may lead to increases in the "artificial intelligence" aspects of the computer, but it is highly speculative to predict new computer capabilities which will be sufficiently basic and powerful to cause the development of a new outlook on business problems or a restructuring of the collective bargaining process.

Negotiating a labor agreement can scarcely be identified as a well-defined business system. On the other hand, the bargaining process is certainly a part of a highly complex informational system. Before we answer the question regarding computer applications in this field, it is important that we do some basic research with regard to the total informational system. Only then can we decide whether the technique and methodology are pertinent and effective.

I believe this is what our survey respondents implied when they indicated a posture of exploration and investigation. All would probably agree that the rate of progress of information technology in collective bargaining will be partially a matter of technological feasibility and partially a matter of economics. There is a third barrier — and an important one — which must be handled. This is the barrier of human acceptance and interpersonal relationships.

Additional References

"Computer Sits in on the Bargaining," *Business Week*, September 10, 1966, p. 154.

Norbert J. Esser, "The Computer — A Challenge to the Personnel Profession," *Personnel Journal*, Vol. 44, No. 6, June 1965, pp. 292–294.

Woodrow L. Ginsburg, "Labor Turns to the Computer," *IUD* Agenda, Vol. 3, No. 9, September 1967, pp. 26–30.

John F. Griffin, "Management Information Systems — A Challenge to Personnel," *Personnel Journal*, Vol. 46, No. 6, June 1967, pp. 371–373.

Daniel E. Knowles, "The Personnel Man as Business Systems Engineer," *Personnel*, Vol. 41, No. 2, March/April 1964, pp. 41–44.

John R. McNulty, "Computers May Have To Be Used To Keep Up With The Unions," *Canadian Personnel and Industrial Relations Journal*, Vol. 14, No. 1, January/February 1967, pp. 4–6.

Charles A. Myers, "New Frontiers for Personnel Management," *Personnel*, Vol. 41, No. 3, May/June 1964, pp. 31–38.

Elaboration and Discussion

Caples   When I agreed to prepare this paper, my assignment was to try to find out what, if anything, was being done by management regarding the use of computers in bargaining; and, beyond these current applications, I was given the license to state my own views and speculations for the future. Of course, at the present time there has not been very much written about this and so I decided I would try to find out from a group of companies directly what they had been doing. I selected for my sample the one hundred largest manufacturing companies in the United States as well as twenty-five companies in each of five other industries: transportation, finance, utilities, merchandising, and insurance. With this cross section I wanted to find out basically two things from them. First, what was the current practice of these companies in the use of electronic data processing for bargaining; and second, what suggestions might they have as to the prospects for future applications?

The response which I received was reasonably good, I think, although every once in a while I was a little startled when I got a letter back stating that the expense of filling out questionnaires or collecting this kind of data is too expensive and that they would have no part in it. I sometimes wonder how we are going to get better information when we run into this lack of cooperation.

In looking into these computer applications in bargaining, they break down into three phases: the preparation; the actual bargaining — being locked in a deadly embrace, as John L. Lewis used to say; and the administration of the contract.

On the preparation, I believe there is considerable merit in using the computer's storage and retrieval ability to find out what is going on within an industry, within the country generally, and possibly we will even get to the point where we can use it to deal with problems of foreign competition. We would then be able to do some kind of an analysis which would tell us how our people compare with other workers.

As to the administration of the contract, I see considerable merit in feeding in data regarding the occurrences of grievances in the mill. This might include information such as where they occur, which foreman is involved, on which shift they occur, and any other kind of retrieval data which will help you see how you are administering the contract. In particular, it can help you to make sure you are reasonably uniform in your application; and that, I point out, is no mean feat when you are spread around the country or around the world.

As to the bargaining itself, I have real doubts as to what, if any, use can ultimately be made of the computer. One of the reasons is that so often the things upon which you make your final decisions are purely subjective judgments, in spite of the fact that the parties agree on the data.

I will use an example we had in the last bargaining in steel in 1965. We had a demand to give everybody the absolute right to retire after thirty years of service. The cost of such a demand could be figured two ways. We could take the cost if everybody retired the minute they had completed thirty years of service; or we could take the cost if nobody retired under it. The difference in cost between the two was 22 cents an hour. To nobody's surprise, the union said it would cost nothing and the company said it cost 22 cents; but where the issue was finally settled was purely a matter of judgment.

In my opinion, there are so many things like this that you can't really use the computer to accomplish much in this area. If you want to take the time to work out a mathematical model, you have to consider several factors. These include the use of the computer time and the programmers' time, compared to the so-called profit items that are competing for this same time. Is the expense justified when you consider that for every bargaining you would probably have to set up a new model and the longest that any of these would work would be, at most, three to five years?

In thinking about using computers for bargaining, it brings to mind something that Don Straus brought up earlier. Back in the earlier days of the use of computers, we ran some figures through our computer for use in the current steel bargaining; but the union would not accept our figures. The only way we resolved the matter was to feed the same data through the computer at Carnegie Tech. The results then became acceptable because the computer was neutral. I am happy to say that they were still the same. It pointed out the absurdity of this, but we finally came to the conclusion that the only way we were going to satisfy the union rank and file about the mystery of the computer was that they had great faith in Carnegie Tech's computer and not very much in Inland Steel's.

Anonymous   Was it a union-made computer?

Caples   No, it wasn't. In fact, it was an IBM computer.

In getting back to those applications not directly connected with bargaining, there are still significant costs to be considered. I think the costs of collecting and maintaining the necessary data are substantial. Interestingly enough, in making inquiries of companies which have done a great deal of collection of personnel data, I have yet to find a company that entered into the collection process after making a cost survey as to what the cost of the data would be. They all went into it for some other reason. Either they had computer time available or they didn't figure the cost first. Some even said, "We didn't know what the cost was beforehand; but if we had to do it again, we wouldn't." I don't know of any company that is keeping such data that is not happy with its system; but I would like to find one that went into it on a cost basis first. Unfortunately, this is almost impossible to find.

There are a few other applications I would like to mention and then I will stop. I think that the analysis of costs under past contracts and their relationships to the costs of the contract you are working on could be very useful. You might get a better idea of the relative costs of the various packages and through this process be better able to piece together an acceptable contract.

In an industrywide or joint bargaining effort, a very real application is the cost of the contract to each of the individual companies. Particularly when you get into the fringe benefits, there are probably no two steel companies that have the same employee age distribution, the same service distribution, and so forth; and, of course, these factors are going to affect the costs of pensions, vacations, and a variety of other things. So where you have these kinds of variable costs, it would be valuable to find out the cost impact on one company in relation to another so that compromises can be worked out on the management side. Of course, such information on costs as a function of employee profiles is also very useful for intracompany analyses.

Bigelow   In your study, did you find anybody who had done anything about putting his contracts into the computer in full text?

Caples   If my memory is right, three percent of the companies had programmed their own contracts so that where they had a variety of contracts they could pull out information and make comparisons. None of them had anybody else's contract on the computer, however.

Bigelow   Was this full text or just an index or summary?

Ginsburg   I doubt if anybody has the full text. That is a mammoth job. We have summaries of contracts on the computer which are useful when we are trying to search for a particular clause. In this way we can determine the frequency of occurrence of an advantageous clause quite readily; and if anybody wants the full text, it is available in-house. But I don't know of anybody yet who has taken the whole text and put it on the computer.

Myers   One thing that you commented on in your paper that interested me is the point you made as to the unstructured character of bargaining. You quoted Herbert Simon, who has written extensively about the nature of unstructured tasks and the science of the artificial. I can recall his saying about eleven years ago that within ten years a computer would be programmed that would win the world chess championship unless forbidden to do so by the rules. Well, it turned out he was a little optimistic about this, but in a Phi Beta Kappa lecture about a year ago, he did say that conceivably there isn't anything a man can do that eventually a computer can't do.

Caples   I can think of one thing real quickly.

Myers   I stand corrected. I meant in terms of thinking, not acting. He may still be optimistic, but as I look at the field of management, it is moving so fast that we shouldn't be too confident that the unstructured things of today won't become the structured and programmable things of tomorrow.

Now collective bargaining is probably one of the last of these areas because of its unstructured character; but the idea of a collective bargaining game, or of simulating possible alternatives, I can see as a possibility for the future. That is, management could feed alternative possibilities into the computer and be provided with informational replies based on a program that assumes that certain things happen. This is the way that some of the systems in the defense area work and you might get some results that would be useful.

Caples   I asked one of our programming people to read my paper before I presented it and his reaction was, "Well, one of the problems in using computers for bargaining is that you must state the logic of your position to a degree that somebody can program it — and my guess is you don't know the logic of your own position." This was something that I could not argue with him about very much.

The progress we are now making in computer applications is all in things upon which, rightly or wrongly, we can agree upon the assumptions. They are all things in which you have fairly well-defined problems and fairly definite data. In the case of bargaining, you don't.

Penchansky   This is not necessarily so. Probably the most important aspect in the ability to use the computer is that it can generate data so quickly that you begin to get distributions of possible outcomes.

The implication of your remark is that to use computers, we have to have decisions under certainty. But I really think that computers can also be used where there is uncertainty of individual decisions.

Daniels   I think you are making a mistake about the nature of the collective bargaining process when you say this, because in the collective bargaining process you are dealing with a number of variables which deal with the emotions of a large group of people.

Penchansky   What says that these can't be quantified?

Daniels   The computer cannot be programmed to consider all of the alternatives that the membership would consider and whether or not they would ratify what was worked out at the bargaining table, nor can it consider all the alternatives that management would consider at the bargaining table. You just can't put in the emotions that are involved. As Bill Caples says, you can have all the facts in the world but you still end up with a judgment factor.

Penchansky   But you could put some weights on these emotional factors. I think what Myers is saying is that you can use weights in developing a computer simulation.

Caples   How much weight would you put on the fact that the president of the union wants to stay in office and a number of district directors want his job? And what weight do you put on the business agent of your local union, who is an ambitious guy and will do anything to sabotage the contract because of a personal stake? I have some grave doubts as to whether you can quantify these things.

Penchansky   What weights do you put on them now?

Daniels   Can you quantify muscle?

Penchansky   Sure, they do it all the time.

Daniels   I mean, can you quantify the extent to which I am prepared to call a strike where it is a function of about 450,000 variables?

Penchansky   You are referring to the 450,000 union members, I presume. Are you saying that each of these people operates independently and there aren't any patterns to their response?

Daniels I say 450,000 variables. I am exaggerating, of course.

Penchansky A large number isn't frightening.

Daniels Perhaps I speak out of a colloquialism of being a practitioner. I just wonder whether, in my own twenty-five years of experience, I was ever able to express at the beginning of a bargaining session, in any quantitative terms, precisely what the muscle relationship was going to be at the critical point where we decided whether or not there was going to be a strike. What takes place in the process of collective bargaining — you call it emotional and I call it muscle — is that the relationships in the process itself are in a constant state of flux.

Penchansky You assume that you are going to get a single answer. I am not saying you are going to get an answer out of the computer; what I am saying is that in building a model — let's drop the word model — you will develop relationships among the factors that are going to be important in this bargaining. You take into account a range of factors. I think one of the real advantages in trying to get somebody to build a model is that the process itself of building the model may help you to make better judgments, qualitatively if not quantitatively.

Daniels But that range is impossible to determine at the beginning. Very often I find that an important factor in negotiations is who is sitting on the other side of the table, what is he like, and how does he react. This is something you don't know until you go through the process. I can tell you in advance that if I sit down and deal with certain management lawyers, the possibility of a strike is fifty percent, with some it is eighty percent, with some a hundred percent, and some zero percent.

Caples I know Arthur Goldberg. I have heard him make speeches and then had to bargain with him, and I didn't recognize the same fellow.

Anonymous You must accept the fact too that in collective bargaining one of the ways really to get off the track is to have so much information that you come into negotiations with a preconceived idea of where you are going to go. One fellow is so loaded with data that he can flood you with exhibits. This interrupts the communication across the table and you never get on the track.

   The computer approach assumes that logic is very important. I don't know much about bargaining, but in my twenty-two years I don't think logic has had much to do with it. Have you ever been in two negotiations where the logic is the same? Have you ever been in two negotiations where you could handle them in the same way? I don't see how you can program this.

Siegel I don't think Penchansky is asking the computer to do the bargaining for him. He is just trying to get some models out of it which would help in preparation. I guess the question is whether or not any models would be useful for preparation.

On another point, I wonder if in your survey you found any companies saying, "We are attempting to develop an overall model of our firm for a variety of corporate purposes, so that when union negotiations come up we can spin off the desired information as a by-product."

Caples If any companies are doing this, they didn't indicate so in their replies. Obviously, everyone wants to get as much use out of their hardware as they can.

I think a point should be made here as to the importance of planning. Lots of times you will go through the planning stage and then never put anything on the computer because you have already found out all you want to know. I have always felt that planning and preparation account for about ninety percent of where you come out in bargaining.

For example, just take the issue of contracting out work in the steel industry. We had to go back over every instance of contracting out work in over fifteen years to find out what we had actually done before we could start bargaining. We had to find out what was done in the plant, what was done out of the plant, what skills were available, and so forth. There was a tremendous amount of preparation that had to be done. Now if you had this information in the computer somewhere, and could retrieve it quickly, it would be great. I am just not sure that the cost of maintaining the data would pay out.

Cole You spoke in your paper of the use of the computer in grievance handling and arbitration. Was that merely for information gathering or for some other purpose?

Caples As you know, we have done an analysis of our grievances in which we went back to every grievance, every arbitration, and found out what happened. We have the department, the contract clause, the relative frequency with other departments on this contract clause, and what not; but our investigation of grievances has really been sort of thin.

For instance, what of the human factors? Is it the foreman that is the problem? Do people work indoors or outdoors? What are the ages of the people? The makeup of the people is very important and we have very little of it. There are all sorts of things that would be useful to know if you had data available. This is the sort of thing to which I think the computer will lend itself. If you have an extensive enough data system on your people, you will be able to pinpoint sources of grievances that you just couldn't do otherwise.

Straus I would like to ask a question. I have a feeling when I listen to you and Woody Ginsburg talk that it is a little like the work on the atom under the Chicago stadium. Here is a new tool with a tremendous potential down the line. It isn't a question of whether it is going to be used or not; it is already being used to an ever-increasing extent by both union and management. The question is for what purpose.

To carry the analogy a step further, is EDP like the atom in that it can be used for peaceful uses or for purposes of war? As I hear you two talk, it seems it is being used for war, with each side getting ready to do battle at the bargaining table. I wonder whether we are likely to get into a kind of data overkill or an EDP megaton stalemate. Or is there a possibility as you look down the line a bit that people in a more enlightened age might be willing to explore the joint uses of EDP?

What I want to ask is this. In your opinion, is the possibility of the joint use of EDP attractive to you in terms of coming to an agreement quicker, or does EDP seem to be such a lovely weapon that you prefer to go down the route you are following at present with it being an expensive tool for gathering figures and marshaling arguments?

Caples As I said, there are three phases in the use of the computer: the preparation, the bargaining, and the administration. In two of those I can see a real use for this joint approach; but in the third, the actual bargaining at the table, I see some trouble.

Straus In your analogy of using the computer at Carnegie Tech because it was neutral, I think this example misses the point. It is the programming that is the important area. Isn't it at the point of input that you would have to have joint cooperation?

Caples This is where the assumptions you make become so important. On a lot of things, we use our actuarial tables and exchange data with Murray Latimer on pension plans and we don't have any quarrel on these assumptions. We use U.S. Steel's computer for this or somebody else's and nobody objects. But on other things there is still the emotional reaction. These are some of the things that we are working on together with the so-called Human Relations Committee.

Daniels In your survey, did you find any change in the form in which unions asked for data from employers before negotiations? I ask that because there are just beginning to be some very fascinating legal problems that are arising under the NLRB as to whether or not a trade union, in demanding the material that it is entitled to before negotiations, can also make demands not only for the material but for the form in which the material is to be presented. I use apoplexy as a bargaining weapon and I am planning to give it to one of our employers very soon. I intend to ask for the data I need, not in the usual form, but on tape. I wondered if in your survey you had come across that?

Caples We didn't ask that question on the survey and so we have no information.

Bigelow There was a case in Connecticut some years ago where the UAW, I think it was, asked for some information and got it on tape. The Court made the company give them a printout. Of course this is just the reverse of your question.

McLean In talking about the unions' data banks and the companies' data banks, I wonder if you have any evidence of the existence of a third party, namely the Government, in furnishing data to both parties. To what extent do you think that labor and management would be willing to use the Government as a single source for data that both groups could contribute to and draw from?

Caples I think in answering that question, I am probably not representing the views of the majority of management, for I have always felt that it would be much better if a great deal of these common data were available from a Government data bank. This is from the standpoint of cost of collection, extent and completeness of the data, and everything else. But my guess would be that most management people would think there is too much Big Brother in this. I draw this conclusion from the time when the Employment Service wanted to keep track of recent college graduates and tried to find out about various levels of skills that companies had. You will recall the reaction to this was so highly emotional and they raised such an uproar that the Employment Service dropped their plans; but I thought it was a good idea.

Anonymous   The 1952 President's Management Advisory Committee made a report on the bargaining process and one of the things they recommended was the joint use of Government information in advance of the actual negotiations. It was thought that the mere joint use of Government facilities would make people more conciliatory and rational in the process of collective bargaining.

Siegel   I would like to go back to an issue we were discussing a moment ago and direct a question to Jay Forrester who has just joined us. The question was raised earlier, Jay, about the effectiveness of modeling and the use of computers to deal with something that is as uncertain, as variable, as emotional, as illogical, as is collective bargaining. In the light of your work with dynamic modeling, how do you feel about the usefulness of this tool in dealing with such matters?

Forrester   It would help to begin with a clarification. In modeling there is no need to attempt a one percent precision. A computer model should be compared to the accuracy of the model that you would otherwise use. The images of social systems you carry in your head, of how people behave and how they react, is a model. These concepts that you already use can be put into a systems model. You can put into a model any process that can be described. The result will be as accurate or as inaccurate as the model you already have in your head. So the making of a model is no more difficult than sitting down and talking about a situation.

Of course, when one starts to put thoughts on paper, he finds often that little has been said and even that isn't very precise. So, when an individual goes through the discipline of model building, he forces himself to be more precise. A model is a difficult taskmaster in showing up ambiguities. Model building forces a better statement of what one believes than would appear in a normal conversational mode.

Having constructed a dynamic model of some social process, the model divulges new information. Although built on plausible assumptions, the model often does not behave the way one expects.

So he discovers contradictions in his thinking; the assumptions do not lead to the expected results. This is because the human mind is not effective in starting with the parts of a system and from these parts deducing dynamic behavior through time. So at the stage of system simulation using a model, one may discover that his proposed solutions are, in fact, a part of the cause of the problem and not a part of the solution; and that the whole system behaves in a very different way than what he would expect.

Recently, I have been developing some models of the city and its growth and decay processes. The reason I started this work on urban processes was the deep conviction, coming out of earlier modeling work, that very often the obvious intuitive solution to improve a system may be at best neutral, and frequently may make the problem worse. Intuition fails and leads to the wrong results more often than not. It is not just bad luck or happenstance. There are basic reasons why people arrive at the wrong conclusions in complex systems when they base decisions on their experiences with simple systems.

Intuition fails in complex systems because our intuitive background has been developed in the simplest possible kind of system, the so-called first-order negative feedback loop. An example is the simple system where you touch a hot stove and jerk your hand away. The pain is related to how far away you are from the stove. Another example is controlling your car to keep it from running off the road. These are simple feedback systems in which the symptoms of the difficulty are close to the effect in time and space. The cause of a trouble is here and it is now.

But in complex social systems, the cause is now no longer close in time and space to the symptoms. In fact, it is usually true that the cause is distant in both time and space. To make matters worse, we frequently look at the complex system and find an apparent cause that *is* close in time and space; but in fact it is not a cause but a coincidental symptom. So, being conditioned to look for a close relationship between cause and effect, the system presents something for us to find. This is the essence of the highly misleading character of complex systems. We have been conditioned by simple systems where the characteristics are almost diametrically opposite to those of complex systems, and so we are methodically misled into drawing the wrong conclusions. It is only in the model of a system that one sees how opposite the effect can be from what one expects.

Time after time we have gone into corporate situations where

there have been some serious problems. We go through the organization and talk to the people and find out what they are doing.
They tell us what they are doing and what they are trying to do.
We check their statements and decide that they are doing what they
say they are doing. Then if we take what each individual is doing
and put it into a computer simulation model of the entire organization, we find that the known actions, when combined, are all that
is necessary to cause the trouble. Those things that are intuitively
correct when viewed separately are the cause of all the mischief
when they are coupled together.

Siegel Bill Caples, in his study of management's use of computers
in collective bargaining, feels that for structured or programmed
decisions, there was really a great deal of help that both company
managers and union leaders can get from this tool; but for unstructured decisions, he feels this tool is a rather meager one.

Myers I think it should be added that many of the practitioners
from labor and management have reflected the view, which many
of us share, that the collective bargaining process is an emotional
one, with mature assumptions being made by each party as to how
the other party will behave. But as to whether these can be quantified in a model I think is a concern of a lot of people and the idea
that somehow computer models would take the place of people in
their setup bothers them.

Forrester Emotional processes can be modeled on the basis of what
you believe to be the reasons that govern emotional response. Unless
you believe that the whole process is absolutely random and capricious and that what you do has no effect at all, you can begin to
establish some of the cause and effect relationships. When you do
this, you have the beginning of a structured system which is the
beginning of a model.

One must be very clear in his reasons for modeling. In general,
one should not try to use a model for making today's crisis decisions.
The kind of modeling I am speaking of is best used to understand
the nature of the system of which one is a part and to understand
which components are most important in its functioning.

About ninety percent of the changes one might make in human
systems will have no effect at all. Apparent roads to improvement
often make matters worse. On the other hand, there are those critical
places where changing something will cause the system to react favor-

ably. Pressures radiate from such effective control points, not so much because people have changed, but because they respond differently when they see things happening differently around them.

Appendix: Comments Accompanying the Questionnaires

Note 1   Problems Encountered in Using Computers

Respondent
Number   Comments

001   The frequency of use for much negotiations data is not great enough to amortize the cost of programming, loading, updating, and machine time.

005   Relatively few — as we make limited use of computers.

017   Most divisions have their own computer systems; hence, there is a variety of hardware and software systems in the corporation which tends to hinder the transmission and interchange of information.

021   This is not a completely accurate statement because our raw data are programmed to provide recaps relevant to the analysis, so the hand methods are quicker only when we have the recaps to work from our final analysis.

022   Keeping data and other information closely guarded.

023   Capricious and conflicting anticipated demands limit usage in demand analysis.

025   Data for represented employees are not kept separate from nonrepresented employees and therefore must be specially broken out.

028   At present, lack of real-time capability to provide immediate information.

034   State of art not advanced enough to be of any real help.

035   Limitations of computer time, programmers, programming time, and specialized type of data needed. Employee data are available in our EDP system and tabulations are prepared periodically on disability absence, pension credits, life insurance coverage, age, service, etc., but we are not able to obtain a set of data relating to an individual employee.

037   In some cases (d) applies. However, the basic problems are utility, programming, and high cost of computer and programming time.

044   Availability of manpower capable of sorting and assembling data and reference materials for input to EDP systems.

049   Problems are of inexperience. Better planning and advance preparation needed.

052   Presently available equipment — IBM 1401 card is main limitation. Delivery of IBM 360 not anticipated until sometime in 1968.

053   Need someone in the systems area more familiar with the contract, benefit provisions, etc., to facilitate structuring of useful programs.

056   Basic data not current. Lack of real-time capability.

057   Most data needed are available, but many are not in a usable form.

Note 2   Use Made of Computers During the Bargaining

Respondent
Number   Comments

001   Current population of jobs; average rates by group seniority lists, special pay provisions for total bargaining units, etc.

002   Analysis of costs of benefits based on such elements as age, length of service, pay rate, etc.; analysis of effects of demands in such areas as seniority protection, wage increases, S.U.B. all done by hand from regular or special reports.

004   None.

008   Bargaining is on a division or plant basis — not centralized for the corporation. Special runs are made as needed, based on personnel and benefit information which computers handle in normal course of business at the division.

017   Limited use to date during actual bargaining.

021   Normally, prior to negotiation the raw data and recaps have been completed; but there may be special programs run on the computer if we don't have the information necessary for the situation.

022   Keeping information confidential.

023   Only as checked.

025   We use the computer to develop cost data of possible offers or union demands.

029   Used to the extent of data availability.

036 Used primarily to compute cost of various proposals which could be included in final settlement.

038 Varies widely depending on subject matter under consideration.

044 Occasional statistical summaries are generated for analysis by hand.

048 Limited use in collecting historical data in various categories and increments to test eligibility, amount of benefits, etc., in evaluating cost of certain proposals or changes in present benefits.

049 Not too effective to date — still learning. Need to develop programs, models, and data banks ahead so can act fast during actual bargaining period.

053 As need arises, past routine reports or special runs are obtained to make computations and estimates pertaining to bargaining issues.

057 Where data are available, programming and computer time is made available for special reports on top priority.

059 Used to generate gross data from source data already available on tape through simple distributions requiring minimum programming time. Data punched into cards for EAM sorting.

Note 3   Use of Computers and Relationship with Union

Respondent
Number   Comments

001 Periodic reports to unions are compiled in tabular form, i.e., seniority, excess, status reports, dues deduction, etc.

012 They recognize that many of our costs have been developed through computer use — such as pension and health and welfare costs. Particularly pension costs.

021 Company furnishes union with relevant data for bargaining and reasonable requests for information by the union are considered by the company.

025 The cost data developed by the computer is one of a number of considerations in developing our bargaining policies.

032 Use the results of the analyses we make in discussion with union to the fullest extent possible. We show data but not analyses.

044 Cooperate with union in planning special analyses relevant to issues in the bargaining.

048   Most of our use of computers is confined to those reports developed in response to union requests.

049   We use results but do not indicate to union method used to develop our information.

050   Share data but not analyses.

059   Data runs provided the union on request as required.

Note 4   Estimated Union Use of Computer

Respondent
Number   Comments

001   Major units have access to IUD Data Bank regarding national issues, e.g., employee benefit plans, rate structures, seniority practices, etc. I am not aware of the extent to which they use this service.

004   Heretofore — very limited. Future?

005   We see little evidence that computers are used extensively, although published reports indicate that OCAW participates in the IUD computer facility.

006   Unless the union first gets the data from the company (the union lacks the data sources to do a very effective job of using computers to analyze some data).

008   The IAM is presently developing computer applications for future use, including contract clause analysis.

015   Meat Cutters developing system that can analyze company, industry, or geographic location.

021   The unions depend almost wholly on the company-furnished information.

022   Use certain data published by International.

029   Union has requested limited data in punched card form. No understanding reached on this matter at this time.

032   The union does use computers to analyze data. Where readily available we share data with union upon request.

035   National organization is working on programs but local union has not used data in bargaining to date.

037   The development and analysis of union statistics on computers would, in my estimation, lack accuracy at the source. Input picked up on participating firm (this would be an even more difficult way for unions to obtain accurate data), wage and fringe surveys are difficult for management accuracy.

039   CWA [Communications Workers of America] has installed a Univac 9300 which will be used for analyzing contracts to highlight targets for improvement in future negotiations. Will also be used for more accurate cost estimates of contract demands.

048   In limited areas where they receive detailed reports they seem to be able to arrive at conclusions which are difficult to repudiate.

052   Locals use some generalized data furnished by AFL-CIO which are probably developed by their EDP setup.

057   Has been used only to compare various company contract provisions.

059   Do not know — have seen no evidence of detailed studies.

066   In our 1967 negotiations, IBEW used data from other labor agreements which they obtained from computer file maintained by the IUD of AFL-CIO.

067   At this time, use appears to be confined to actuarial studies and analyses.

068   Benefit data (pensions, insurance, seniority) may sometimes be placed on a computer by a union.

Note 5   Future Plans for Use of EDP in Bargaining

Respondent
Number   Comments

001   No major programs. May add subroutines to existing programs for more detailed information.

006   We plan to consider developing capabilities to accumulate data needed in making cost estimates of wage and fringe benefit modifications that may become bargaining issues.

009   Running wage summaries; personnel affected by changes.

015   Computers will be of no significant value to us unless we must bargain through coalition bargaining.

019   We are giving consideration to using computers to obtain basic personnel data (sex, age, service, marital status, dependents, etc.).

025   We plan to develop models for local units which will facilitate our local bargaining, particularly in the chemical business.

029   Total planning is incomplete, but extensive use is contemplated. Data source development is receiving high priority.

031   Cost and union demands and develop mathematical models to project impact of union demands.

037   Develop more auxiliary programs as output from payroll master records. Mainly, in the area of employee benefits.

040   More sophisticated personnel history data.

044   Hope to develop a catalogue of grievance, arbitration, and contract clause references for cases internal to company.

048   Attempt to anticipate type of union demands and, to the extent feasible, build basic data in computers for future reference as needed.

053   In the process of developing a program to record and store centrally extensive information about all corporate grievances and arbitration decisions.

057   Include basic data in usable form. Make more prenegotiation computations.

058   Plan to create a computer file containing personnel information, plus payroll and accounting information, concerning individual employee.

059   Develop models to reduce time lags and programming requirements; test use time-sharing with simple programming.

060   None formulated, however, considering further use of computers for benefit plan data and intracompany labor agreement analysis.

063   Presently reviewing possibility for grievances. Whole matter under study and all potentials are being considered and evaluated to assist in bargaining preparation.

065   Having available current and historical wage, attendance, and other known factors available in tape records.

067   Studies under way to determine areas of maximum benefit and utilization of new techniques such as time-sharing. Work now in process to broaden utilization of information presently available.

Note 6   What Limitations, If Any, Do You See on the Use of Computers in Bargaining?

Respondent
Number   Comments

001   Computers have extended capabilities, however, the cost of constructing models and programs for extrapolation and trend

development in collective bargaining *for a single company* is prohibitive.

002 Cost and the response time involved.

003 Availability, high cost, programming skills, and availability of time.

004 Its use in our bargaining will be limited for some time since our diverse operations and unions, as well as contract expirations and provisional peculiarities, do not lend themselves to computer applications.

005 Exact analyses are frequently secondary to reaching an agreement. Competitive considerations often predominate.

006 With respect to development of data with reasonable lead time, no serious problem. However, any computer "output" requiring extensive programming of "input" can be of questionable value at the "11th hour."

008 Frequency of bargaining in a decentralized situation such as ours is not conducive to widespread use except to analyze information contained in memory banks for other purposes.

010 Each of our contracts cover only one location with bargaining units comparatively small in number.

011 Don't know limitations at this time because of limited experience.

012 I don't believe there should be any, as long as the information is used intelligently.

013 (1) Contract issues generally are not of a mathematical nature, (2) contract comparisons have not been so complex as to warrant EDP approach, and (3) costing formulae have been developed over the years which do not necessitate sophistication of EDP.

016 Very little restriction.

017 Effectiveness of computers is to a degree tied to management's ability to predict demand areas and hard core issues.

019 Feel their use for the present would be limited to obtaining basic personnel data, as indicated above.

021 They cannot aid in the full scope of bargaining — their function is pretty much limited to the economics, costing, etc.

023 Use of computers presupposes considerable advance understanding of the problem scope, availability of accurate input, reliable factor weighting, and logical resolution of problems — somehow these elements still are rarities in the bargaining process.

024 Time element.

025 Their effectiveness really depends upon the soundness of the assumptions fed into them. To a great extent, this depends upon noncomputer considerations.

026 We don't use to any great degree so really unable to comment on limitations.

029 Don't know.

031 Cost versus value.

032 Time limitations for data gathering and preparation of information during the course of bargaining.

033 Because of the sophistication of the computers, none that we anticipate.

034 None.

035 Limitations of computer time, programmers, programming time, and specialized type of data needed.

036 (1) Availability of data in machine language, (2) retrieval of information on a timely basis.

037 Payroll oriented statistics and master records on tape as opposed to benefit records and/or employee or personnel oriented records and programs.

038 Time required to program computer to analyze and cost unanticipated union demands made during bargaining — validity of output only as good as validity of input data.

039 Difficulty involved in obtaining specific data not readily available and programming time.

040 None.

043 Preparatory work prior to negotiations, statistical analyses, etc. work fine during negotiations; but time factor, programming, and compilation of basic data in usable form many times is different in the middle of negotiation sessions.

044 Time of programmer and time on the computer make it too slow for many of the problems involved in analyzing a particular proposal in contract negotiations or administration of labor contracts. Beginning in 1968, we anticipate improvement via more sophisticated systems.

045 Machine time limitations and difficulty in programming fast enough to keep pace with tempo of bargaining.

047 When we estimate what the computer should do for us, we must never forget it is only an extension of the human mind. In other words, it can do no more than the human mind, or a

collection of human minds working together. The difference is solely that the computer carries out operations in a fraction of the time the human mind would require. Thus, it can speed maneuvers in bargaining.

048   Reliable source data may not be readily available, particularly layoffs, vacations, sickness, etc. Also there is often a lack of sufficient notice to prepare necessary information either in source document or computerized reports. Too often we must do these things on a "crash" basis. Absence of sufficient historical data currently stored in files prevents better use of machines under such circumstances. Use of machines will be limited to amount of source data which are normally accumulated for other purposes and which are already available on a current basis when the need for such data becomes known during negotiations.

049   No ultimate limit. Problem one of learning how to handle this new tool quickly and accurately.

051   (1) Degree to which we were sufficiently foresighted to feed relevant data to the computer; (2) degree to which we have speedy access to the computer.

052   (1) Economics of maintaining certain extraneous data. (2) Data comparability with other company setups. (3) Problems in data security.

053   Real-time limitations are perhaps the most obvious: don't have the capability to get information of a special and often ill-defined nature as rapidly as needed.

056   Availability of computer time when required.

057   Required data not available. Programming too time-consuming to be of use.

058   Limited only in that the data must first be fed into computer.

059   (1) The time required to develop programs limits use in quick changing situations. (2) Primarily limited to aggregative data.

060   Availability, and the expense for small bargaining units.

063   Wide variety of subjects and the nature of them do not appear to be readily adaptable for computerization as value judgments must constantly be made.

064   Little application where only a few employees are involved, can analyze problems by hand from available records.

065   Many items are of a specific nature and do not lend themselves readily to computer operations.

067   The use of computers in bargaining would be virtually limit-
      less providing all basic data are in storage and programs were
      prepared for anticipated demands.
068   Now only used to support positions where data are readily
      available. If data become easily available, they will be used to
      a greater extent.

Note 7   What Do You See Overall as the Prospects for the Use of
         Computers in Collective Bargaining?

Respondent
Number   Comments

001   They have possibilities for frequent use on a co-op basis by
      many employers or unions if standard models and programs
      were available on a share basis.
002   An ever increasing use of computers.
004   Overall, I believe the prospects will be proportionately de-
      termined by the extent to which coordinated and/or coalition
      bargaining will be permitted by management, the courts, and
      Congress.
005   We have not experienced a critical need for greater usage of
      computers in our negotiations. We plan to be alert to such
      use if and when the need does arise.
006   In dealing with a large and sophisticated union which asks
      for extensive data which it deems necessary to negotiate in-
      telligently and where the union represents a large number of
      your employees, it will probably be essential that the data
      gathering process be computerized.
007   Increased use by companies to "cost out" union demands,
      management proposals, and final settlements.
008   Groups of employers will probably pool their resources or
      share computer use at a central location to make applications
      economically feasible.
010   If multiplant bargaining develops in chemical industry, more
      use will be made by companies of computer data.
011   A wide distribution of usage in all levels of negotiations.
012   (1) Better relation to operating costs — that is, the impact of
      negotiations can be more readily predicted; (2) changes in
      bargaining strategy may be accomplished more rapidly by be-
      ing able to assess costs of a new set of circumstances.

013 Costing of increasingly complex employee benefits, such as SUB Hospitalization–Surgical, Sickness & Accident, etc.

015 Very slow growth for companies like ours with large numbers of small individual bargaining units. If we become involved with coalition bargaining, we will be forced to use computers.

016 Visualize use of model with emphasis on evaluation of long-range impact of proposal.

017 As bargaining issues become more complex, both management and the union will utilize computers more extensively to develop more and better information for resolving these issues.

018 Very little. We are a multiplant, multiproduct company and bargain with many unions on a local plant basis only.

019 Should be good — for basic personnel data (sex, age, service, marital status, dependents, etc.), employee benefits, and pensions.

021 It will continue to improve in its use because of its ability to provide more up to date information on our employees, more accurate costing of union demands and company proposals, and speedier and more efficient access to information needed in "crisis bargaining."

022 Growing.

023 Management can refine its cost analysis techniques and can minimize predictive error. In the event of government intervention or third party proceedings, computerized data could be persuasive. Briefly, they will be of assistance technically but not in relations between parties.

024 In multi-union relationships the prospects for use of computers is essential.

025 Their main use will be in cost analysis of complex issues, e.g., pensions and other benefit programs.

026 Little use in our own situation.

028 Ultimately the development of mathematical models and the use of simulation techniques will greatly increase the value of EDP in this area.

029 It is our intent to greatly expand computer use in bargaining. Since we are in the early development stages, it is difficult to conclude the total use and value.

030 It appears that computers will become a very important part of future collective bargaining.

031 Definite conclusions reached sooner.

032 Foresee expanded use. The amount of information which can

now be made available by the use of computers will assist in analyzing proposals, making counter proposals, and providing cost data.

033 In view of the anticipated coordinated bargaining approach by unions and the need for knowledge of our conglomerate company, there will be extensive use of computers both in preparation for bargaining and during bargaining itself.

034 Computers will become a way of life in collective bargaining and will be used not only in preparing for negotiations but also during negotiations.

035 Little prospects due to limitations of computer time, programmers, programming time, and specialized type of data needed.

036 We look for significant increases in the use of computers by both the companies and unions in preparing for negotiations and during negotiations.

037 Costs, after the fact, can be obtainable from payroll statistics. As far as projections of costs are concerned, neither business nor engineering (math) programming is sophisticated enough to handle estimations.

038 Increasing use anticipated.

039 If the trend in our industrial structure toward consolidation of diversified businesses and coordinated bargaining continues, expectations would be that unions will increase their use of computers. As their techniques become more refined and a greater awareness of the uses to which such data can be put is achieved, computer utilization will increase. Management will also tend to employ computers more extensively in its bargaining preparations both as a refutation of union demands and as a support of its own proposals.

040 When program methods became available, we will have a better measure of cost of demands, of offers, and of settlements.

043 Increased use as more data become available and as more programmers are trained.

044 Useful for compilation of statistics, case-reference catalogues, and projections or model building, but not generally a substitute for judgment factor or policy development.

045 Hopefully a substitution of computer calculation for existing hand methods. We do not expect the computer to analyze political aspects of bargaining nor to bring imagination and judgment to the bargaining table.

047 The immediate prospects are not good for more extended use of computers in the bargaining process, per se. They will improve only to the extent that rationality in bargaining increases. However, as use of computers is extended further and further into the *normal* operations of companies they can be made to yield, ancillary to these operations, more complete, more detailed, and more rapidly retrieved information about the company itself. Thus, the company would be enhancing its one important advantage over the union in bargaining proceedings, namely, the knowledge of its own operations.

048 The company and the union may some day use computers to a greater extent to properly evaluate effects of contract changes and proposals.

049 Use will steadily increase. Both companies and unions are learning new uses. IUD's use and coordinated bargaining will speed development.

050 Extensive use, if for no other reason than the sheer volume and increasing complexity of the data to be accumulated and analyzed, both electronically and by hand.

051 Since it appears that most compensation and personnel data will be maintained on tape within the next 5 to 10 years insofar as large companies are concerned, the computer should replace most of the current manual analyses in the preparation for bargaining and to a somewhat lesser extent during bargaining.

052 (1) Provide quick historical data retrieval and analysis in relation to current issues on more detailed basis; (2) help make more accurate projections of cost items and effect of changes in contract provisions.

053 If data base can be enlarged to include information about all bargained-for employees, there would seem to be a great deal that could be done in area of costing union demands, evaluating alternative settlement options, and projecting the future impact of union demands.

056 Gradually improving and expanded use as more data converted to machine records form.

057 Limited to (b) above. Unions are political in nature and demands are tailored to satisfy employees.

058 Can be very valuable, subject to the requirement mentioned previously in Item 6 above.

059   Greater use in preparation for bargaining; use during bargaining will increase only as techniques are developed for faster programming and data retrieval.

060   Use will increase particularly if companywide or industrywide bargaining spreads.

062   Slow but sure growth.

063   Certain advantage in compiling statistics and in making cost analyses of union proposals.

064   Little or none in this area or industry.

065   Increased use in gathering detailed items and costs where union demand is known ahead of actual bargaining.

066   We foresee more sophisticated prenegotiation studies in such areas as grievance analysis, experience under specific contract provisions, and industry wage and fringe comparisons. We also foresee increasing use of computers during negotiations to evaluate proposed changes.

067   Computers in collective bargaining represent a virtually untapped and limitless information potential which, when more fully utilized, will also serve to minimize time delays and human errors arising in the costing of packages and specific proposals. Projections of demands will provide the ability to analyze, before agreement, the future impact of these demands.

068   Restricted at this point in time.

069   Great waste of time and effort.

Note 8   General Comments

Respondent
Number   Comments

012   We are, and have been for several years, in the process of getting on line company-wise so as yet we do not use computers in a sophisticated manner for collective bargaining. The largest single group we have in bargaining involves 12,000 employees and 10 contracts so we do not have a similar bargaining situation as at Inland.

035   Employee data are available in our EDP system and tabulations are prepared periodically on disability absence, pension credits, life insurance coverage, age, service, etc.; but we are not able to obtain a set of data relating to an individual employee.

046 Computers are used mainly in preparation for negotiations in the multiple units.

051 Make limited use of the computer in either preparation for bargaining or during bargaining. This results from the fact that we have not yet placed employee relations data on tape comprehensively and uniformly throughout the company. A contributing factor is that we bargain on a local plant basis. Bargaining on this basis, we have not been motivated to compile employee relations data centrally to the degree that companywide bargaining would have dictated. Presently, we are in the midst of a broad computer utilization study, including personnel and employee relations functions. It is expected that all employee compensation and benefit plan data will be computerized within five years and that this development will produce much greater use of the computer by industrial relations people.

052 At the present time, we are not utilizing computer applications either in the preparation of collective bargaining nor directly in bargaining. We have just recently begun to utilize computers effectively in the Industrial Relations Department. At the present time, we are directing our efforts toward the use of computers in developing a skills inventory for manpower development and replacement purposes, and in the employee records area. We have utilized computers sparingly for years in collecting data with respect to wages and status of personnel as well as to compute paid absences, such as holidays, vacations, and other similar benefits. When computer time becomes available, and dependent upon priority of computer applications, we anticipate a broader use of computers in the collective bargaining process. For example, we anticipate a better information retrieval system which would provide us necessary information relative to grievance activity. This would provide grievance frequency experience by department or division as well as by subject matter. Also, this would tell us the disposition of each case and the respective positions of the parties as well as the provisions in the union agreements applicable. Such would be valuable in analyzing major problem areas in union agreements. Further uses are anticipated in analyzing prior negotiations transcripts, personnel policies and practices, and extra contractual agreements with the unions. We also anticipate being able to utilize computers

for the review of personnel policies and practices and union agreements in other companies. In addition, we would anticipate further expansion of data pertaining to the status of employees, job classifications, wage rates, benefits, and other pertinent information which we would consider to be essential for intelligent collective bargaining.

056   In general, we have found that our need of computer application has increased with each bargaining cycle. The most important use at present is the availability of programmed basic information for labor groups, enabling us to develop various cost and distribution factors needed for management review and bargaining table presentations. I believe, however, that as the complexities of our flight crew contracts tend to increase we will be required to make more sophisticated use of our data reduction facilities.

Simulation of Union Health and Welfare Funds

G. M. Kaufman and R. Penchansky[1]
Assisted by Byron Marshall

Introduction and Background

Introduction

The nation's private health, welfare, and pension plans are a natural object of study for economists because of the sheer size in number of people they cover and in the amount of dollars invested and expended in the course of managing them. When coupled with the fact that the typical manager of such funds has, at most, a primitive understanding of the effect of management policy decisions on many key aspects of his fund's financial behavior — in a sense defined more carefully below — the study of the behavior of financial variables of funds as a function of managerial policy is a fertile field of study for operations researchers as well as economists.

The purpose of this article is to describe the preliminary portion of such a study of fund management policy. We chose to begin by examining the health and welfare benefit plan of a union in the building trades. There were several reasons for this choice, the primary ones being: first, the cyclical nature of employment in the building trades makes it particularly difficult to trace out the implications of policy changes on the fund's financial behavior by heuristic or intuitive modes of reasoning; second, a managerial policy is, in this particular instance, effectively described in terms of a set of well-defined quantitative variables; and third, at least a

[1] We wish to express our gratitude for financial support from the Graduate School of Business, Harvard University; the School of Public Health, Harvard University; the School of Public Health, University of Michigan; and the Sloan School of Management, M.I.T.

121

portion of the raw data needed to do such a study was available for the plan we examine here.

We began our study with the suspicion that fund trustees in the building trades are dramatically over-conservative in specification of eligibility rules and benefit packages because of their desire to avoid the possibility of fund insolvency and the unavailability of any method for accurately specifying how the probability of fund insolvency changes with changes in the rule and the benefit package, as well as with changes in the dollar reserves of the fund. Consequently, our effort was two-pronged:

1. To build a reasonable first-order model of fund financial behavior that enables us to measure in a rough way the effect of diverse policies on fund financial behavior.

2. To provide the fund trustees with a workable tool for measuring quantitatively the effect of policy changes.

Background

Private health, welfare, and pension plans for employees have grown phenomenally in the past two decades as attitudes toward social insurance and welfare programs have changed in the United States. The legal requirement to bargain over fringe benefits established under the National Labor Relations Act and tax legislation allowing managements to deduct the cost of these benefits in their tax computations have fostered this growth. Union interest in fringe benefits was sharpened during World War II and the Korean action when wages were frozen. As wages and living standards have risen steadily in the years since, the unions have felt less pressure to secure cash gains and have sought new areas in which they might secure improvements for their membership. Often their efforts have centered on increasing the "security package" of their members.

The growth of benefit plans in the building trades has lagged behind their development in general manufacturing, primarily because the characteristics of the industry create particular problems for employee benefit programs, but also because the leaders of the trade unions involved preferred wage increases to fringe benefits for the members. Few health and welfare programs existed in the building trades before 1952, when a decision of the Construction Industry Stabilization Commission taken during the Korean action permitted employers to contribute up to seven and one-half cents per hour for fringe benefits. Because wages were frozen, unions directed their attention toward securing these contributions in their bargaining with employers.

Today thousands of health and welfare plans operate in the building trades and serve as the major source of funds for the medical care expenses of most of the 3,500,000 workers in the industry. Generally these plans are established when agreement is reached on an employer contribution during the bargaining between union locals and their respective employers' association or associations. The amount of the employer contribution is specified in the contract usually as either so many cents per hour or as a percentage of wages, and the number of hours to which the rate will apply is also given. The rate and the amount of work the employer offers determine how much money will be available for the plan.

These plans face not only the problems that affect all union-employer health and welfare plans, but also unique difficulties arising from the nature of the industry. Industry characteristics that have posed special problems for building trade plans and delayed their growth include:

1. The variable nature of employment, with seasonal and other fluctuations preventing the development of a job identification with any one employer and causing periods of unemployment for most industry employees.

2. The casual nature of employment, with frequent movement of employees in and out of the industry and from area to area.

3. The bid and contract nature of business, with changes in the location and manpower needs of the employer as well as movement of employers in and out of the industry.

4. The craft basis of employment, with many different trades operating in a single area.

5. The varying and generally limited geographical jurisdictions of local unions, with labor-management negotiations usually taking place at the local level.

Under these circumstances, employees have no direct identification with a single employer and benefit programs cannot be established on an employer-employee basis. The movement of employers from area to area, and the instability of smaller firms in the building trades, are further reasons why benefits cannot be provided through an arrangement under which each employer covers his own workers. Only a stable organization with which employees have a continuing relationship can handle the financing and provision of health and welfare benefits.

Federal legislation has also influenced the structure of health and welfare plans in the building trades. Theoretically, unions might serve as the stable organizations through which fringe benefits could be provided; and unions did, in fact, collect contributions and provide benefits under the first plans established in the building trades and other industries, such as the longshoring and maritime, that have similar problems. This system was ruled out, however, by Section 302 of the 1947 Labor-Management Relations Act (Taft-Hartley).

The 1947 legislation prohibited payments by employers to unions for other than certain fringe benefits, and required fulfillment of three major conditions if fringe benefit payments were made. First, a formal agreement between the employers and the employees (the union) was to be signed; second, a formal trust was to be established for the management of these payments; and third, the trust was to be controlled by equal numbers of employers and employees. The collective bargaining agreement establishing employer contributions presumably satisfied the first requirement. The second and third introduced what was then a novel phenomenon — a legally established and continuing joint union-management trust to administer the collection of money and the provision of benefits.

Not only have the characteristics of the industry brought about a particular form for the provision of benefits but they have caused particularly difficult decision problems for the trustees responsible for the health and welfare plans.

The movement of both employer and employee from job to job and area to area, and the casual and variable nature of employment, mean that a man's eligibility for fund benefits cannot be based solely on a particular job. As a result, a system of rules has been established under which a man becomes eligible for benefits if he works a minimum number of hours for any employers under contract during a given period. He may, by working the minimum number in a current period, become eligible for benefits at a future date, or he may have earned current benefits because of hours he has worked in the past. The minimum number of hours, the period during which they must be worked, and the length of time a worker remains eligible vary greatly from fund to fund.

Essentially, the goals of fund trustees are to provide benefits for the "workers active at the trade," to use the maximum sums available for current benefits, and at the same time to maintain fund solvency. Their decisions concerning eligibility rules, the amount of money that will be spent for benefits per eligible worker, and the sum of money to be held in reserve determine the fund's financial position. Because of the fluctuations in employment in the building trades, however, the trustees can never predict in advance just how many men will be working, the number of hours they will work, and how many of them will be achieving eligibility. Consequently, they can never be sure exactly what their income or expenses will be at any one time.

When increased expense, reduced income, or inadequate reserves threaten the fund with insolvency, the trustees can strengthen the fund's position by changing the eligibility rules to reduce the number of beneficiaries, by shortening the period during which members remain eligible, or by cutting down on the benefits available. All of these solutions have been used by various funds, but each one reduces the effectiveness of the health and welfare plan. Changes in eligibility rules and reduction in benefits undermine the employees' confidence in the fund, and may lead to their purchase of coverage outside the fund. This in turn may cause unrest in the union and internal political difficulties, as well as possible over-insurance. Even when a plan is running successfully, many members prefer to receive the amounts contributed by employers in cash rather than benefits. When their confidence in the benefit plan is undermined by a series of changes in eligibility and benefits, they will certainly prefer the cash. Frequent changes may, in fact, lead to the termination of the plan.

In rather simplified terms, the essence of fund management lies in control of the money flowing into and out of the fund. The flow of income into the fund during a particular period is determined largely by the contribution rate and the working hours to which the rate applies. It is also, of course, affected by earnings from investment of reserves and by reciprocal agreements between funds.

Money flows out of the fund primarily for the purchase or provision of benefits and for operating expenses. The amounts spent on benefits, assuming that these are purchased rather than provided directly, depend on the premium rate paid to the insurance company and the number of eligible workers. This last, in turn, depends upon the number of members who work the required number of hours called for by the eligibility rules. The operating expenses of the fund are determined by the size of the fund, the type of administration, the efficiency of the administrator, and the range of functions performed.

The timing of flows of money into and out of the fund is an important determinant of the fund's financial position. Since the eligibility rules generally provide for future benefit coverage on the basis of hours worked in a current period, current income pays for future benefits, at least theoretically. The timing of money outflows is affected not only by the number of workers who become eligible, but by the length of time over which coverage is continued. The eligibility rule and the period over which benefits are payable create a future liability for the trustees, even though their legal liability continues only so long as there is money in the fund.

Not infrequently, more money is flowing out of the fund than is being replaced by income into it. For this reason a reserve sum of money is needed to serve as a reservoir which can be tapped to meet expenses and to maintain solvency. The reservoir may also enable the trustees to adjust eligibility rules during periods of depressed employment conditions to provide for the continued coverage of workers active in the trade but not currently employed. In some funds this reservoir is initially created by provisions specifying that benefits will begin only after the fund has been collecting income for some period of time. Figure 1 is a rough summary of the way that contribution rate, premium rate, and an eligibility rule interact with hours worked to generate dollar flows in and out of the fund.

Inevitably, fund trustees find themselves in a sort of three-cornered tug-of-war as they seek a mixture of eligibility rules and benefit package which will balance their conflicting goals:

1. To provide the maximum amount of benefits possible per eligible employee.

2. To cover as many active workers in the trade as possible.

3. To ensure that the fund remains solvent.

The sources of conflict among the goals are obvious. If the eligibility rule is very stringent, few employees will be covered, but the benefits per covered employee can be generous. Alternatively, if the eligibility rule is not made more restrictive, and yet the benefits offered eligible employees are expanded, the fund runs a higher risk of insolvency if no increase in contributions takes place.

If the trustees are to trade off among these three goals most effectively, they must have a clear understanding of the way the elements involved interact. If, for example, workers are required to work ten more hours to become eligible for benefits, exactly how many employees would then fail to achieve eligibility? And how much would the odds of the fund's becoming insolvent be de-

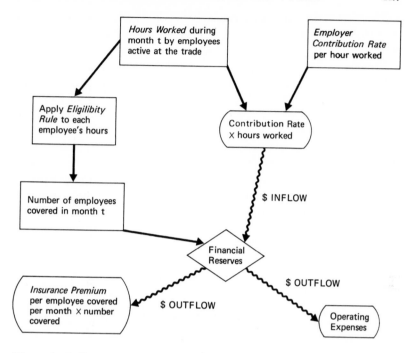

Figure 1   Inflows and outflows of financial reserves of a union health and welfare fund.

creased? In sum, what the trustees need is a clear idea of the *quantitative* impact of a variety of combinations of eligibility rules and benefit costs. They need to know not only whether or not a change in expenditures for benefits or in the eligibility rule will achieve one of their goals to a greater or lesser degree, but they also need to know how much of each of their goals would be achieved or sacrificed were they to make the change. As matters now stand, however, this sort of careful analysis of the interactions is not ordinarily undertaken; and as a result, many health and welfare plans are not meeting, as well as they could and should, the goals for which they were established.

Even though the trustees can make a multiplicity of choices among combinations of eligibility rules, expenditures for benefits, and fund reserve requirements, some aspects of the way these interact are evident. Increases in benefit expenses, for example, will always mean increased expenditures for the fund if all other aspects of fund operation remain the same. And, given the usual spread of working hours among members, a reduction in the number of hours needed for eligibility will also mean increased expenditures because there will be a larger number of eligible workers.

Because of the great number of possible combinations, and the wide variety of possible results, it is almost impossible for the trustees to know exactly how one change, or several changes, will affect all the other aspects of fund operation. If, however, a set of mathematical statements can be created that accurately depict the essentials of fund behavior, then a computer could do in a short time, and reliably, what individual trustees would find impossibly complicated. The simulation model described in this paper attempts to depict the essentials of fund behavior in such a fashion that the interactions described above may be determined.

Simulation Study

We shall divide our discussion into eight parts:

> Goals
> Work Patterns
> Model Building
> Parameter Estimation
> Output
> Validation
> Experimental Design
> Summary

We postpone a careful mathematical discussion of our assumptions and of properties of the model to the Appendixes.

Goals

Our goal is to *describe* how the probability of fund insolvency and how the random quantities "number of workers covered in month t" and "dollar reserves in month t" for $t = 1, 2, \ldots, T$ are influenced by the choice of

1. Initial reserves R in the fund,
2. Length T of the planning period,[2]
3. Premium rate r per covered employee,
4. Contribution rate k per hour worked by an employee active at the trade, and

[2] By "planning period" we mean the sequence of months during which we will simulate behavior of the fund's financial reserves.

5. Form of eligibility rule applied.

Ultimately, we wish to base this description on predictions of the as yet unobserved *future* hourly work patterns in a given trade or labor jurisdiction. Such a description is clearly more useful to the trustees as a guide to policy choice than one based only on historical data, but it presupposes the existence of a model for predicting future work patterns. No such model exists for the jurisdiction we examine here, so at this juncture we choose to "divide our difficulties" and to restrict our effort to building a reasonable first-order model of work patterns based on historical data alone. At a later date we plan to extend our analysis, and to imbed this initial model in a larger one encompassing an entire local construction industry.

In spite of these limitations and the rather incomplete nature of the simulation experiments we have performed to date, we have been able to draw some useful conclusions about policy choices. Also, we feel that the model reported here, while not complete, provides a useful starting point for investigation of the behavior of other union health and welfare funds.

Work Patterns

The basic unit of data for any given year is the number of hours worked by a given worker in each month. The jurisdiction we examine here records such data on punched cards for each worker active at the trade. We transferred data on approximately seventeen thousand individual workers for the year 1962 from punched cards to magnetic tape;[3] and, in addition, recorded certain summary statistics for the years 1964 and 1965. A typical block of data on tape is shown in Table 1.

Some obvious features of these data are: first, if any employee works *this* month he is on the average much more likely to work *next* month than if he did not work this month; second, if he did not work this month, it is more likely than not that he will not work next month; and third, the number of hours worked by an employee who works during a given month is highly variable.

These observations led us to compute two sets of statistics for each year: *transition counts* and *relative frequency histograms* of hours worked per month by employees working more than zero hours in that month.

[3] This turned out to be an unbelievably time-consuming job because of the poor condition of the cards.

Table 1 Hours Worked by Individual Workers.

Identification Number	Jan	Feb	Mar	Apr	May	June	July	Aug	Sept	Oct	Nov	Dec
10 40681	38	69	170	147	0	0	0	0	0	0	0	0
10 98004	0	0	273	134	0	0	0	0	0	0	0	0
11 07216	18	0	0	0	0	0	0	0	0	0	0	78
11 27787	0	0	0	33	178	185	190	241	165	114	166	4
11 40681	0	0	0	0	0	0	10	82	0	0	55	0
11 40684	0	0	0	0	160	178	121	124	161	120	40	142
12 46091	66	84	0	0	0	0	0	0	0	0	104	72
12 47816	144	0	0	125	229	188	172	196	202	233	157	85
20 32482	0	0	0	0	155	20	0	0	0	0	0	0
20 36293	0	0	0	144	106	0	0	0	0	0	0	0
20 92490	104	152	142	135	0	200	144	35	177	141	148	176
21 08806	136	38	0	0	0	8	152	200	58	24	153	175

Table 2   First-Order Transition Counts.

		1962			1964			1965	
		Wa	NWa		W	NW		W	NW
		Feb			Feb			Feb	
Jan	W	.7035	.2965	W	.7920	.2079	W	.7587	.2412
	NW	.0610	.9390	NW	.0850	.9150	NW	.0635	.9364
		Mar			Mar			Mar	
Feb	W	.5570	.4430	W	.8324	.1675	W	.8514	.1485
	NW	.2166	.7834	NW	.1280	.8719	NW	.1420	.8579
		Apr			Apr				
Mar	W	.9173	.0827	W	.8424	.1575		.	
	NW	.2456	.7544	NW	.2164	.7835		.	
		.			.			.	
		.			.			.	
		.			.			.	

a "W" denotes the state "work" and "NW" the state "did not work."

For 1962, 1964, and 1965 we computed for each month the number of workers who worked in the preceding month and the number who did not; then among those who worked last month we computed the proportion who also worked *this* month, and repeated the calculation for those who did not work last month. A sample of these proportions is displayed in Table 2, and we shall call them *first-order transition counts* since the proportions for a given month are computed by examining the state "work" or "not work" of each worker in the immediately preceding month. Thus, in February of 1964 of those who worked in January, 79.20 percent worked in February and 20.79 percent did not, while among those who did not work in January, only 8.50 percent worked in February and 91.50 percent did not. These transition counts are subject to seasonal cyclicality and vary from year to year.

It is possible to compute higher order transition counts. Table 3 displays such a count, a *second-order transition count*. Each employee was classified into one of four categories; e.g., "worked in January, worked in February," "worked in January, did not work in February," etc. Then we computed the proportion who worked in

March for each category and repeated this computation for each month. The data shown imply that whether or not a given employee works in, say, March, depends not only on whether or not he worked in February, but also on whether or not he worked in January as well.

Table 3   Second-Order Transition Counts for 1962.

		W	NW
		January	
	(W, W)	.815	.185
⎰November⎱	(NW, W)	.456	.544
⎱December⎰	(W, NW)	.167	.833
	(NW, NW)	.077	.923
		February	
	(W, W)	.730	.270
⎰December⎱	(NW, W)	.568	.432
⎱January⎰	(W, NW)	.090	.910
	(NW, NW)	.053	.945
		March	
	(W, W)	.508	.392
⎰January⎱	(NW, W)	.277	.723
⎱February⎰	(W, NW)	.387	.613
	(NW, NW)	.191	.809
		April	
	(W, W)	.941	.059
⎰February⎱	(NW, W)	.895	.104
⎱March⎰	(W, NW)	.291	.709
	(NW, NW)	.236	.764
·		·	
·		·	
·		·	

In addition to transition counts for 1962, 1964, and 1965, we computed the relative frequencies of number of hours worked in each month for those who worked in that month; e.g., Table 4 displays a set of such relative frequencies for 1965. In Table 5, we show for each month the mean number of hours worked and the variance of hours worked. Again we can see that both means and variances show a seasonal effect.

Table 4   Relative Frequencies (in Percent) of Hours Worked in Each Month of 1965 by Employees Working More Than Zero Hours in That Month.

Number of Hours	Jan	Feb	Mar	Apr	May	June	July	Aug	Sept	Oct	Nov	Dec
0 to 20	3.3	3.5	3.8	3.8	2.9	3.1	2.9	2.6	3.2	2.6	2.7	3.2
20 to 40	5.6	6.1	6.6	6.1	4.2	4.6	4.3	4.3	4.8	3.2	4.3	5.1
40 to 60	4.8	4.4	4.2	4.7	3.1	3.9	3.3	3.2	3.7	2.8	2.9	4.2
60 to 80	6.1	5.6	6.4	5.9	4.4	4.0	4.2	4.2	4.2	3.9	4.0	4.9
80 to 100	6.1	5.2	5.2	6.3	3.9	3.9	4.0	3.6	3.5	3.0	3.8	4.4
100 to 120	8.9	8.3	6.8	8.7	5.5	6.3	7.2	5.8	7.6	7.0	10.0	7.3
120 to 140	9.8	12.6	6.0	14.0	6.6	6.3	7.2	5.8	7.6	7.0	10.0	7.3
140 to 160	27.8	37.8	17.2	28.2	27.1	21.9	31.1	23.2	30.9	31.8	32.0	22.2
160 to 180	11.3	9.9	13.1	10.5	17.1	11.9	10.7	15.4	12.6	11.3	13.6	15.3
180 to 200	11.0	3.0	18.2	7.8	12.8	22.5	14.8	17.1	14.3	15.3	15.1	17.9
200 to 220	3.4	1.3	7.4	1.9	6.0	6.4	5.8	9.1	4.8	7.2	3.1	4.7
220 to 240	.6	1.0	2.3	.7	2.9	2.3	2.7	3.0	1.8	3.0	1.2	1.3
240 to 260	.4	.2	.6	.3	1.3	1.0	1.2	1.3	.8	1.7	.4	.6
260 to 280	.2	.2	.6	.3	.7	.6	.5	.7	.4	.6	.2	.4
280 to 300	.2	.2	.4	.2	.4	.3	.4	.4	.4	.7	.2	.2
300 to 320	.2	.2	.2	.3	.3	.2	.4	.3	.3	.6	.2	.2
320 to 340	.1	.1	.2	.2	.2	.2	.2	.2	.2	.3	.2	.1
340 to 360	.1	.2	.3	.2	.2	.1	.2	.2	.2	.2	.1	.2
Above 360	.2	.1	.7	.1	.3	.5	.3	.4	.5	.3	.3	.2
	100.0	100.0	100.0	100.0	100.0	100.0	100.0	100.0	100.0	100.0	100.0	100.0

Table 5 Percent of Employees Active at the Trade Working Zero Hours in the Jurisdiction, and Mean and Standard Deviation of Hours Worked per Employee Working More Than Zero Hours.[a]

Month	Percentage of Employees Not Working			Hours Worked for Employees Who Worked					
				Mean Hours/Employee			Standard Deviation		
	1962	1964	1965	1962	1964	1965	1962	1964	1965
Jan	67.61	69.45	64.88	132	143	132	42	65	56
Feb	73.09	69.90	69.23	125	144	128	47	66	52
Mar	69.17	65.99	63.97	131	143	144	36	68	67
Apr	54.74	57.07	54.20	131	143	129	37	70	55
May	48.37	49.75	46.77	146	162	150	42	73	59
June	46.76	46.20	42.86	139	154	150	42	65	59
July	47.89	47.07	42.69	147	158	148	43	67	61
Aug	48.12	47.05	42.68	146	165	154	44	73	58
Sept	47.93	47.93	43.59	143	151	145	44	65	60
Oct	50.17	53.61	46.71	147	160	143	42	81	59
Nov	52.16	57.84	52.15	133	148	143	45	62	58
Dec	58.11	70.51	64.37	137	131	143	40	70	53

[a] This tabulation includes only those employees who worked in at least one month of the year.

Model Building

Our model of the behavior of financial reserves of the fund may be conveniently separated into three parts: a submodel that generates the number of hours worked by each employee active at the trade in each month of the planning period, a submodel that applies the eligibility rule in force to the sequence of hours worked by an employee and determines those months during which he is covered by the plan, and a submodel consisting of a set of accounting equations which operate on the output of the first two submodels to generate changes in dollar reserves from month to month. The flow diagram of Figure 2 is a convenient way of summarizing in broad outline the manner in which the model might be used to generate a sample realization of monthly changes in reserves.

In order to use the model we must make a number of explicit, unambiguous assumptions about:

1. The process which determines whether or not a given employee works in month *t* or not (step one in Figure 2*a*), and if he does work, the number of hours that he works (step two in Figure 2*a*),

2. The length of the planning period (step three in Figure 2*a*),

3. The number of employees active at the trade (step four in Figure 2*a*),

4. The eligibility rule to be used (step five in Figure 2*b*),

5. The accounting function which operates on the number of employees covered in a given month to generate the dollar outflow in that month (step six in Figure 2*b*), and

6. The accounting function which operates on hours worked in a given month to generate dollar inflow in that month (step seven in Figure 2*b*).

The model is described in a rigorous mathematical fashion in Appendix A. Here we shall informally state our assumptions, beginning with a discussion of the type of eligibility rules we shall consider. We next outline the basic accounting equations used to generate dollar changes in reserves once the hours worked by each employee in each month have been given, and follow with a discussion of the submodel for generating the hours worked.

While some of these assumptions may seem unduly restrictive, it is possible to change them in a way that renders the model more realistic — at the cost of further complicating the analysis. Nevertheless, an examination of simulated data shows that the essential

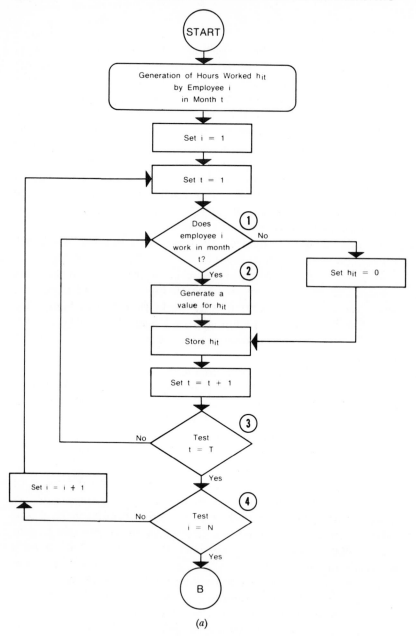

(a)

Figure 2   Flow diagram.

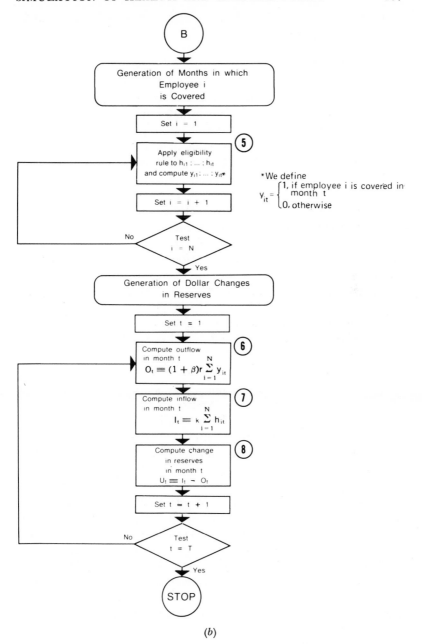

(b)

Figure 2   *Continued.*

attributes of the behavior of fund reserves seem to be captured by the model we present.

ELIGIBILITY RULES

Among the host of possibilities for eligibility rules, we choose, in this initial analysis, to examine the behavior of two classes of rules that are fairly common in the construction industry. The first class is typified by the following quotations from fund policy statements.

1. (*a*) "Insurance terminated at end of month following any three consecutive calendar months during which employee has less than 180 hours of employment."

(*b*) "Insurance terminated at the end of calendar quarter next following any three consecutive calendar months during which employee has less than 180 hours of employment."

Each possible rule of the above type may be characterized by three numbers: the number of previous months that hours are counted towards eligibility, the number of total hours required, and the number of months that coverage is in force for an employee being covered.

Another class of rules which frequently occurs is:

2. "Insurance terminated at the end of month following any three consecutive calendar months during which have less than 40 hours in *each* month."

The latter class of rules demands that a worker work in *each* of three consecutive months to be covered, whereas with 1(*a*) or 1(*b*), the total hours required for coverage can be met (in principle) by a worker who works in only one of three months. As one would expect, this class has a quite different impact on behavior of the financial reserves of the fund over time.

At this point, it is important to ask what the effect of choice of an eligibility rule on a worker's pattern of hours worked will be. While this is impossible to determine in a rigorous way from the data we have available, there is reason to believe that work patterns are not totally independent of the eligibility rule, as workers near the eligibility limit will make special efforts to meet it and the union business agent may attempt to spread work to keep employees eligible. In large funds this effect is considered inconsequential; however, in small funds facing a declining employment scene, it may have some importance.

The form of eligibility rule may, however, significantly affect employer cheating. A low limit rule tends to minimize workers' bothering to check to see that credit for all hours worked is paid into the fund by the employers. At the other extreme, a banking system which builds up reserves of hours over many months and which an employee can use for later periods tends to maximize employee interest in seeing that correct hours are reported and paid for.

EMPLOYER CONTRIBUTIONS

In a similar vein, the contract clause setting requirements for employer contribution may also affect these patterns; e.g., a clause that sets an upper limit of forty hours per week per employee for contribution purposes encourages overtime scheduling, whereas a clause specifying time-and-a-half contributory hours for overtime discourages it. We shall regard the contribution rate as fixed over the time period (planning horizon) covered by our model, although as a negotiable item it can be increased at one or more points in time if the planning horizon is long enough.[4]

ACCOUNTING EQUATIONS

We shall assume that the employer contribution rate, k dollars per hour worked by an employee active at the trade, and the premium rate, r dollars for covering an eligible employee for one month, are both fixed for the T months over which we examine the behavior of financial reserves. The *change* in dollar reserves from one month to the next is, under this assumption, simply k dollars times the total number of hours worked in the jurisdiction by employees active at the trade less r dollars times the number of employees covered in the month. We may symbolically characterize these dollar changes in terms of k, r, and for $t = 1, 2, \ldots, T$ as follows:

$$U_t = -rn_t - \alpha_t + k \sum_{i=1}^{N_t} h_{it}.[5]$$

where

N_t – the number of employees active at the trade in month t,

n_t – the number of employees covered in month t,

h_{it} – the number of hours worked in the jurisdiction by employee number i in month t, $i = 1, 2, \ldots, N_t$,

α_t – expenses of operating the fund in month t,

U_t – the change in dollar reserves during month t.

---

[4] Again, we can easily build this feature into the model; but for our initial analysis we prefer to leave it fixed.

[5] $\sum_{i=1}^{N_t} h_{it}$ means $(h_{1t} + h_{2t} + \cdots + h_{N_t t})$.

If we begin with reserves R at the beginning of month 1, then at the end of month t, the amount of reserves Z_t in the fund is the sum of initial reserves R and changes in months 1, 2, . . . , t:

$$Z_t = R + U_1 + U_2 + \cdots + U_t.$$

Aside from accounting errors and delayed and/or delinquent collections from employers, we may regard these equations as the *fundamental accounting equations* for the financial reserves of the fund.

While in principle the number of employees active at the trade during month t can be any positive integer, we shall assume that N_t has a fixed value N for each t. We shall also assume that expenses α_t in month t is a fixed percent of total expenditures for premiums during that month. With these assumptions we may rewrite the first equation as

$$U_t = - (1 + \beta) r n_t \, k \sum_{i=1}^{N} h_{it}.^6$$

Assumptions about work patterns

Guided by statistics similar to those illustrated in Tables 2 through 5, we shall assume that the number of hours worked in a given month by employee i active at the trade is a random quantity whose value is generated in two steps: we first determine whether or not he worked; and then, if he did work, the number of hours that he worked.

Provided that we are willing to interpret relative frequencies as probabilities, we might then use Table 2 to assign probabilities. For example, the relative frequencies for 1962 of transitions from "worked in February" to "worked in March" and to "didn't work in March" are .5570 and .4430, respectively. We then interpret .5570 as the conditional probability that an employee who worked in January will work in February and .4430 as the conditional probability that he will not work in February. All other relative frequencies in Table 2 are similarly interpreted under this assumption. If we wish to take into account an employee's work pattern in two preceding months, we may use the data of Table 3 in an analogous fashion.

Once we make such an interpretation we have at hand a characterization of a random mechanism that allows us to generate probabilistically sample realizations of employee work patterns (step one in Figure 2a).

[6] Operating expenses for the fund we examine here average about 6 percent of total expenditures for premiums; i.e., $\beta = 0.06$.

Parameter Estimation

A key assumption underlying our simulation model is, informally speaking, that the conditional probability that employee i works in month t, given his past history of hours worked, depends only on whether or not he worked in month $t - 1$, and is independent of whether or not he worked in months $t - 2, t - 3, \ldots , 1$.[7] In order to simulate the work pattern of employee i, we must assign a number to each such probability for $t = 1, 2, \ldots , T$ as well as specify the (marginal) probability that he works in month $t = 0$. Again informally, we shall call the set of all such assignments that are possible a *parameter set* $\mathcal{P}^*$ and any *particular* assignment $\mathcal{P}$ contained in $\mathcal{P}^*$ a *parameter*. The problem we face here is to decide what $\mathcal{P}$ in $\mathcal{P}^*$ to use when generating simulated data.

Whether or not there is a problem of statistical inference about this parameter set depends on the objectives of our study. For suppose that we wish to use the model to explore what the behavior of reserves would have been during 1964 and 1965 if we had adopted a different eligibility rule than that actually employed. Since we have taken a 100 percent sample of employees active at the trade in 1964 and 1965, we *know with certainty* these proportions. If, on the other hand, we wish to forecast the behavior of reserves under a particular policy choice during the years 1968 to 1973, then it is unreasonable to use relative frequencies or proportions observed during 1965, since these proportions change from year to year.

To forecast meaningfully a parameter set $\mathcal{P}$ for 1968 to 1973, we must devise a model which explains the way in which $\mathcal{P}$ depends on: one, observed values of proportions obtaining during earlier years (such as those in Table 2); two, other observable variables which characterize the level of demand for construction workers during 1968–1973; and three, the subjective judgments of the trustees and their advisors about these variables.

We have not yet begun to construct such a model, and so will restrict ourselves here to an examination of the sensitivity of the behavior of reserves to *changes* in the value of elements of $\mathcal{P}$. We do this by doing a simulation experiment first under the assumption that the value of elements of $\mathcal{P}$ are given in each year by the 1962 column in Table 2 and then repeating the experiment using the 1965 column. While this is a poor substitute for a bona fide forecast of $\mathcal{P}$ insofar as predicting future performance, it is very useful as a

[7] See assumption II of Appendix A for a precise statement.

device for generating an understanding of fund behavior as a function of model parameters; and this is perhaps equally important.

A similar commentary can be given for the parameter set of the probability function of hours worked by those who work in a given month. Again, if we are willing to interpret relative frequencies as probabilities, Table 4, for example, gives us the probability an employee who works in month t of 1965 works more than h and less than or equal to $h + 20$ hours for $h = 0, 20, \ldots, 280$. With these probabilities in hand we may construct a submodel which uses them to generate the hours worked in each month by each employee who works in that month.

Henceforth we shall let the symbol H denote the set of cumulative functions of the random quantities "hours worked by those who work in month t" for $t = 1, 2, \ldots, T$.

In addition to the form of the eligibility rule, parameters that must be specified are: N – number of employees active at the trade, k – contribution rate per hour, r – premium rate per covered employee per month, R – initial dollar reserves at $t = 0$, T – number of months to end of run, a parameter set $\mathcal{P}$ for transition probabilities, and for $t = 1, 2, \ldots, T$ the parameter set $\mathcal{H}$ of the cumulative function of the random quantity "hours worked by a given employee in month t." Each of these parameters may be freely specified within its domain of definition, and in particular (with the exception of R) may be made dependent on "time" t; e.g., we could specify that $k = \$0.10$ for months 1 through 24 and then increase to $k = \$0.125$.

Output[8]

The output format is variable and includes a variety of reports which may be used to check the internal consistency of calculations and to explore tactical problems in digital simulation. (We shall discuss some of these problems in the next section.)

To illustrate, consider a fund where $k = \$0.10/\text{hr.}$, $N = 20,000$, and the eligibility rule is "an employee must have worked 180 hours or more in the past three months $(t - 3, t - 2, t - 1)$ in order to be covered in the month $(t + 1)$ following the present month t.[9] We

---

[8] Our model is programmed in FORTRAN II and the experiments reported here were run on the Harvard Computation Center's IBM 7094 digital computer. The nature of our model is such that there is no particular advantage to using one of the many special simulation languages available; e.g., GPSS, DYNAMO, SIMSCRIPT, or GASP.

[9] The fund we are discussing imposes a one-month hiatus in order to give the accounting system time to process accrued hours.

assume that for each of the five years the probabilities of transitions between states "work" and "not work" are as in the 1962 column of Table 2, and the means and variances of hours worked are as in the 1962 columns of Table 5. At $t = -24$ we assume that 41.89 percent of the employees work and 58.11 percent don't work. Accounting for dollar flows begins at $t = 1$.

The premium rate $r = \$9.84$ and is chosen so that the *mean* change in reserves averaged over all sixty months is zero. Initial reserves are set at $152,250 — approximately 10.5 percent of the sum of the mean of total premiums paid plus operating expense during 1962.

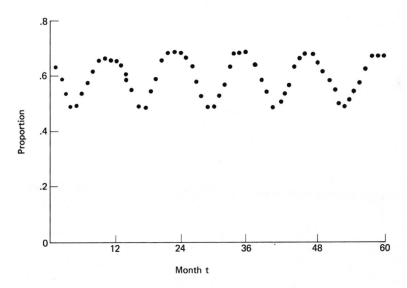

Figure 3   Mean proportion of employees active at the trade covered in months 1–60 with eligibility rule of Type 1 requiring a total of 180 hours in past three months to be covered "next" month.

A portion of the output for this run is displayed in Figures 3, 4, and 5 and some of its prominent features are summarized below.

NUMBER OF EMPLOYEES COVERED

The average proportion of employees covered in months 1 through 60 varies seasonally between approximately 0.46 and 0.67 with a seasonal low occurring in April or May and a seasonal high occurring in September through November. With $N = 20,000$ employees active at the trade, the variance about these proportions is so small that the maximum marginal probability of any given proportion deviating by more than ± .003 from its mean is less than 0.005.

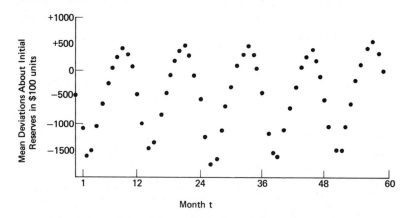

Figure 4   Mean deviation in reserves in Rule 1 at 180 hours: premium rate $10, Contribution rate $.10/hour, $N = 20,000$.

Amount of dollar reserves on hand

The means of dollar reserves fluctuate seasonally between an approximate high of initial reserves plus $49,000 in November and an approximate low of initial reserves less $160,000 in March. Marginal variances of dollar reserves are small enough so that with initial reserves of $160,000 or more, insolvency — *if* it does occur — will occur with probability close to 1 in March. We may paraphrase this statement very roughly by saying that seasonal fluctuation in the means of dollar reserves is with very high probability a numerically larger source of variation than are random fluctuations about these means.

Probability of insolvency

Figure 5 shows how the probability of insolvency varies with increasing initial reserves R expressed as a percent of the mean of one year's total expenditures for premiums and operating expenses. Thus in March ($t = 3$ on Figure 4), we see that the mean reserves in the fund are less than zero. Since the variance of dollar reserves is small, we would conjecture that insolvency will obtain at $t = 3$ with high probability. Figure 5 substantiates this conjecture; the proba-

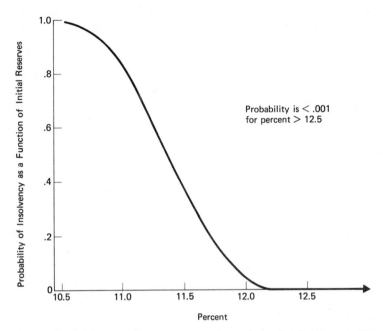

Figure 5   Initial reserves as percent of one year's total mean outflow.

bility of insolvency is found to be .986. This probability decreases *very* rapidly with an increase in initial reserves, however; and an increase of only 2 percent to 12.5 percent reduces the probability of insolvency to less than .001! Again, the marginal variance of dollar reserves at $t = 3$ is so small relative to the size of mean reserves that this fact is intuitively obvious.

Validation

There is no consensus among experts as to what constitutes an adequate test of the validity of a simulation model. In fact, there is no consensus as to the meaning of validation.[10] Most will agree that it has to do with measurement of the degree to which a model

[10] See James L. McKenney, "Critique" (of Naylor), *Management Science: Application Series,* Vol. 14, No. 2, October 1967, pp. B-102–B-103.

T. G. Naylor and J. M. Finger, "Verification of Computer Simulation Models," *Management Science: Application Series,* Vol. 14, No. 2, October 1967, pp. B-92–B-104.

W. E. Schrank and C. C. Holt, "Critique" (of Naylor), *Management Science: Application Series,* Vol. 14, No. 2, October 1967, pp. B-104–B-106.

is an accurate representation of the real-world system being modeled
and so we shall loosely interpret the process of validation to mean
performance of a series of experiments and tests designed to accomplish three tasks: to show the degree to which assumptions about
relations among model components accurately reflect relations
among elements of the real system these components represent; to
test the degree to which data generated by the model conform to the
observed data from which the model was formulated; and to test
the degree to which data generated by the model conform to yet-
to-be-observed data (forecasting).

Some typical questions having to do with the validity of our model
are:

1. Are the work patterns of *different* employees statistically independent, as the model assumes?

2. Must an accurate model of transitions between the states "work"
and "not work" be at least second-order, or is the assumption that it
is first-order reasonable?

3. Will a dramatic change in the benefit package and eligibility
rule induce a change in work patterns in the jurisdiction?

4. The submodel of dollar inflows and outflows represented by
the first accounting equation is an aggregated submodel, composed
of a combination of N disaggregated submodels of individual employees. Do we need to validate the submodels of hours worked by
individual employees in order to guarantee the validity of this
model?

In Appendix B we describe a statistical test of independence of
employees' work patterns, and on the basis of the results of this test
conclude that there is no evidence of strong interdependence.

The central idea motivating the second question is this: a necessary but *not* sufficient requirement for validity is that data generated by use of the model replicate the "essential features" of the
set of data from which the model parameters and numerical values
of relations among model components are derived — provided that
this set of data is "large enough." "Essential features" and "large
enough" are in quotes because, in practical applications, what features are essential and how much real data are necessary depend on
the end use of the model. We can show that within 1962, 1964, or
1965 our model can accurately replicate what we regard as essential
features; i.e., the numerical values of transition counts and the
numerical values of relative frequencies of hours worked. This is
in a certain sense a tautological statement, since we have constructed

a model with these features and there is no problem of parameter estimation. (We have a 100 percent sample of the population whose work patterns we are modeling.)

Under certain circumstances it is possible to use observed data to check the internal consistency of model assumptions. For example, in Table 5 we display for 1962, 1964, and 1965 the percentage of employees in each month who do not work. If our postulates about transitions between states "work" and "not work" are reasonable, then we would expect that *in the long run,* the probability that an employee will be in the state "work" in any given month does not depend on whether or not he is presently working or not. Stated in another way, the *proportion* of workers active at the trade who work in a given month in the long run does not depend on the proportion presently working. This may be seen by interpreting the entries of the 1962 column of Table 2 as conditional probabilities and then computing the probability that if a worker, say, worked in January that he will work j months from January for very large j. In fact, we find that for j larger than 30, a table such as Table 6 has rows that differ only in the fourth decimal place! To illustrate we display in Table 6 the results of such a calculation for $j = 13$, . . . , 28. The probabilities in Table 6 differ only in the fourth decimal place from those displayed in the 1962 column of Table 2 and so confirm our conjecture, demonstrating that this portion of our model is consistent with observed data in a certain special way.

We have no way of determining in a precise way the effect of changes in the benefit package and/or eligibility rule on work patterns; but, as stated earlier, we conjecture that within the limits of the rules and values of the premium rate we consider here, such changes are second-order and can be neglected.

Finally, since we are concerned with the aggregate behavior of dollar reserves, we need only concern ourselves with the validity of the model of the *sum* of hours worked per month implied by our assumptions. Our model replicates actually observed sums well and, in our judgment, is satisfactory for the use to which it is put.

Experimental Design

In the language of experimental design, we shall call the probability of insolvency, the probability function of number of workers covered per month, and reserves in the fund per month, *responses.* Initial reserves, premium rate, contribution rate, and eligibility rule will be called *factors.* Our object is to investigate functional relation-

Table 6 j-Step Transition Probabilities.[a] The first row of each block contains the probability that an employee works in month j given that he worked in month 1, and the complementary probability. The second row contains the probability that he works in month j given that he *did not* work in month 1, and its complementary probability.

		Month j		Proportion not working in month j from Table 4
		$j = 13$	(Feb)	
		W	NW	
	W	.30067	.698002	
Jan				.6945
	NW	.30021	.698679	
		$j = 14$	(Mar)	
		W	NW	
	W	.339631	.658969	
Feb				.6599
	NW	.339168	.659432	
		$j = 15$	(Apr)	
		W	NW	
	W	.428706	.569794	
Mar				.5707
	NW	.428416	.570084	
.		.		.
.		.		.
.		.		.
		$j = 27$	(Apr)	
		W	NW	
	W	.427991	.569311	
Mar				.5707
	NW	.427990	.569312	
		$j = 28$	(May)	
		W	NW	
	W	.501028	.496174	
Apr				.4975
	NW	.501028	.496174	

[a] Calculations assume that for $t = 1, 2, \ldots$ transition probabilities for month t to month $t + 1$ are the same as those for month $t + 12$ to month $t + 13$.

ships between responses and factors. Each of the factors just labelled is *controllable* by the experimenter; and, to a first approximation, initial reserves, premium rate, contribution rate, and planning horizon are *continuous*. Within each set of eligibility rules of the same functional form, we can regard a portion of the (parameter) set indexing particular members as continuous and unbounded; e.g., "a worker must work X hours in the preceding L months" with X ranging over all numbers from 0 to ∞.

We shall examine only *equilibrium* policies. An equilibrium policy, by definition, sets the expectation of change in dollar reserves over the planning horizon at zero. Thus letting $\tilde{U}_t$ denote the random quantity "change in dollar reserves in month t" for $t = 1$, 2, ..., T and defining $E(\tilde{U}_t)$ as the expectation (mean) of $\tilde{U}_t$, an equilibrium policy has the property $E(\tilde{U}_1) + \ldots + E(\tilde{U}_t) + \ldots + E(\tilde{U}_T) = 0$. The reason for restricting our attention to equilibrium policies is that nonequilibrium policies are more likely than equilibrium policies to lead to either larger and larger expectations of dollar reserves as time passes, or to insolvency with very high probability — both of which defeat the purpose of the fund.

We report here the results of the first of several blocks of experimental runs we shall perform. This initial run is designed to give us an indication of the functional form of responses for a particular choice of eligibility rule. We plan additional runs designed to reveal how sample size (number of replications of a sequence $U_1, \ldots, U_T$ of changes in reserves), initialization period (number of months simulated in each replication before actual recording of reserve changes begin), and choice of random number generator affect simulated output. We shall also test the change in output induced by assuming that the Markov chain generating transitions between states "work" and "not work" is second-order rather than first-order — although we conjecture that the change will be negligible.

SIMULATION RUNS

The design of our initial block of runs is displayed in Figure 6. It is in effect a factorial design in continuous factors for an eligibility rule of type 1: factors are $(\mathcal{P}, \mathcal{H})$, X, k, R, and T; $(\mathcal{P}, \mathcal{H})$ is set at two "levels," X at two levels, k at three levels, R at between fifteen and twenty levels, and T at ten levels. Thus the total number of combinations of factor levels considered is roughly $2 \times 2 \times 3 \times 20 \times 10 = 2400$. By appropriate nesting of computer subroutines and application of a multivariate central limit theorem we are able to reduce the total time required for implementation of this design to approximately 55 minutes on an IBM 7094. A brute force simulation

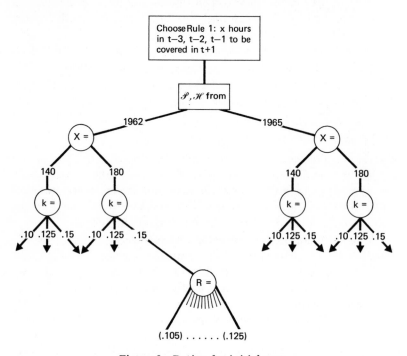

Figure 6   Design for initial runs.

experiment using the basic model as outlined in Figure 2 is computationally infeasible. When $N = 20,000$, one replication of a sequence $U_1, \ldots, U_{60}$ with this model would require about 75 minutes.

Table 7 illustrates a convenient way of summarizing some of the features of this block of runs. For six different combinations of rule and contribution rate, we see the amount of initial reserves R needed to keep the probability of insolvency less than .001 over a five-year period under the assumption that $(\mathcal{P}, \mathcal{K})$ for 1962 is the parameter set for each of these five years. Figures 7 through 10 supplement Table 7 and are self-explanatory.

Table 7   Report to Trustees on Rule 1: X Hours Total in Months
$t - 3, t - 2, t - 1$ to be Covered in Month t.[a]

Hours	Contribution Rate	Breakeven Premium Rate	Mean of One Year's Total Expenses	Initial Reserves Needed[b]
140	$0.10/hour	$8.94	$1,460,000	$170,000
	0.125/hour	11.17	1,830,000	220,000
	0.15/hour	13.41	2,190,000	260,000
180	$0.10/hour	$9.84	$1,450,000	$180,000
	0.125/hour	12.30	1,820,000	230,000
	0.15/hour	14.76	2,180,000	270,000

[a] Uses parameters estimated from 1962 for each of five years.
[b] For probability of insolvency < .001 within five years.

A parallel set of responses was generated using as parameter set
($\mathcal{P}$, $\mathcal{H}$) transition counts and relative frequencies of hours worked
for 1965. Since they differ only slightly from those based on 1962
data, we display for comparative purposes only the graph of average

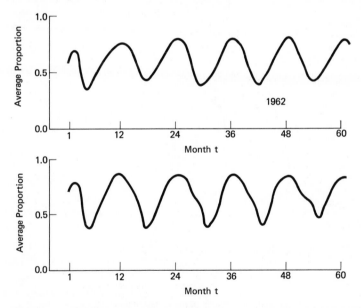

Figure 7   Average proportion of employees active at the trade covered
in months 1–60 with Rule 1: 140 hours in $t - 3, t - 2, t - 1$ to be
covered in $t + 1$. $\mathcal{P}$ and $\mathcal{H}$ from 1962 and 1965 data as shown.

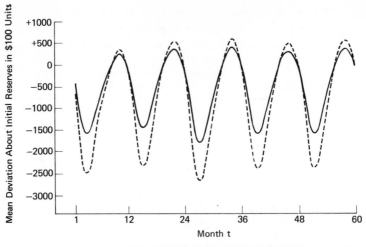

Figure 8   Mean deviation in reserves about R with Rule 1: 140 hours
in $t - 3, t - 2, t - 1$ to be covered in $t + 1$. $N = 20,000$. $\wp$ and $\Im c$
from 1962 data.

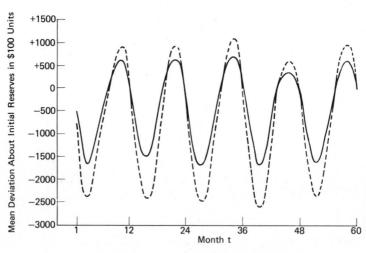

Figure 9   Mean deviation in reserves about R with Rule 1: 140 hours
in $t - 3, t - 2, t - 1$ to be covered in $t + 1$. $N = 20,000$. $\wp$ and $\Im c$
from 1965 data.

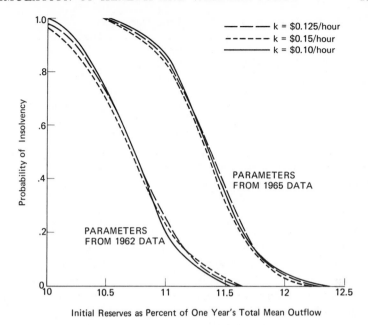

Figure 10   Probability of insolvency as a function of initial reserves.

proportion of employees active at the trade who are covered when $X = 140$ (Figure 7). Comparing plots in Figure 7, we see that the pattern of coverage is exactly the same with both sets of data, the minimum proportion covered occurring in June (0.35 for 1962 data and 0.36 for 1965 data) and the maximum occurring in December (0.84 for 1962 data and 0.89 for 1965 data). A similar comparison of the mean deviation in reserves about R shows that again the 1962 and 1965 patterns match almost exactly, with the maximum deviation occurring in October and the minimum in March. Deviations in reserves differ in amount between 1962 and 1965, however. For example, with $X = 140$ and $k = \$0.15$, the maximum is \$60,000 with 1962 data and \$105,000 with 1965 data, and the minimum is minus \$230,000 with 1962 data and minus \$245,000 with 1965 data. Table 8 shows that this difference is paralleled by a difference in breakeven premium rates, mean expenses, and initial reserves needed for the probability of insolvency to be less than .001.[11]

[11] Figure 10 displays in more detail the manner in which the probability of insolvency varies as a function of initial reserves R expressed as a percentage of one year's total mean expenditures for premiums and for operating expenses.

Table 8   Comparison of 1962 and 1965 Data.

	Breakeven Premium Rate $R	Mean of One Year's Total Expenses	Initial Reserves Needed
1962	$13.41	$2,190,000	$260,000
1965	14.18	2,440,000	270,000

In sum, this partial comparison shows that deriving $(\mathcal{P}, \mathcal{K})$ from 1965 data in place of 1962 data leads to observable but not dramatic differences in simulated output.

Summary

We have informally outlined the structure of a simulation model of fund reserves and shown how it can be used to generate information about fund behavior that can be of real value to trustees in making policy choices. On the basis of the limited analyses done here the following observations appear to be valid for the fund we are examining:

1. *Given* a choice of eligibility rule and premium rate, a substantial change in work patterns is required to induce a significant change in response functions, such as the probability of insolvency as a function of initial reserves R.

2. The probability of insolvency as a function of R is insensitive to changes in the contribution rate k over the range $0.10 to $0.15.

3. An analysis based on forecasts of work patterns over the period, say, 1968 to 1975, would show that the probability of insolvency can be kept below .001 with initial reserves of substantially less than 50 percent of one year's total average expenses.

We *conjecture* rather than state these conclusions because our analysis is built upon an historical data base and is done with an incomplete model which must be subjected to additional tests of validity. The nature of the limitations of this initial portion of a continuing study constitutes an instructive example of some of the strategic and tactical problems one faces in doing simulation experiments and simultaneously points up an important fact about the *process* of simulation: the exercises of data interpretation and analysis and of model building and validation can give useful insight into the structure of a complicated real world system even at a stage in this process when the goals of the study have been only partially achieved.

Elaboration and Discussion

Penchansky This paper deals with decisions made in administering multifirm employee health and welfare programs, most of which are found in the building industry; but the more general effects of these decisions on the bargaining process should be obvious. More importantly, for those of you not interested in this particular narrow subject, I think it is interesting to look at the use of simulation in predicting employment status for particular employees. Some of the technology that Gordon Kaufman developed is useful, I think, in other applications. Therefore, you should think of this in the light not only of the specific use that it will be given in the health and welfare field (we hope), but of its use in broader employment considerations.

What we wish to focus upon here is an attempt to improve the decision-making ability of trustees of health and welfare funds. The kind of decisions that the trustees have to make are usually in three major areas: the eligibility rules for benefits; the amount of benefits to be offered to those eligible; and the reserve level, or how much money is necessary for fund solvency. I will discuss each of these in order.

Basically we have a situation where employers bargain with unions to determine the amount to be contributed by the employer for fringe benefits. To administer these contributions a trust is set up. Since there is no necessary permanent attachment between employer and employee, the normal means of deciding eligibility for fringe benefits (whether full time or part time) which prevail in industries where employment is less casual do not exist here. So eligibility rules are developed which typically state that if a craftsman has worked so much time in the most recent period, say, three months, he is eligible for a certain level of benefits. This eligibility is established even though he worked for a number of employers.

In determining the rules for eligibility, a problem arises concerning the relationship between hours worked and number of employees. Under some circumstances, the work could be concentrated among a small percentage of the union membership; in other cases, it may be more or less equally distributed. Thus for a given number of total hours worked, the number of workers eligible might be widely different, depending upon this distribution pattern.

So there are two uncertainties here. First, how many total hours will be worked by the workers in the jurisdiction of this fund; and second, given the eligibility rule, how many workers will this rule allow to become eligible for benefits?

The second major decision which must be made is how much should be spent for the benefits for those people who become eligible; $3 a month or $30 a month? Also, we have a situation where past or current work means future eligibility, so the trustees face the possibility that there will be periods of time where the expenses of the fund will exceed the income. To allow for this eventuality they build up a reserve pool. The question is, how much reserve will be needed to assure fund solvency? As can be seen, these factors are interrelated.

In determining the size of the reserve, it would appear that the longer the period an employee is eligible for benefits the greater the amount the trustees should hold in reserve. To test this notion I plotted a graph for all the funds for one union in the United States to attempt to establish a correlation between these two variables — and there was no relationship. Most of the trustees have set up their reserves on the basis of suggestions from their health and welfare consultants who use various rules of thumb, such as you should always have one year in reserve or two years in reserve and so on.

For instance, there is a fund where one of the key people had the idea that the fund should hold two years' total expenses in reserve because the day might come when the union would not settle with the employer and so there ought to be enough money in the fund to carry it for two years in the absence of any further employer contributions. If you were to ask him what is the probability of this happening, he would be unable to answer. He saw this as the ultimate possibility, and so has built up and is holding two years' total expenses in reserve. And you would be amazed how many funds in the United States have *more* than two years' total reserve.

In order to establish a more reasonable figure, you must estimate how much employment will decline in the next two years, say, 30 percent, before the Federal Government will step in and take remedial action. Or, over the next five years, what is the greatest decline in employment which can be reasonably expected in this area? These will give a pretty good upper limit. You can then set your income and expenditures accordingly.

It should be pointed out that health insurance is a current benefit. It is generally money which is spent in the same year it is collected.

We are not talking of a pension situation. This should be kept in mind in considering the level of fund reserves.

Most of the health and welfare funds are very small. In fact, that is one of the problems. There are something like thirty-two different carpenters' funds in the State of Massachusetts alone. This creates a number of problems. There are very high administration costs and very high insurance costs. There is also the problem of workers being ineligible for benefits because half their time was credited to one fund and half of their time to another, with neither fund being credited with sufficient hours to establish eligibility.

Because of the high administrative expenses which these small funds face, it is my estimate that in the average building trade fund 40 cents of every dollar goes for administration cost and only 60 cents goes for the purchase of benefits. In one-third of the funds in the United States I would venture that over 50 cents on the dollar goes for administrative cost.

Anonymous What is the composition of this overhead cost?

Penchansky Let's take a fund of five hundred men as an example. I would say that in a fund of this size they would probably be losing over 5 percent, maybe even 7 or 8 percent, in employer non-payment. In a larger fund, it is even harder to keep control on the employer's contribution. The internal administrative costs would run about 10 to 12 percent and the insurance cost for five hundred men would add another 10 to 12 percent. This totals to 25 or 30 percent, so perhaps my figure of 40 percent is a little high.

Daniels If you don't mind a dissenting footnote, in the apparel trade the administrative costs are running from 3 to 8 percent; and our experience also has been that as we consolidate and merge funds, our costs go down and the number of employer defaults goes down rather than up.

Penchansky Are you including your insurance costs?

Daniels We are self-insured.

Penchansky There are self-insurance costs which must be considered. The reason I say that employer nonpayments increase with increasing size, at least in the building trades industry, is that when you have one local and one fund, the business agent sees the fund as being *his* and thus is very conscientious about assuring employer contributions. As soon as you have three or four locals with different agents all in one fund, they tend to say, "Let the other guy take care of it." They won't call their employees out on strike in order to enforce the health and welfare payments; they would rather let it go. I don't have any statistical data on this; but from my talks with fund administrators and business agents, when a fund has only one or two locals in it, the agents do a better job of controlling employer contributions than when you have ten or twelve business agents. They would much rather keep their men on the job than strike the employer over benefit payments.

In coming back to our simulation, since almost all the funds use the services of large consultants, we see the possibility that the consultants, most of whom have computer systems, could install a system similar to the sort we have devised. This would contain a series of variable rules and decisions so that each client could simulate the financial characteristics of his fund and thus make his annual decisions about benefit payments and reserve levels more intelligently. This is the specific objective of our model, but there is an even broader one in terms of health and welfare plans.

When the client begins to use this model and sees the effect that the number of employees in the fund has on the amount of reserves that are required, this may be an important factor in getting funds to start to consolidate. As the number of workers in a fund increases, you get increasing stability and so the financial reserve level can be lower; also, you get decreased administrative costs. Hopefully, these facts will lead to greater consolidation. So, not only do we see this model being useful for consultants in assisting fund administrators in making better health and welfare decisions, but as they begin to use it, they will see the advantage in moving to larger plans.

McLean You look to the consultants to provide this service. Do you see any evidence that the insurance companies themselves might begin work in this area in order to gain a competitive advantage and thus eliminate the consultant?

Penchansky No, not really. I would hate to see the insurance companies provide too much of this service because I think one of the things the funds have to get away from is their close identification with the insurance companies.

Bigelow Why?

Penchansky Because I think the funds in the building trades have been much too narrow in their perspective of what to buy, how to administer the benefits, and the whole concept of eligibility; and the insurance companies are not going to help them in these areas.

Kaufman Let me begin my part of the discussion by restating the objectives of this study. First of all, our objective was to build a model which would enable us to judge explicitly the effects of different policy choices on the part of trustees of these funds. It is virtually impossible to be explicit and accurate about these choices unless you have some kind of careful model of what is going on because there are simply too many factors at play and there is a great deal of uncertainty inherent in the work pattern.

In order to make something like this work, we have to separate the process of building a model of a fund's behavior from the problem of projecting present work patterns into the future so that the model can be used to impute future experience. We simplified the matter for the purposes of this study by using historical work experience, collected from over eighteen thousand workers in three different years (a 100 percent sampling), and assumed that this work experience would serve as a basis for examining different policy choices by the trustees.

As you might guess, this process of gathering month-by-month data on eighteen thousand workers is not a trivial problem and it was particularly difficult because of the condition of the card records. Nowadays, many funds record their data on magnetic tapes, so the collection process should be a much easier task in the future.

It is probably worthwhile to say something very quickly about simulation. Simulation is the process of building a model of a real-world system, taking care to verify that the components of the model match components of the real-world system and that the relationships among these components in the abstract model accurately mirror the components in the real world. You must make sure that the data you originally used to build the model fit the attributes of the parameters which are contained in the model. Then this model is used to generate data which can be interpreted as if they were occurrences in the real world. In other words, what you are doing is using an abstract symbolic model to generate hypothetical experience, in this case the behavior of union health and welfare funds. Even with a very limited number of choices among the contribution rates, forms of the eligibility rule, and effects of changing work patterns, there are some 450 combinations to look at to get a feel for the structure of what is going on. I think that the sheer tyranny of large numbers will convince you of the utility of a device like this.

Let's take a look for a moment at the kind of thing that you might want to provide the fund trustees. Let's suppose that in consultation with the trustees we wish to examine the probability of insolvency within a period of five years if we use a certain eligibility rule. Say, for example, that an employee must work a total of 140 hours in January, February, and March in order to be covered in April; and the contribution rate by the employers is 10 cents per hour. What will be the probability of insolvency?

For the purposes of this initial study, we say that insolvency occurs if the fund starts off with a certain amount of money and, at some point within the five years, the changes in the fund cause the amount of initial reserves to dip down to zero or below. It should be noted that we can define insolvency in any other way that you like within the context of this model.

Of course, you would never let this situation happen. As soon as you saw the reserves were dipping down, you would change the eligibility rules or go back and try to renegotiate a higher contribution rate from the employers.

In any event, the breakeven premium rate is the insurance premium that you can pay for each employee who is covered in order that the average of the inflows and outflows, which are highly cyclical, will balance out to zero over the five-year period.

You might ask, why look at a breakeven premium rate? Well, let's assume that the work patterns are fairly consistent, although cyclical, throughout the five years. Using this assumption, you find that the breakeven premium averages out to be $8.94. Therefore, if you pay out $15.00 in premiums, in three or four years you will use up your reserves; or alternately, if you cut down to $4.00, you would be pyramiding them upward. In both of these cases, these policies would defeat the purpose of the fund.

Anonymous Did you put a factor in for increases in premiums or changes in work patterns?

Kaufman No, I didn't; but in this model you are welcome to manipulate any figure that you choose. As you will see, it is complicated enough as it is.

In looking at the probability of insolvency as a function of initial reserves (Figure 10), there is something that is very interesting in this, isn't there? We see that only about 12 percent of one year's total expenses are needed to assure fund solvency; and, as Roy [Penchansky] was mentioning earlier, many trustees presently keep as much as two years' total expenses in the fund as a reserve.

Realizing that there are any number of work patterns which are possible, we might want to double this percentage to twenty-five. Then the probability of insolvency would be considerably lower than one out of a thousand and the reserves could still be reduced by several hundred percent. It is with this kind of thing that you can begin to see how the model can be very useful.

Anonymous How sensitive would the breakeven premium rate be?

Kaufman The breakeven premium rate has nothing to do with insolvency per se. It is merely that premium for which the average change in the reserves of the fund is zero over the planning horizon. Of course it is clear that if I fix a certain eligibility rule and fix a contribution rate, the premium rate then determines the probability of insolvency. That is what I have done in this illustrative example because it seemed like a reasonable thing to do.

Mills You haven't specified what craft these data refer to; but when you look at other crafts, these cyclical patterns aren't pervasive in the industry at all. Now I know that this doesn't have anything to do with the validity of your model or the use of this kind of technique, but I think it is important to state that for the construction industry generally there is a tendency to maintain the average number of hours worked per month over the whole year and to level employment much more than you have indicated.

Penchansky This study is of the laborers and they have a more seasonal pattern than boilermakers, but probably no different than bricklayers. In fact, the bricklayers might be worse. Each trade has a different pattern and our theory is that you could build a new pattern for each area of the country. The patterns will also change given the level of construction in an area.

Mills It seems to me that one of the things you start with in this model is the number of men available or working in this jurisdiction. And this is the really hard thing to predict because it is not only a function of the current supply, both in terms of composition as well as size, but it is also a function of availability from other industries. And you must predict this number in order to use this aggregate model.

Kaufman If you assume that a certain number are available, it simplifies the process; but this raises another possibility I would like to comment on. If you think that there are going to be fluctuations in the number of workers in a trade jurisdiction and you are not really clear on how to go about precisely predicting what the effect of this is going to be on the fund behavior, then I think the model becomes useful because it enables you to look at a large number of possibilities for differing numbers of people in the jurisdiction within, say, a two-year period and see what happens.

Anonymous This goes back to the point that the model can be extremely useful even if it doesn't predict exactly. Through simulation, you can see, out of all the things that could affect the model, which things are important in terms of what happens. Even though it is only relative, you are in much better shape in order to plan intelligently.

Mills I don't think that estimating the number of people is that tough a problem. The business agents I have had contact with can tell you a year or two in advance where their workers are going to go or where their workers are going to come from. If you use all the men in the state and not only those currently active, you could consider this as the potential labor force, at least for the purpose of the simulation.

Kaufman Let me push on now and start to show you what some of the results are.

This graph (Figure 10) gives you the probability of insolvency with initial reserves of one year's total average expenses. The figure is 1.4 million dollars for a 10-cent monthly premium, 1.9 million dollars for a 12-cent premium, and so on. What I have done is express this reserve as a percent of one year's total expenses. But you will notice that in terms of these percentages, there is very little difference in their behavior. If I get down below 10 percent of total expenses, I am going to get into trouble; I don't have enough money as an initial reserve. However, as I move up only about 3 or 4 percent, I have so many workers in the fund that the law of large numbers comes into play. The problem of insolvency drops dramatically, in this case to only 0.1 percent or somewhat less than one in a thousand. You will also notice that whether contributions are 10, 12, or 15 cents makes very little difference. Of course, these are expressed as percentages; in dollar amounts they differ by hundreds of dollars.

Well, let me stop with the graphs here. I could show you some quite different experiences with another eligibility rule as well as some printouts I have for some 1965 data, but we ought to get some discussion in and so I won't bother. Obviously you want to be very selective in the kind of things you choose to show to trustees and consultants and perhaps I haven't been selective. I have tried to give you a general view of the process that we went through in developing the model, the things we took into consideration, and the kind of applications that quantitative analysis of this sort can be used for.

Anonymous Did you consider the impact of one major variable on another?

Kaufman No, we did not. The problem is you have to decide whether to work within a given, limited set of parameter values in building a model or in a framework which is in a certain sense more flexible and covers a wider domain. In other words, the problem you are posing is similar to the problem that we faced in deciding about our transition counts and whether they should change as a function of variables in the construction industry as a whole. At the present stage, they do not. In fact, it is not clear to me how you go about that.

Penchansky It is clear to me. I think a simple solution to get a first look at this is to take different parts of the United States with different work levels in relation to numbers of men available. Then you compare these across regions, taking several factors into account, and decide whether they are similar difficulties and where the difficulties lie given different work loads.

Kaufman Perhaps, but that was a good question. We are just getting started and there are a lot of loose ends.

Penchansky This is another reason why we think the best way to handle this type of thing is through the health and welfare consultants. For instance, someone like Martin Segal has over five hundred plans throughout the United States. He alone could collect the data that would be needed. He could set up one central system similar to insurance companies' actuarial tables. Someone who is dealing with five hundred of these analyses a year could be quite precise; whereas we are dealing with only one trade union at one point of time, and therefore are not.

Anonymous In going back to the subject of this morning, what are the possibilities of setting up a model for collective bargaining?

Kaufman As Roy Penchansky pointed out, this welfare fund simulation is very special. This particular application happens to be something that one can easily encompass with a quantitative model because there are not nearly the intangibles floating around that you find in the usual collective bargaining fight among men. This is why it seemed to us that this special case is a very useful way to get started. Other applications, such as a collective bargaining simulation, would be considerably more complex.

Anonymous I take it you did this analysis for a particular union with a union trustee in charge?

Penchansky No, you have to have union *and* management as trustees.

Myers Perhaps this simulation might be an example of a way in which a model could be useful to these joint trustees and in connection with possible future decisions in bargaining.

Penchansky The implications on bargaining decisions become quite obvious because the employers are always saying, "Your reserves are too high; why do you want another 2 cents?" And the union says, "We need another 2 cents because we know that business is going to decline." This happens all the time.

Myers As a result of this model?

Penchansky No.

Anonymous Wouldn't the union say, "Our reserves are too high so we had better reduce our eligibility requirements to make more men eligible," while management would say, "Let's keep this higher reserve and not fiddle with it"?

Kaufman Let me point out that when you are building up reserves and patterns change dramatically, everybody assumes that when employment declines we are going to need more reserves. This is not necessarily true. It depends on the fund's early accumulation, the eligibility rule, the amount of premiums paid, and the work patterns.

Lesieur In thinking about getting a group of trustees to understand and use this model, I recall a meeting we had with Kaiser. Edgar Kaiser and the rest of management were all in seventh heaven because this plan we had worked out had been translated into seventeen different languages. And then one of the shop stewards who was there asked, "When are you going to translate it into English?" This probably wasn't the right attitude but it really came from down deep.

I think if I were a trustee I would be most concerned about this 40 to 50 percent administrative cost. If you are really going to move in and do something for people, it seems to me that if something were done about these high administrative costs and their causes, you might have quite a different reception for your model building. If I were a trustee of one of these funds, I sure would want to move in on that 40 to 50 percent.

Penchansky But the trustees haven't shown any interest in reducing these costs.

Anonymous Why don't you make a model and say that with it you can cut administrative costs by 20 or 25 percent?

Kaufman One way that this could be done would be to take five, seven, or ten of these small funds and show what the experience would be if they were amalgamated.

Anonymous I am not sure that amalgamation is the answer, although you may be right. I have experience in a couple of these funds in the building trades and one of the huge administrative costs was the problem of the independent who was not a member of the association. (This is the union which has signed an individual contract and yet pays into the association fund.) And every time you change the trustee agreement you have to get practically unanimous agreement from all of these independent participants. The inflexibility and a lot of the high administrative costs of the funds that I am familiar with is caused by having to deal with these independents. I suppose in your study they were all in the association?

Kaufman The ones we talked with were.

Penchansky The independents are actually a very small part of the problem.

Anonymous We found them to be quite substantial in our area.

Anonymous Have you tried this out on the consultants? What is their reaction?

Penchansky The consultants in this field don't want to hear anything, to be honest. However, I did talk to one in California who at that time was administering funds covering seven million people and had set up a computer service to handle them. He claimed they had set up various formulas to try to deal with some of these problems.

Many of the trustees sit down and really try to work these things out. They see the problem but are faced with the difficulty of not knowing what kind of effect a change in the eligibility rules will have. I think most of these trustees are well enough aware of the issues. You show a business agent the trend which the model shows and he says, "Sure, that's quite logical." So I don't think the problem is getting them to understand it.

Anonymous Look, if that is really true, why don't they do something about administration, where you can get almost a dollar more benefits for each dollar reduction in costs? What makes you think they are going to get excited about something that will allow them to reduce reserves somewhat, the ultimate effect of which on benefits is really pretty small? How much more benefits can you buy by leaving eligibility rules the same and cutting reserves?

Penchansky It would only give you more money for a short period of time. The cost of administering funds is for the most part a structural problem. It flows from the size of the fund and the nature of the jurisdiction. Basically, the building trades bargain locally and the funds are set up as a parallel to the bargaining units. This structural problem, of having many small funds, is the cause of these ridiculous expenses. Let me explain.

There are a lot of funds in Massachusetts that have four hundred workers and have a full-time administrator. It is absurd. I can take you to a dozen funds within twenty miles of here that are running funds where they have an administrator with only five hundred workers. These are what I call structural constraints, which are different from managerial constraints. They are a matter for education and consultants could play a significant role. But they are playing it on the conservative side.

Mills I would like to comment on Professor Myers's question on the impact on collective bargaining. My first comment refers to the question of whether using models like this one would really affect the bargaining process. I think there is clearly an implication that they would. Just to give you an example, in 1960 in Detroit, the Carpenters couldn't open their contract for wage negotiations, so they opened it on the health and welfare side. They were successful in bargaining an increase in benefits from 15 cents an hour to something in the neighborhood of 45 to 50 cents an hour, the whole intention being to pick up in fringe benefits what they couldn't get in wages.

An even more important point than this, in considering the impact of the computer on bargaining, is that there is being constructed through the funds a vast amount of data on the working conditions. The data that are collected in connection with the health and welfare funds are very interesting. I think at the moment there is a kind of moratorium on this information because of its potential effect on bargaining. In fact, I know the Department of Labor has received letters from fund administrators asking the Secretary of Labor if he can use his influence on either the unions or management to enable them to look at the data.

Anonymous What stops trustees now from looking at the data that are collected for the fund?

Mills They can't get the rest of the trustees to let them do it. There are some things they get to look at but the detailed information is not given them.

Penchansky It isn't available.

Kaufman I have to agree with Quinn; it is all there. But let me make Roy's point in a different way. There is a great deal of inertia in the management of these funds. It is not that the data are not available at the microscopic level to someone who wants to go in there and use them, but they are usually collected in such a fashion that they require a great deal of time and expense in order to get them in shape for a trustee to look at them and make any sense out of them.

Appendix A *Mathematical Recapitulation of Assumptions, Model, and Simulation Strategy*

A.1 Terminology and Restatement of Objectives

In our development we shall be concerned with several interrelated sequences of random variables (rvs): we begin with these definitions: for $t = 1, 2, \ldots, T$ and for each t, $i = 1, 2, \ldots, N_t$,

N_t — number of employees active at the trade in month t,

h_{it} — number of hours worked by employee i in month t,

n_t — number of employees covered in month t,
U_t — change in dollar reserves in month t, and
Z_t — amount of dollar reserves in month t.

We shall assume that $\{\bar{h}_{it}, i = 1, 2, \ldots, N_t; t = 1, 2, \ldots, T\}$ is a sequence of rvs, each with range set $R^+ \equiv [0, \infty)$, that $N_t = N$, all t, and that subsequences $\{\bar{h}_{it}, t = 1, 2, \ldots, T\}$ are mutually independent with common probability law indexed by $(\mathcal{P}, \mathcal{K}) \in \Theta$, with Θ a parameter set to be specified in detail later.

An eligibility rule may be defined as a map e from the range set $\underbrace{R^+ \times \ldots \times R^+}_{T \text{ times}}$ of a generic $T \times 1$ rv $\bar{h}_i \equiv (\bar{h}_{i1}, \ldots, \bar{h}_{iT})^t$ to $\underbrace{C \times \ldots \times C}_{T \text{ times}}$ where c denotes the event "covered," $\bar{c}$ its complement and $C \equiv \{c, \bar{c}\}$. The number n_t of employees covered in month t is simply the number of times the event c obtains at t. Thus once we have specified the probability law of the $\bar{h}_{it}$s, a choice of an eligibility rule e induces a probability law for the sequence $\{\tilde{n}_t, t = 1, 2, \ldots, T\}$. In turn, given operating expenses α_t in month t for $t = 1, 2, \ldots$, contribution rate k, and premium rate r for each t, the probability law of $\{\tilde{U}_t, t = 1, 2, \ldots, T\}$ and that of $\{\tilde{Z}_t, t = 1, 2, \ldots, T\}$ may be deduced from the *joint* probability law of $\{\bar{h}_{it}, i = 1, 2, \ldots, N_t; t = 1, 2, \ldots, T\}$.

The trustees may choose k, r, R, T, and an eligibility rule e from the set $\mathcal{E}$ of rules that are allowed. Consequently, we define the set $\mathcal{A}$ of *acts* available to the trustees with generic element a, as the set $\{(e, k, r, R, T) | e \in \mathcal{E}, k > 0, R \geq 0, r > 0, T \in \mathcal{J}\}$ where $\mathcal{J} = \{0, 1, 2, \ldots\}$.

Letting $\theta \equiv (\mathcal{P}, \mathcal{K}) \in \Theta$ it is clear that

1. the probability law of $\bar{h}_i$ depends only on $\theta \in \Theta$;
2. the probability law of $\tilde{n} \equiv (\tilde{n}_1, \ldots, \tilde{n}_T)^t$ depends on $(\theta, e) \in \Theta \times \mathcal{E}$;
3. the probability law of $\tilde{U} \equiv (\tilde{U}_1, \ldots, \tilde{U}_T)^t$ and that of $\tilde{Z} \equiv (\tilde{Z}_1, \ldots, \tilde{Z}_T)^t$ depend upon $(a, \theta) \in \mathcal{A} \times \Theta$.

Our objectives may now be summarized like this: given (a, θ) consider

(i) the probability $P_T(a, \theta) \equiv 1 - P(\tilde{Z}_1 > 0, \tilde{Z}_2 > 0, \ldots, \tilde{Z}_T > 0)$ of insolvency occurring within months 1 to T inclusive,

(ii) the expected waiting time $E_T(a, \theta)$ to insolvency conditional on solvency occurring at $t' \leq T$,

(iii) the mean vector $\bar{n}$ and variance matrix $\text{Var}(\tilde{n}) \equiv \mathbf{V}_n$, and

(iv) the mean vector $\bar{Z}$ and variance matrix $\text{Var}(\tilde{Z}) \equiv \mathbf{V}_Z$.

How do (i), (ii), (iii), and (iv) change with changes in (a, θ)? In order to put interpretive meat on the bones of the above statement of objectives we must give an explicit, detailed structure to the probability laws of the $\tilde{h}_i$s. We do this in the next section.

Using a multivariate central limit theorem we then show that if we let $N_t = N$ for each t, as $N \to \infty$ the rv $\tilde{\mathbf{Z}}$ is asymptotically Normal, and use this result to develop an efficient Monte Carlo procedure for estimating $P_T(a, \theta)$ and $E_T(a, \theta)$.

A.2 Assumptions

Our initial formal assumption is

I. For time periods $t = 0, 1, 2, \ldots, T$ the number of workers active at the trade is N.

While not strictly true, this assumption seems to be a reasonable first-order approximation and simplifies the calculations a good deal; e.g., Cramer's theorem in A.3 is directly applicable. The Monte Carlo routines are in no way dependent on this assumption, however, and the limit theorem we use can be modified to encompass the cases where N changes in a known fashion with t or N at t is a random variable with very "large" mean and finite second moment. We prefer to proceed in this initial study unencumbered by the need to specify behavior of N as a function of t.

Our second assumption characterizes the work pattern of a generic employee as a two-part stochastic process: transitions from month to month between the states "work" and "not work" are assumed to be generated by a finite Markov chain with nonstationary transition probabilities (assumptions II a, b, c); conditional on being in state "work," the number of hours that he works is generated by use of a second stochastic process (assumptions II d, e).

Although the work patterns of employees differ so dramatically that any attempt to model the behavior of an *individual* employee must take into account his particular work attributes, we choose to make the simplifying assumption that a sample realization of hours worked for, say, employee i in periods $0, 1, 2, \ldots, T$ is generated according to the *same* model as a sample realization of hours worked in periods $0, 1, 2, \ldots, T$ for worker $j, j \neq i$. The reasons are fourfold: first, we are ultimately interested in the sequence $\{\tilde{Z}_t, t = 0, 1, 2, \ldots, T\}$ and a sample realization $(Z_1, \ldots, Z_T)$ is essentially a weighted sum of $N \ (> 18,000)$ individual employee sample realizations, as we shall see; second, asymptotic Normality of $\tilde{\mathbf{Z}}$ will hold whether or not this

simplifying assumption is made provided that we assume mutual independence *between* workers; third, this simplification is a realistic
compromise forced by the tyranny of large numbers; and, fourth, as
reported earlier, the models we posit here give a good first-order approximation to the aggregate data of Tables 2–5.

In the sequel we shall alternate between discussing a "generic
employee" and "employee i" whichever terminology is most convenient. We define for employee i

$$
S_{it} = \begin{cases} 1 & h_{it} > 0 \\ & \text{if} \\ 0 & h_{it} = 0 \end{cases}
$$

and make the following assumptions about hours worked:

II. (a) The $(T \times 1)$ rvs $\tilde{\mathbf{S}} \equiv (\tilde{S}_{i1}, \ldots, \tilde{S}_{iT})^t$, $i = 1, 2, \ldots, N$, are
    mutually independent and identically distributed.

   (b) For each i, and for $\xi_t \in \{0, 1\}$

$$
P(\tilde{S}_{it} = \xi_t | \tilde{S}_{i,t-1} = \xi_{t-1}, \tilde{S}_{i,t-2} = \xi_{t-2}, \ldots, \tilde{S}_{i0} = \xi_0)
$$
$$
= P(\tilde{S}_{it} = \xi_t | \tilde{S}_{i,t-1} = \xi_{t-1}) \equiv p_{\xi_t \xi_{t-1}}^{(t)}.
$$

   (c) The marginal probability $P(\tilde{S}_{i0} = 1) \equiv P_1^{(0)}$ is given; and
    $P_2^{(0)} \equiv 1 - P_1^{(0)}$.

   (d) The $(T \times 1)$ rvs $\tilde{\mathbf{h}}_i$, $i = 1, 2, \ldots, N$, are mutually inde-
    pendent and for each i the set $\{\tilde{h}_{it_j} | 0 \leq t_j \leq T, \tilde{S}_{it_j} = 1\}$ is
    a set of mutually independent rvs; i.e., the subset with ele-
    ments $\tilde{h}_{it_j} | \tilde{h}_{it_j} > 0$ is a *conditionally* independent subset of rvs.

   (e) For fixed t, the set $\{\tilde{h}_{it}, i = 1, 2, \ldots, N \text{ and } \tilde{S}_{it} = 1\}$ is a
    set of mutually independent and identically distributed rvs
    with common cdf F_{h_t}. We label $\{F_{h_t}, t = 1, 2, \ldots, T\} = \mathfrak{K}$.

In sum, II says that hours worked by employee i are independent of
those worked by employee j if $i \neq j$ and that whether or not employee
i works or not in month t and if so, how many hours he works may be
visualized as generated in two steps: first, generate a value of $\tilde{S}_{it}$; if
$\tilde{S}_{it} = 0$, set $\tilde{h}_{it} = 0$, if $\tilde{S}_{it} = 1$, generate a value of $\tilde{h}_{it}$ according to the
probability law represented by F_{h_t}.

For notational convenience we define

$$
\mathbf{P}^{(t)} = \begin{bmatrix} p_{11}^{(t)} & p_{10}^{(t)} \\ p_{01}^{(t)} & p_{00}^{(t)} \end{bmatrix} \quad \text{for } t = 1, 2, \ldots
$$

while for $t = 0, 1, 2, \ldots$, we define $P_1^{(t)}$ as the marginal probability
that an employee works in month t, and label $(P_1^{(0)}, (1 - P_1^{(0)})) = \mathbf{P}^{(0)}$.
We then have

$$P^{(t)} \equiv (P_1^{(t)}, (1 - P_1^{(t)})) = P^{(0)} \prod_{\tau=1}^{t-1} \mathbf{P}^{(\tau)}.$$

It can be shown that $\{\tilde{S}_{it}, t = 1, 2, \ldots, T\}$, a finite Markov chain with nonstationary transition probabilities, is cyclically ergodic if we assume that for each t, $P^{(t)} = P^{(t+12)}$; that is, for $\tau = 1, \ldots, 12$ there exists a $\pi_\tau \equiv (\pi_{1\tau}, \pi_{2\tau})$, $\pi_{1\tau} + \pi_{2\tau} = 1$, $\pi_{1\tau} \geq 0$, such that for any $\epsilon > 0$ no matter how small, there is a T_0 such that $|P_1^{(12t+\tau)} - \pi_{1\tau}| < \epsilon$ for all $t > T_0$.

The final two assumptions are

III. Operating expenses α_t in month t are a fixed fraction β of premiums rn_t paid in t; k and r are constant for $t = 1, 2, \ldots, T$.

IV. The change in dollar reserves U_t in month t is

$$U_t = k \sum_{i=1}^{N} h_{it} - (1 + \beta)rn_t \quad \text{for } t = 1, 2, \ldots, T.$$

A.3 Asymptotic Normality of $\tilde{Z}$

If we define

$$y_{it} = \begin{cases} 1 & \text{if employee } i \text{ is covered in } t \\ 0 & \text{otherwise} \end{cases}$$

for $i = 1, 2, \ldots, N$ and the $T \times 1$ rvs $\tilde{\mathbf{y}}_i = (\tilde{y}_{i1}, \ldots, \tilde{y}_{iT})^t$, then $\tilde{n}_t = \Sigma_{i=1}^{N} \tilde{y}_{it}$ and we may write

$$U_t = \sum_{i=1}^{N} [kh_{it} - (1 + \beta)ry_{it}].$$

Thus letting $\mathbf{x}_i \equiv (h_i^t, y_i^t)^t$ for $i = 1, 2, \ldots, N$, $\mathbf{I}$ be the $(T \times T)$ identity matrix, and $\mathbf{A}$ be the $(T \times 2T)$ matrix $\mathbf{A} = [k\mathbf{I}, (1 + \beta)r\mathbf{I}]$, we obtain

$$U = \sum_{i=1}^{N} \mathbf{A}\, x_i.$$

As assumption II implies that the rvs $\tilde{x}_i$, $i = 1, 2, \ldots, N$, are mutually independent and identically distributed, the problem of computation of $P_T(a, \theta)$, $E_T(a, \theta)$, $\tilde{\mathbf{Z}}$, and $\mathbf{V}_Z$ is essentially one of finding certain properties of sums of mutually independent, identically distributed rvs $\mathbf{A}\tilde{x}_i$, $i = 1, 2, \ldots, N$. We have immediately that $E(\tilde{U}) = N\mathbf{A}\bar{x}$, $\text{Var}(\tilde{U}) = N\mathbf{A}\mathbf{V}_x\mathbf{A}^t$. In turn, since $Z_t = R + \Sigma_{\tau=1}^{t} U_\tau$, defining T as a $(T \times T)$ triangular matrix with 0's above the diagonal and 1's on and below the diagonal and $(T \times 1)l = (1, 1, \ldots, 1)^t$, we have

$$\mathbf{Z} = Rl + \mathbf{TU}.$$

Thus, $\tilde{\mathbf{Z}} = Rl + N\mathbf{TA}\bar{x}$ and $\mathbf{V}_Z = N\mathbf{TAV}_x\mathbf{A}^t\mathbf{T}^t$.

We may regard $\tilde{Z}$ as a sum $\Sigma_{i=1}^{N}\,\tilde{\omega}_i$ of mutually independent rvs $\tilde{\omega}_i$ with common mean $\bar{\omega} = (R/N)l + \mathbf{TA}\bar{x}$ and common variance $\mathbf{V}_\omega = \mathbf{TAV}_x\mathbf{A}^t\mathbf{T}^t$. The following theorem implies that $N^{-1/2}\Sigma_{i=1}^{N}\,(\tilde{\omega}_i - \bar{\omega})$ converges in distribution to a Normal cdf with mean O, variance $\mathbf{V}_\omega$.

Theorem (Cramer):[12] Let $\tilde{\boldsymbol{\delta}}^{(l)}$, $l = 1, 2, \ldots, n$ be a sequence of mutually independent $m \times 1$ random vectors. Let $\tilde{\boldsymbol{\delta}}^{(l)}$ have mean vector O and variance matrix $\mathbf{V}_\delta^{(l)}$ with generic element $V_{ij}^{(l)}$, $1 \le i, j \le m$ and left tail cumulative function F_l. Suppose that as $n \to \infty$ the following two conditions are satisfied:

(i) $\dfrac{1}{n} \sum\limits_{l=1}^{n} V_{ij}^{(l)} \to V_{ij}$, $1 \le i, j \le m$, where the $V_{ij}^{(l)}$ are not all equal to 0, and

(ii) $\dfrac{1}{n} \sum\limits_{l=1}^{n} \displaystyle\int_{||\delta|| > \epsilon/n} ||\boldsymbol{\delta}||^2\, dF_l \to 0$ for every $\epsilon > 0$, where $||x|| \equiv (x^t x)^{1/2}$.

Then the cumulative function of $n^{-1/2} \Sigma_{l=1}^{n} \tilde{\boldsymbol{\delta}}^{(l)}$ converges uniformly to a Normal cumulative function with mean O and variance matrix $\mathbf{V}_\delta$.

This theorem is in fact stronger than we actually need in that it provides sufficient conditions for the asymptotic Normality of $\tilde{Z}$ when the $\bar{x}_i$s are NOT identically distributed; i.e., we could relax the rather unrealistic assumption that the $\bar{x}_i$s are identically distributed and still exploit the fact that $\tilde{Z}$ is asymptotically Normal, although this maneuver gets us into computational difficulties when we wish to calculate an approximation to $\tilde{Z}$ and $\mathbf{V}_Z$.[13]

As N is huge ($N > 18,000$) relative to the dimension of $\tilde{Z}$ (the maximum T we consider is $T = 60$), we may invoke the theorem here and regard $\tilde{Z}$ as Normal for all practical purposes. Then $\bar{Z}$ and $\mathbf{V}_Z$ serve to characterize fully the probability law of $\tilde{Z}$, and we can compute as described below.

A.4 Simulation

While it is in principle possible to compute $\bar{x}$ and $\mathbf{V}_x$ directly, as we pointed out earlier, the computations are very involved and might very well require more computer time than the method of estimating $\bar{x}$ and $\mathbf{V}_x$ we are about to describe. When coupled with the fact that no easy analytical expression for $P_T(a, \theta)$ and $E_T(a, \theta)$ exists even when it is

[12] Harald Cramer, *Random Variables and Probability Distributions,* Cambridge Tracts in Mathematics, No. 36, Cambridge, 1937.
[13] We can no longer obtain a Monte Carlo estimate of $\mathbf{V}_Z$ in the simple fashion described in A.4.

assumed that $\tilde{Z}$ is Normal, these difficulties lead naturally to the following tactic: for each (a, θ),

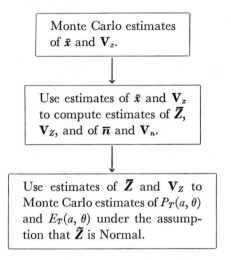

Monte Carlo Estimation of $\bar{x}$ and $\mathbf{V}_x$

To estimate $\bar{x}$ and $\mathbf{V}_x$ for a given (a, θ) we generate a sequence of values of mutually independent random variables $\tilde{x}^{(1)}, \ldots, \tilde{x}^{(\nu)}$, identically distributed according to the probability laws described in assumption II.

We then compute

$$\bar{x}(\nu) = \frac{1}{\nu} \sum_{j=1}^{\nu} x^{(j)} \quad \text{and} \quad \mathbf{V}_{x(\nu)} = \frac{1}{\nu} \sum_{j=1}^{\nu} (x^{(j)} - \bar{x}(\nu))(x^{(j)} - \bar{x}(\nu))^t$$

and use $\bar{x}(\nu)$ and $\mathbf{V}_{x(\nu)}$ as estimates of $\bar{x}$ and of $\mathbf{V}_x$. Any one of several laws of large numbers can be appealed to as a pragmatic justification for use of these estimates — provided ν is large enough. We chose $\nu = 2000$ in the runs reported here.

Monte Carlo Estimation of $P_T(a, \theta)$ and $E_T(a, \theta)$

The asymptotic Normality of $\tilde{Z}$ enables us to make Monte Carlo estimates of $P_T(a, \theta)$ and $E_T(a, \theta)$ by generating, say, J sequences of T independent Normal random variables, identically distributed with mean 0 and variance 1, and then transforming each sequence appropriately. This affords a reduction of order N in the number of random numbers we must generate over the number that would be needed for a brute force simulation, for x_i has $2T$ components and one sample realization of $\tilde{Z}$ is, in effect, a sum of N x_is.

We proceed like this:

(1) Find a nonsingular $T \times T$ matrix $\mathbf{D}$ such that $\mathbf{D}\mathbf{D}^t = \mathbf{V}_\mathbf{Z}$.

Repeat these steps J times:

(2) Generate T values $u_1, \ldots, u_T$ of Normal random deviates each with mean 0 and variance 1.

(3) Defining $\mathbf{u} = (u_1, \ldots, u_T)^t$, compute a value $\mathbf{Z} = \mathbf{D}\mathbf{u} + \bar{\mathbf{Z}}$.

(4) If there is at least one component of $\mathbf{Z}$ less than 0, insolvency occurred. Record whether or not insolvency occurred and if so, the value of the index t for which first passage of a component Z_t of $\mathbf{Z}$ through 0 occurs.

After J replications of (2), (3), and (4), we compute

$$\bar{\rho}_J = \frac{1}{J} \sum_{j=1}^{J} \rho_j \quad \text{and} \quad \rho_J^* = \frac{1}{J(J-1)} \sum_{j=1}^{J} (\rho_j - \bar{\rho})^2$$

where

$$\rho_j = \begin{cases} 1, & \text{if insolvency occurs at } j\text{th replication} \\ 0, & \text{otherwise.} \end{cases}$$

The statistic $\bar{\rho}_J$ is an unbiased estimate of $P_T(a, \theta)$ and ρ_J^* is an unbiased estimate of the variance of $\bar{\rho}_J$ prior to observing it. Here we can again use the weak law of large numbers to give us a rough idea of the behavior of $\bar{\rho}$: if the true value of $P_T(a, \theta)$ is ρ_0, then as $0 \leq \rho_0 \leq 1$,

$$P(|\bar{\rho} - \rho_0| \geq \epsilon) \leq \frac{\rho_0(1 - \rho_0)}{J\epsilon^2} \leq \frac{1}{4J\epsilon^2}.$$

In a similar fashion we can estimate $E_T(a, \theta)$. Let $J' = \{1, 2, \ldots, J\}$ be the set of replication numbers, with J_R the subset of J' with elements consisting of the replication numbers at which ruin occurred, define γ as the number of elements in J_R and for $j \in J_R$, let t_j denote the time in number of periods elapsed to first passage of an element of $\mathbf{Z}$ through 0. Then an unbiased estimate of $E_T(a, \theta)$ is

$$\bar{t}_J = \frac{1}{\gamma} \sum_{j \in J_R} t_j, \quad \text{and} \quad t_J^* = \frac{1}{\gamma(\gamma - 1)} \sum_{j \in J_R} (t_j - \bar{t}_j)^2$$

is an unbiased estimate of the variance of $\bar{t}_J$.

Appendix B   *A Test of Independence of Employee Work Patterns*

Our model posits[14] that the rvs $\tilde{h}_1, \ldots, \tilde{h}_N$ are mutually independent and identically distributed. Now in each h_i replace positive elements

[14] We define $h_1 = (h_{11}, \ldots, h_{1T})$ and $S_1 = (S_{11}, \ldots, S_{1T})$.

by a 1. This maps h_i into a vector of 0's and 1's; e.g., row 1 of Table 1,

$$h_1 = (38 \ 69 \ 170 \ 147 \ 0 \ 0 \ 0 \ 0 \ 0 \ 0 \ 0 \ 0)$$

is mapped into

$$S_1 = (1 \ 1 \ 1 \ 1 \ 0 \ 0 \ 0 \ 0 \ 0 \ 0 \ 0 \ 0).$$

Clearly, if $\tilde{h}_1, \ldots, \tilde{h}_N$ are mutually independent and identically distributed, then so are $\tilde{s}_1, \ldots, \tilde{s}_N$. As a consequence, a necessary (but not sufficient) condition that $\tilde{h}_1, \ldots, \tilde{h}_N$ be mutually independent is that for fixed t,

$$P(\tilde{S}_{it} = 1 | \tilde{S}_{jt} = 1) = P(\tilde{S}_{it} = 1 | \tilde{S}_{jt} = 0) = P(\tilde{S}_{it} = 1)$$

for $i \neq j$ and *all* $t \in \{1, 2, \ldots, T\}$. We tested whether or not this holds using a "Run Test" [15] structured like this: consider for fixed t the sequence $\{\tilde{S}_{it}, i = 1, 2, \ldots, N\}$ and assume that this sequence is a stationary Markov chain with $P(\tilde{S}_{it} = 1 | \tilde{S}_{jt} = 1) \equiv p_0$ and $P(\tilde{S}_{it} = 1 | \tilde{S}_{jt} = 0) \equiv p_1$. Let the null hypothesis H_0 be "$p_0 = p_1$," and test this against the alternate hypothesis that $p_0 < p_1$. Then randomly choose a *column* from data such as that displayed in Table 1 and within this column randomly select samples of size $n = 20, n = 30$, and $n = 40$.

P-values or levels of significance for tests of this sort are tabled[16] and we found these significance levels: for $n = 20, 0.520$; for $n = 30, 0.283$; for $n = 40$, approximately 0.9. We repeated this test once again on a different column and found for $n = 20, 0.817$; for $n = 30, 0.282$; for $n = 40, 0.809$. We conclude that there is no strong evidence in favor of rejecting the hypothesis that $p_0 = p_1$, but *repeat* that $p_0 = p_1$ is a necessary but *not* sufficient condition for our assumptions to hold. Lacking any obvious indication of strong interdependence between the $\tilde{S}_{it}$s, for $i = 1, 2, \ldots, N$ we chose to proceed under the assumption that in fact the $\tilde{s}_i$s and the $\tilde{h}_i$s are independent.

[15] E. L. Lehmann, *Testing Statistical Hypotheses*, New York: John Wiley and Sons, 1959, pp. 155–156.

[16] See F. C. Swed and C. Eisenhart, "Tables for Testing Randomness of Grouping in a Sequence of Alternatives," *Annals of Mathematical Statistics*, Vol. 14, 1943, pp. 66–87.

The Computer in Dispute Settlement:
A Panel and General Discussion

Panel Members: George W. Taylor,
David L. Cole, and John T. Dunlop

George Taylor When you start to figure what it is people are trying to maximize, which is really what you are talking about when
you build models, I get jolted when I think of this story, which I
heard from the mayor of Mechanicsville, New York, when I was
working recently on Governor Rockefeller's Commission.

The mayor of Mechanicsville was in great distress because, in his
little town, they needed a primary school very much; and it had to
go on the ballot to be authorized. He was about ready to submit
the bond issue to the voters when the local fire department, a volunteer fire department, sent in a group of people. They insisted that
the mayor put on the ballot the authorization for a ten-story snorkel,
which is a water tower that can douse a fire on the top of a ten-
story building. The mayor thought he had the convincing argument
against this in that there wasn't a single building in the town over
five stories high. The volunteer fire department was not deterred in
the slightest and insisted that it go on the ballot for the voters to
decide. And lo and behold, the voters turned down the school building and voted for the snorkel. In talking to the mayor, he said to
me, "You don't understand. Up in our neck of the woods, all the
volunteer fire departments from all around have a contest every year
on Labor Day; and with a ten-story snorkel, we are sure to win the
blue ribbon."

I must say that the role of the volunteer fire department in
American life, both socially and politically, has never really been
delineated; but this is sort of what you get into when you start to
assume that certain objectives are to be maximized. I would never

176

have even considered putting a snorkel in a survey of the development needs of that particular community, but evidently other people have different values about these things than I have.

If you look upon these new techniques as instruments of persuasion — and just that — then something useful can be developed. I think the usefulness is going to depend on just how they can be developed for persuasion and to save face. Face saving, I have observed, and all the other factors that go into it, is not just an oriental characteristic. Also, I think the usefulness of these approaches in administering inanimate objectives is obvious; for many administrative purposes there is a clear benefit. I think there can even be a usefulness in mediation, although I am not sure how this can be made possible.

For example, there is this data bank that is being compiled by the Industrial Union Department with its emphasis on uniformity. I would like to see added to it for particular situations, not only the fact of nonuniformity, but the reasons for the nonuniformity. They might be valid and they might not; in many cases, one can explain the differences very well. In the early days of the War Labor Board, we would go on a uniformity binge for a while, and then along would come a demand for restrictions to maintain historical differentials. You have to play between these two extremes. I think you have to analyze things qualitatively to find the reasons for these differentials.

There are some conceptual problems that can't be oversimplified. I had this impressed on me in the last railroad craft dispute a year ago. In that industry, the shop craft people had been uniform for years. Indeed, for over thirty years they had had the same kind of wage increases that had occurred for the operating personnel. At first, it was a cents per hour increase; and more recently, it was a percentage increase. And suddenly they found they were out of whack with the rest of the labor market. In other words, by looking at the railroad industry as a separate entity, a greater disparity was created. If you wanted to keep a work force, you had to deviate from the uniformity of the railroad industry; and I thought the machinists had a very valid case in stating this.

This same thing occurred in the New York Transit Authority. Transit was always considered as a unit with an industrywide relationship. Then the Transit Authority sold their power plant to Consolidated Edison and immediately those employees got a big wage increase as they adjusted to the area rate. As a result, the rest of the employees began wanting to get away from this industrywide wage pattern and they started talking about having a wage based on the tight local labor market.

So my first point is that uniformity is not necessarily an end in itself. This uniformity notion could be a starting point, but I would want to look qualitatively at why there has been this difference. Are the reasons for it valid or are there changes that are necessary in view of the current situation?

In general, then, these data banks can be useful in many, many cases. But I am not so sure that, among some of the smaller firms, they won't cause more trouble than help, because the reasons for differences might not be too readily apparent or not easily available to the investigator. In using this bank to deal with a particular problem, you need a way whereby its uniqueness can be brought into the equation. There is usually a unique factor that you have to deal with and you can't get this from a general bank of information.

I think one of the most important questions before us is a very simple one: what do you pay wages for? The answer used to be very simple when I studied economics. Obviously you don't pay people for time not worked. But now people start coming around with different answers to this question. Nowadays, some of the skilled workers point out, at least implicitly, that if you're entitled to all the calories and thermal units you need for doing nothing, such as is the case with welfare or with this new idea of a negative income tax, what are you entitled to if you do something very important for society — and are in very scarce supply as well? There is a shift in what you pay wages for. As we know, economic theory has been very good on the demand side; but it has never been very good on the supply side.

Myers Suppose in one of your mediation disputes, you had a data bank similar to Woody Ginsburg's; but, in addition, it had all the up-to-date data on past agreements and on the competitive situation. If these data were instantly retrievable, or retrievable in a short time, would it help you get a meeting of minds or is there such a matter of principle that the facts wouldn't help?

George Taylor I think they might. Of course, there are political matters too. There is no doubt about the fact that in the copper situation, the merger of the Steel Workers and the Smelters was a new factor in the picture. And how you would bring this into the equation quantitatively, I don't know.

Myers   It leads to more uniformity.

George Taylor   Certainly there was a demand for this, but it seemed to me that it wasn't a very viable one.

I don't think it is too useful to look upon this data base as a general purpose tool. I think somehow or other it must be made into a special purpose tool which can zero in on a particular situation, not with a view of providing the answer but as a tool for trying to achieve a meeting of the minds.

Cole   I must say I agree with the last statement very much. I think the time has come that we need some new tools. It isn't that the old tools haven't been pretty good ones and haven't served us pretty well; it is that we are in a period of irrationality in labor relations, and it is the worst I have ever seen. I have had my most colossal failures recently because I am a rational person and the parties don't want rationality. It is not a "me too" kind of society we are in any more; it is quite the contrary. People want to know what the other fellow has done so they can outdo it. It is a muscle society.

You have the problem of the union movement having no more worlds to conquer. They are not being exploited. You have fair trade and union security and the local people feel left out of the parade and they are asserting themselves. We see this in the frequent rejection of negotiated settlements. We see it in a great variety of contexts. To suggest that we can have another centralized tool that will tell the parties what is right will lead, I think, to the wrong results. It will lead to more reaction.

I think that the defeat of Dave McDonald or Jim Carey is another manifestation of this independence of the locals. They want to get away from centralized direction and centralized control. In most industrial areas they no longer have to worry about organizing and about picket lines and so they have nothing to do. I really think that this is a factor that has to be reckoned with.

It has never been the procedures or the techniques. There was a time that the Government and certain mediators were held in some degree of respect. I think this is at a minimum now. People have gotten very sophisticated and they are not impressed by George Taylor or me or anyone else. If they think the traffic will bear another nickel, they don't care what the consequences will be. And there are others who are becoming more reactionary than formerly because they don't think that reasonable and constructive labor relations are delivering the results.

Bill Caples was telling me during the recess about a situation out at Inland Steel. They were having an epidemic of grievances at one time and so they tried to institute a program to expedite the handling of these grievances that would be an expression of their good will. The program went in but the epidemic continued and few grievances were settled. Then there was a change in the local administration and the number of grievances went down and the number of settlements went up. The same people were there but with new local leadership. There was no change in anything that was really tangible, but there was a change nevertheless that cannot be discounted.

I can certainly tell you that in my experience with International Harvester, it was not a change in the contract that helped us get away from the eight thousand grievances that were pending; it was the change in the disposition of the parties. Everybody finally looked at one another and said, "Let's try something new."

When I think about the use of strikes to settle disputes, the controversy on public employment comes to mind. Do public employees have the right to strike? Is the right to strike inseparable from collective bargaining and is this the only means for settling wage and salary disputes in public employment? People like Ted Kheel have been advocating the right to strike for almost all employees. He states the proposition that you can't have genuine collective bargaining in the public sector unless people have the right to strike.

If this is so, it would be counter to everything we have been discussing here. The right to strike and the force which strikes represent is contrary to what the facts might reveal. In every sensible labor-management system, certainly every one that has been codified in courts of law, there is a provision for finding the facts. This fact finding is almost universally advocated; and yet the right to strike is felt necessary to make a fair deal. Philip Murray used to refer to this resorting to strikes as the process of trying to get the "last lousy nickel." These were his words.

I once asked him why his negotiated settlements were never rejected. He replied, "Very simple. The President would send for me and Ben Fairless and say, 'The country can't stand this. It has nothing to do with pay but we just can't stand a strike.' So they would lock the door on us and we would settle. Then I would go back to my people and say, 'The country can't stand a strike and so we settled.' I would say to my Wage Policy Committee, 'I don't know what we could have got if we struck, maybe another nickel; but I thought this deal for eight cents was the best we could get short of a strike. I want you to vote not on whether we could get that last lousy nickel, but on whether you have confidence in my judgment that this is what we could get without a strike.' And they would support me." This seems to be a thing of the past. We don't see this kind of leadership. We are seeing rank and file leadership.

Myers I would like to ask you a question, Dave [Cole]. Beginning with the War Labor Board days and when you were head of the Federal Mediation and Conciliation Service, you have had access to facts, sometimes before the mediation process, sometimes during it, which were relevant to the dispute. Do you feel if you had a data bank similar to the one the IUD is developing, or if you had information on prior grievance and arbitration settlements by industry or area such as Bill Caples was suggesting, if you had ready access to this information from a computer data bank, do you think it would facilitate the mediation process?

Cole On the face of it, you would think it should; but actually I don't think it would. Only on the one condition that both parties want it and would develop it jointly would it be helpful; then it would be a wonderful tool. Of course, facts alone will not cause a settlement. In the newspaper situation, it wasn't the lack of information or facts that prevented us from settling the dispute. The facts were perfectly evident and clear. No computer could have told us any more than we already knew about the situation, the economics of it, and so on. That wasn't what prevented us from settling; it was the experience of the last four or five years that led the union to believe that muscle would prevail — and it did. They got pretty much what they wanted, except they killed the newspapers. I don't think a bank of information would have made any difference.

Ginsburg I agree that facts alone won't settle situations that aren't going to be settled. There are such other key factors as interunion rivalry or key union positions or who knows what between the management and union. Those of us who have been in the game can cite situations where things change overnight.

One of my favorite examples is U.S. Rubber, where they used to have a hundred wildcat strikes in a year. Suddenly it stopped. What happened? The company simply said, "From this point on, we are going to start enforcing the discipline of suspension for those who participate in such strikes." As a matter of fact, the union leaders themselves had been urging the company to live up to its responsibility in this area for some time. So in this case there was not any new aggregation of facts which caused the change.

However, I would suggest that there are many situations, particularly in smaller unions, where a data bank could be helpful. These people frequently don't have access to all the facts or only have small research staffs who can't always stay on top of recent developments. Also, information on area patterns is not as easily attainable by the bargainers for these small unions. This is where we are hoping we can be helpful.

Bigelow   I wonder if I might raise a question in connection with what Mr. Cole said about his feeling of disenchantment with centralized information files and also about what someone earlier talked of in the setting up of profiles on union members. Has anybody given any thought to the privacy of the individual? In other words, how is a union member in, say, Indiana going to feel about the fact that the International has data on how many children he has and other personal information?

Myers   This is a very interesting point. I think data processing, as a technique, has to be centralized; but how the data are used, whether centrally for control or to assist the parties in the field to do a better job, this is a crucial issue.

Daniels   Most representatives could get this kind of information if they stayed in a location long enough, but they could cut down the time in learning if they got this beforehand. For example, in any shop with a health and welfare plan, a representative could easily find out how many dependents each of the members had. It isn't a question of privacy, it is of understanding the membership. How many are females? How many are younger than twenty-five? This gives you an insight into the group that you are going to be working with.

The importance of this goes even further when you consider that a lot of our people are considering bargaining for scholarship benefits. A vital question, for example, is how many people have children who would be old enough to go to college in the next four years. You could spend hours talking about this; but if you don't know the facts, you don't know a thing.

Bigelow   I can see a number of advantages from your standpoint, but I am still raising the point. There has been a considerable amount of discussion in Congress on taking the information from the Census Bureau and from the Internal Revenue Service and putting it in one huge file. The life insurance companies already have much of this sort of information and now you will have it also. Has any thought been given in the labor-management field to the issue of privacy?

Cole   Of course, the employers have had this information all along. I haven't heard any discussion of this in union quarters. Do you have anything specific in mind?

Bigelow   No, I don't; but you indicated some disenchantment.

Cole   Yes, but not on this issue.

Straus   We have heard a lot recently about the rank and file turning down an agreement once it has been negotiated because they didn't fully understand it. Have there been any situations where the computer has been programmed to print out what the total impact of the settlement is for the union membership?

George Taylor   Dave Cole, Johnny Dunlop, and I were in on the negotiations at Kaiser and I am sure that the package could not have been sold except for the job that was done in communicating it to the people. In this case, it was not computerized. With the modifications that had been made, everybody thought the workers would turn it down. But Marv Miller and some of those with him talked to the people, not in terms of what a wonderful contract it was but by showing them where they fit into it and explaining what it would do for each individual. It was very carefully done. In my judgment, it takes this kind of explanation to the people to sell a contract, not with generalities but with specifics.

Cole   There is a great deal of information that is disseminated to the employees from month to month. It is broken down into very simple lists of items, in quite some detail, which look complicated to a nonparticipant, but the participants can read them very, very well.

Myers   This isn't produced by computer?

Dunlop   Oh, yes, it is. You couldn't run without it.

Cole   The original information on the contract was done by simple word of mouth with every question that anybody could raise gone over one by one. It was a rather heavy sell the first time; but in the renewal recently, it was a much softer sell. The vote was still almost three to one in favor of the new contract in spite of all the publicity that it was going to be turned down.

Myers   Much of what we have talked about so far has been concerned with the union group providing better data for their people and the management group using data processing to prepare for their side of the negotiations. But we really haven't had any examples of the joint use of data banks, either prior to the bargaining process where positions are formed or during the process when both parties may need access to a data bank.

Dunlop   There has been some of this, although I don't actually know whether a computer was involved. In the modern world, I would assume it would almost have to be involved. One of the very important elements that contributed to the early negotiations and the settlement of the Armour agreement about a year ago was the fact that they agreed on a joint set of pension and health and welfare experts. These fellows agreed upon a set of cost estimates and these estimates provided the basis by which it was then possible to reach an agreement. The negotiators were able to get these data very fast. The fact that the joint experts agreed on the figures made it much easier for the negotiators to reach agreement and for the bargaining table to become a forum for the discussion of areas of disagreement, without having to argue over facts.

Straus   But what of selling a somewhat abstract pension plan to the rank and file?

Dunlop   That is a different problem. While in negotiations everyone had better be certain of their facts and all the nuances in them, I am not sure that I want each side to be as accurate with the facts when they are reported to the constituency. I am very serious about this. It may be important for the union to emphasize certain aspects of the settlement and thump its chest and claim it got something else than it really did. The employer may wish to do the same thing in saying it was able to maximize other kinds of dimensions. These things are very technical.

We have had this problem on the Council of Economic Advisers. People say we need to have a system for settling on the facts so we can put down a number for the settlement as being worth so much. I am not so happy about that. I think there are problems that each side faces and they ought to be given a certain amount of leeway in their public statements — but the men who did the negotiating had better know just what the facts are.

Mason At the time of the merger of United and Continental Airlines, didn't all the parties have the facts, and yet wasn't settlement still a problem?

Cole That is right and it is completely relevant. There wasn't a fact that wasn't known to the parties, including all the pilots. After all, these pilots are not illiterate. They can read and are accustomed to relying on instruments and even not seeing where they are going; but when it was attempted to apply logic to the matter of their seniority number, all reason went out the window. They all cried, "What happened to my number?"

Mason It illustrates what John [Dunlop] is saying. It makes a difference how you explain the proposed settlement to the membership. And it makes a difference whether you are saying it to the Continental or the United membership.

Meyers As I sit here and listen to this discussion, I don't think any computer is ever going to do the collective bargaining, because I don't think you can put much of what is essential into the equipment. For example, a particular plant I know has two unions, both international, one representing around a thousand people and the other barely a hundred. For years the company always settled with the big union before the little one, and the packages were generally pretty much the same. But the little union contained more of the skilled people, so under the table they negotiated the proper wage scales between jobs. However, the members of the little local got quite disturbed and said, "We never negotiate our contract; somebody else always does it for us. This year we are going to do it for ourselves." Well, they did it; but when they went back to their membership, they couldn't sell it because there was more money for the higher skills and less money for the lower skills and this was the part that they had always taken care of under the table. As a result, they had a strike.

I think each case has its own specific kinds of arrangements which are peculiar to the conditions and which allow people to live within this environment. I don't know how you can feed these things into a computer. I think the tool is a very useful and even necessary one, but I don't think there is any substitute for leadership. There is no substitute for sitting down and discussing what you must do and where you must go and what you need in order to obtain the support of the people. This job must still be done and I don't think there is any machine that can do it.

Zack   On the question of information access, I think in the field of public employment, a data bank would be helpful. In school board negotiations, for instance, there has been no experience in the past either in negotiations or the developing of data. There is a great rivalry developing among the school boards in communities as to the wage rates for teachers. Ultimately I think this is going to be a very dangerous thing for the whole educational system.

   I have been involved in the mediation of a couple of these contract negotiations; and when I tried to get ratification by the rank and file, I found they just don't know what the comparative rates for other communities are. They say, "X community got a 50 percent dental program and you didn't get that for us," without considering what the rest of their package is worth. If there were some way in which the State Education Department, either alone or in conjunction with the National Education Association (NEA), could develop a data bank on what the settlements are as they take place in these small communities, including their value on the basis of the total cost and the number of people in the different salary ranges, I think this might be a great help to a mediator. Not only would this help in arriving at a settlement which is in line with prevailing conditions, but it should help in getting ratification because you are dealing with an intelligent group who can say, "On the whole, we see we are coming out pretty well."

Cole   I think there is a great danger in that the teachers are just now feeling their new strength. Until they learn that the strike is not the means for arriving at equity, they are going to strike. Every strike has been successful; unlawful, but successful. In fact, the more unlawful the strike, the more successful it has been. I think we have to get some rules into the game, either to rely on the strikes and the muscle that this implies or on the rule of reason with economic standards. But they are not ready to accept this yet.

Myers   What if you had some intermediate steps for fact finding?

Cole   That might be very helpful.

McLean   My question is an outgrowth of one of the major concerns of the conference on computers and management that was held here two years ago. At issue was the design of management organizations and the problem of corporate centralization. It has been suggested that computer systems can, in a sense, be neutral. They can promote either greater decentralization or greater centralization of management structure, depending upon the wishes of the designers.

Now we find that data banks are being built up centrally within the labor movement in order to provide a service to the smaller locals who are unable to create and maintain data banks of this sort on their own. I am wondering to what extent this development will cause a centralization of the labor movement, with more and more power being concentrated in the international headquarters. It is frequently said that with knowledge comes power; might not these centralized data banks be the source of such power?

Myers   Bill [Caples] suggests in his paper that the greatest usefulness for a data bank system would be where there is a centralized bargaining system. He said the more centralized the bargaining, the greater the advantage of having a computer system. You can turn this question around and say, if you have a centralized data bank with provision for information retrieval, will this lead to more centralization for bargaining?

Cole   Well, to the extent that we expect the parties to rely on this data bank and on what the machine produces, to that extent you narrow the area in which they can negotiate and play an active part; and they don't want these limitations. The use of facts can be very valuable; but the question is, are people ready for facts, whose facts should they be, and how should they be presented and developed?

Dunlop   I have always thought that there are some kinds of situations in which the computer has a comparative advantage and its advantages are greatest when you can get joint agreement in its use. But apart from this area, I think it is most likely to be useful in questions where large masses of data are relevant; and in my view these are likely to be in situations where you have substantial manpower questions.

For example, I think that the study which the Railroad Commission did in providing data with respect to length of service and age profiles by occupation and by length of service, data which had never previously been available and which could not have been made available aside from a mass data handling system, this use of computers opens up new approaches to old problems. I think it is not enough to look at a problem and ask, can new data shed light on old problems? Instead, I think these data open up new ways of going about some of these old problems. We would not have been able to approach many of the problems about retirement and of estimating manpower requirements and so forth without these data.

Myers   On that Railroad Commission, it occurs to me that we might have been able to show the Locomotive Engineers' representative that the proposed wage rates *did* benefit some of his members even though it hurt him personally on his run.

Dunlop   It seems to me that there is a whole series of problems related to the movement of manpower, for example. If you are trying to stabilize employment — the kind of thing Vernon [Jensen] is talking about in the New York docks and my own interest in construction — the problems that are associated with the fact that you have 3.2 million people working in the construction industry on the average and yet 5 million people working at sometime during the year, you can't look at the problems of who these people are and what are their characteristics in the absence of this sort of data handling equipment. So it seems to me that there is the opportunity to open up new problems for us mediators.

This new set of tools opens up a new dimension, but there is still the fundamental question of whether these tools can be fruitfully used. This depends very much on the attitude and skills of the parties and on the mediators themselves.

Uses of the Computer in Contract Enforcement: The ILGWU Experience

Wilbur Daniels

It occurs to me that I have the definitive reply to all the young men who yesterday saw the computer replacing me as a negotiator. Many years ago when I first began to negotiate my own wage settlement with the then President of the International Ladies' Garment Workers' Union (ILGWU), I asked for an outrageous amount as a bargaining tactic and, much to my amazement, I got all of it. My instinct as a gentleman was to say, "President Dubinsky, thank you," but my instincts as a negotiator warned me against any such unqualified gesture. So instead I said, "Thank you, Mr. Dubinsky," but before I knew it, we were in a heated argument concerning my wage increase. I thought it wasn't enough and he thought it was too much.

He could never get used to the fact that I have two relatively short names; and so, for over twenty years, I have been known to him as Wilburdaniels. "You know, Wilburdaniels, when I was your age I didn't make as much as you do." So I used my instant retrieval and cited five or six others of my age who were making more than I. I did that about as quickly as any computer could. I had prepared myself. He circled me, looked at me, and said, "All right, Wilburdaniels, the argument you won; but more money you are not getting."

That is my answer to the computer substituting for the negotiator. The computer will supply facts but it will never replace the subtlety of human relations or the balance of economic power.

When I accepted this invitation, I said I would come only if I were permitted to spin fantasies. I will deal, therefore, only to a very limited extent with the actual experience of the ILGWU with

189

computers. The much greater part of my talk will be concerned
with the plans of the ILGWU to use computers.

We do have computers both at our international headquarters
and at many of the larger locals and joint boards. They are used
primarily now for internal housekeeping purposes, to compute the
payrolls, to take care of dues, to check on our census, to print retirement fund and Supplemental Unemployment Benefit (SUB) checks,
and so on.

To a very limited extent, they have begun to be used for the
enforcement and the policing of collective agreements. The need for
new enforcement techniques stems from the unusual conditions in
the apparel industry which provide relatively easy opportunities for
contract violations. The nature of the industry gives rise to the need
for a constant lookout for violations of the agreement. It has resulted, I suppose, in a kind of mass paranoia which we manifest in
our search for contract violations.

We have an enormous auditing staff whose purpose basically is to
check the records of employers to make sure that the major provisions of our agreement are being enforced. That staff, even though
it is probably the largest in the trade union world, is, nevertheless,
absolutely insufficient in number.

What is the nature of the women's apparel industry? Despite the
recent growth of giant firms in the industry, it is still largely made
up of very, very small enterprises; the average establishment employs under forty employees. There are about twelve thousand
separate establishments with which we deal and there is a very
large turnover among employers. In some branches of the industry,
the annual turnover rate is 20 to 30 percent. It is an industry with
a predominantly female labor force and is characterized by a relatively high turnover in that work force. The industry is one in
which the worker is paid primarily on a piecework incentive program. There are craft minimum rates; but since it is basically a
piecework industry, there are generally no classification wage rates.
The product, of course, is not at all standardized. The industry is
less and less concentrated in metropolitan areas and more and more
dispersed all over the country.

The records that many small employers keep are often elusive,
inadequate, or inaccurate. Much depends on which set of records
you get: the one the employer keeps for himself, the one he keeps
for his partner, the one he keeps for his mistress, or the one he

keeps for the Internal Revenue Service. We often have our choice, and the efficiency of our auditor depends on which one he selects. This is by no means true of the giant firms which are publicly owned and have acquired a tailored respectability.

My own special interest in the use of computers in enforcing agreements has developed from my particular responsibility at the ILGWU to negotiate and administer agreements with the giant women's apparel companies. We have so-called master agreements with over a dozen such firms. They are by no means typical of the industry. Instead of employing forty workers in one small plant, they employ as many as five, six, or seven thousand employees in fifteen or sixteen plants scattered over the country. Their record-keeping techniques are unlike most of the industry and are basically those of the twentieth century. They have begun to use computers in their own work for payroll purposes, for billing purposes, and indeed they have even begun to use computers for some of their production techniques. They have begun to use computers for making patterns on cloth and for sizing, the latter being the grading of the patterns so that the garment that your teenage daughter wears in size five gets graded up by the computer to a garment that your wife wears — hopefully — in size twelve. Computer techniques have been developed so that they can take a particular style and crank out the variations required for each of the sizes.

But this is by no means typical. The industry is still made up of the small businessman to whom advanced technology is largely represented by the ball point pen. There is a corresponding lack of enthusiasm for computer techniques and advanced technological means among many union officers.

It is by no means an accident that the use of the computer in union offices will correspond very largely to the sophistication of the industry in which that union has jurisdiction. I don't think it is an accident that the Machinists and the Communications Workers are among the pioneers in the use of computers. To a large extent this reflects the knowledge the officers of those unions have acquired of the use of computers among the employers they deal with.

I should also add that the reluctance of many union leaders to contemplate the use of computers is due not just to their lack of familiarity with the techniques but to their bewilderment at the strange kind of language that computer technicians use. I think if I were to use the language that we have heard here with most union officials, I would be "generated" right out the window. It is not a language familiar to them. It is a language we are going to have to introduce in some other form.

Nevertheless, despite the fact that the garment industry is one made up primarily of small businessmen and union officers to whom a computer is a somewhat disturbing mystery, we have begun to use a computer right now for some enforcement purposes and hopefully we will, in the not-too-distant future, begin to use it for many other enforcement purposes. These purposes, present and future, can roughly be divided into the following fields:

1. The checkoff of union dues and, as a by-product of that, a profile of union membership;

2. The enforcement of the earnings provisions in our agreements;

3. The enforcement of piece rate provisions;

4. The enforcement of contributions to benefit funds provided for in the agreements; and

5. The enforcement of three related areas — those provisions in the agreement which deal with nonunion work, with contracting out, and with the prohibition against runaway shops.

We will be getting into one area of computer use in a rather peculiar way. We distribute, at considerable cost, a newspaper twice a month. Part of that cost is wasted by having newspapers returned because the member isn't a member any longer, or she has moved, or she has changed her name. Through many trials and errors we have found — and this has not yet been implemented but is about to be implemented — that we can use some of the computer techniques to get basic information about our membership to make sure they get our communications. Once you start getting something as simple as a name and address, it really isn't that much harder to find out age — well, women sometimes are a problem — marital status, number of children, length of employment in the industry, prior union affiliation, the craft and branch of the industry, and social security number. The use of this information is obvious for internal housekeeping purposes; for negotiations; and, if I may say so, for political purposes. That is area number one.

Area number two involves earnings. Our agreements provide for a variety of guarantees. To begin with, they provide for minimum wages; that is, minimum guarantees to each individual worker. These minimums will be either a craft minimum to an experienced worker or a progression which leads up to the craft minimum for a newly hired worker. In a piecework agreement, there are other guarantees which are basically additional minimums expressed as minimum yields to a craft, rather than to an individual. For example, "Piecework rates for sewing machine operators shall be set to yield no less than $2.50 an hour." Sometimes these provisions get to be more sophisticated. Sometimes the yield is not limited to a craft as a whole but to a section. "All dart makers shall have piece rates that shall yield no less than $2.50 an hour." Even this can get more sophisticated. "All dart makers with two years' experience shall get not less than $2.60 an hour."

There is a basic difference between a guarantee for a flat minimum and a guarantee to a group of workers; that difference turns on the ease of self-enforcement for each. It is easy enough for a worker to know that she is not being paid $2.50 an hour. It is not quite that easy for her to know that her group, her craft, or her section is not making $2.50 an hour. It is in those areas where enforcement of guarantees is not as easy as with flat minimums for individuals that we find a computer is beginning to help us. In short, it is when the pieceworker doesn't know whether her *group* is "making out" that the computer can be of use to her.

Now of course the way to do this is to check payrolls. But when you have twelve thousand establishments, 70 to 80 percent of which are still in the eighteenth century, it is rather difficult to do a really thorough job of policing. The task of checking payrolls usually has been assigned to us when we have reason to be suspicious, when there is a complaint, or when there is something odd about earnings in the plant; and to a large extent this is still the case. But as the giant firms begin to develop in importance, we are now beginning to change to a routine check. We now get payrolls on a regular basis from our major firms. The payrolls, because they are themselves prepared with computer techniques, are much more accessible for checking by our own computers.

I get a payroll for one week of every month from every one of the firms with which I negotiate. These firms think that I check every one of them. I generate a great deal of noise so that they come in quite regularly; but, as a matter of fact, I check them only on a random sampling basis — but they don't know that. We have not found many willful violations but we have found enough discrepancies that the technique more than pays for itself in back wages that are recovered. It also serves a kind of feedback process. As the computer finds violations and as they are reported back to employees, the employees in turn become much more aware of the need for constant self-enforcement. In addition, it may well be that enforcement of agreement provisions is improved when the local business agent knows that someone at headquarters is looking at some of the payrolls.

There is another area in which the computer has not yet been used for enforcement but about which there has begun to be considerable discussion, that is, in the area of piecework settlement. There are hundreds of thousands of piece rates set in the industry every season. They are spread over three or four or five seasons a year and are used in about twelve thousand different establishments. If you then attempt to impose upon this some kind of uniformity, you can see the enormity of the problem, the fantastic scope of the task. We have tried to do this through a centralized form of settlement of piece rates and through regional guidelines and have had varying success. There is great difficulty in imposing such uniformity, partly because of lack of information and partly because most of the time you are comparing apples and oranges.

But there are some basic standard elements in constructing agreements that we are just beginning to try to put into a form that can be fed into a computer. When we want information, for example, about the rate for making a dart on black nylon cloth, we hope to be able to collect some standard data on that operation by the use of a computer.

A more immediate application than this hope is the actual use we now make of computer techniques to enforce contributions by employers to benefit funds. We have basically three types of funds: a retirement fund and a SUB fund, which are both national in scope, and health and welfare funds, which are local. Almost all the contributions are made in the form of a percentage of the payroll. There are very few cases in which the contributions are dollar amounts per worker. Most of the contribution rates are from eight to fourteen percent of the payroll.

This form of payment requires a very large auditing staff. In the administrative cost of our funds, this probably represents the single largest element. This is so because of the great amount of turnover among employers, because of the small size of the establishments, and because of the way books and records are kept in the industry. If we are to do our job in making sure that contributions are made, there has to be a constant auditing, overseeing, checking, and double checking. The contributions are paid by the employer not only for the payroll of his immediate employees but also for employees of contractors who work for him, so that the scope of the problem becomes even larger. Thus, in addition to our need to check the payroll of the Smith Garment Company, we have to check as well on whether or not Mr. Smith has paid ten percent of the payroll of the Jones Contracting Company.

It becomes a much simpler task for us to feed payroll information into a computer and to begin to match contributions and payrolls so that what was once a very difficult and laborious task for auditors to perform now becomes a much simpler problem when computer techniques are used. We can make cross references very quickly. So if we feed in all the payroll data on the contractors and all the "in-shop" payroll data, we can find very quickly whether Mr. Smith has paid all of the contributions for his employees and for all the employees listed by his contractors. The matching process thus becomes a much simpler one.

The computer has also permitted us to use health, welfare, retirement, and SUB contributions as a cross check on other data. There are pretty well established ratios between payrolls and sales. When we get sales data, we feed these into a computer. But using the principle of exception, the computer will report to us when the ratio seems to be out of line. That ratio will usually be out of line because the work is going to nonunion shops or to unreported contractors or we have gotten wrong information on the type of product made, so that our ratio is wrong. Here again what has been a quite difficult and laborious task has become a much simpler task by using the computer to correlate the various data that we have.

The computer has also begun to be of some assistance to us in enforcing the controls we have sought to exercise over the use of contractors in the apparel trade. Basic to the labor standards in the industry is a set of rather rigid controls about when work may be contracted out, under what circumstances, to whom, for what purposes, for how long, and so on. The effectiveness of those controls, of course, is in direct proportion to the kind of information we can get and use. For example, one of the provisions in our agreement is that an employer may not send work out to a contractor unless all the employees in his inside shop are fully employed. This is easy enough to enforce when the manufacturer has his plant on 35th Street and his contractor is around the corner on 7th Avenue. It is not quite as easy to do, but still relatively simple, when his contractor moves across the river to the wilds of Hoboken or Scranton.

But as you get a dispersal of manufacturing and contracting facilities all over the country, all this becomes harder and harder to do. We have just now begun to correlate the employment records for employers and the employment records for their contractors.

Of course, the day-to-day job still has to be done by the business agent. If I may add a footnote here, despite all of the glamorous use that we make of computers, one thing that I have to emphasize is that the computer is not, cannot, and never will be a substitute for enforcement by business agents, by managers, by vice presidents, by presidents, and by department directors. At best it can be a tool, an aid, but never a substitute; and I suspect that this is generally true not only in the enforcement of agreements but also in the negotiation of agreements. The computer will help the business agent, and head of a health and welfare program, and the union president to enforce the agreement. It helps them with information but they still have to do the basic job.

There is yet another area where the computer has been of some assistance to us. Runaway shops, perhaps to the amazement of some of you, are still a major problem in the apparel industry. It isn't often that I differ with Dave Cole — almost never when I appear before him — but I think he was somewhat optimistic when he said that trade unions have achieved almost all of their goals and that many of them now simply sit back and think up problems to confound their adversaries. I think Dave exaggerated to make his point. There are many unions working in marginal industries — the ILGWU is one of them — where their task is by no means finished and their goals have by no means been achieved.

The apparel industry is one where organizing, for example, has to go on day in and day out if we are just to stay where we are. You have to remember that to start an establishment of ten, twenty, thirty, or forty employees really doesn't take much capital investment. Sometimes $500 and an equal amount of gall is all you need to go into business. And with the assistance given by local communities in the South and elsewhere, all you need is the gall; you don't even need the $500.

Runaway plants are a constant problem to us and here again one of the ways — I emphasize *one* — in which we deal with them is by using the computer to correlate information. Many of the runaway plants are set up secretly during the life of an agreement. To enforce the prohibition against them we try to correlate data that we get from different sources.

This is not a hope but a fact. Our central organizing department has fed into its computer the names of all of the officers of all of the union plants we have. At the same time we have fed into the computer the names of all of the officers of new establishments, as soon as we learn of them. And we do this by going to county records, by getting incorporation papers from states, by reading newspapers, and so on. Here again, what had been a rather enormous task in the past has become much simpler. The computer has now begun to match names and to match companies. The names that we feed in are those of the owner, his wife (often her maiden name as well), his daughter, his son-in-law, and the name of someone who is sometimes euphemistically called his secretary. We also feed into the computer any information that we have about which Southern plant is sending work to which Northern plant. There have been some very interesting results. When we go to some of our more respectable employers, the shock of being faced with some of the information which our computer has revealed is sometimes so overwhelming that it overcomes their opposition to our organizing efforts at their Southern plants. Sometimes, of course, the shock isn't enough; and that is when we use what some people call emotion and others call persuasion.

This is a basic outline of what we are doing and what we hope to do. To some extent, the value of a computer is not only its impact on the information we get, but also its impact on the people who have to do the enforcing. The business agent knows that some place in that ivory tower called union headquarters, information is being fed to his superior. That is helpful. But I want to emphasize that the computer can at best be a supplement or a tool, but never, never a substitute for the human being who has to do the enforcement.

There is one last point that I would like to make. As we gain experience in using the computer for enforcement purposes, this use itself is beginning to have a rather fascinating impact on negotiations. I have mentioned the fact that I now get payrolls regularly from some of our giant firms. The problem is I now have to deal with our programmers. They don't just want payrolls; they want payrolls in such-and-such a form and in such-and-such an order. I now find that when I sit down to negotiate the details of a payroll reporting provision, I have to deal not only with obstinate employers but with stubborn programmers; and my demands upon the employer are to some extent being shaped by the demands of the programmers upon me. So I would predict that as the mechanics of contract enforcement become at one and the same time both easier and more complex because of the computer, we will find that to some extent and in a limited manner — and I want to emphasize both "some" and "limited" — the use of a computer for enforcement purposes may well begin to shape the form, if not the content, of some of the union demands upon the employer.

In my own experience, a union proposal or a tentative agreement with an employer on a proposal has on occasion been abandoned, not because of lack of merit, but because of the difficulty of policing it. To the extent that the computer will make policing easier, such demands may be put back on the bargaining table.

Let me give you a simple illustration. In our industry the aristocrat is the cutter. Let's say that as an apprentice he begins at $1.80 an hour; and after a progression of moves, he arrives at $3.50 an hour, the minimum for an experienced worker. The tendency has been to give that apprentice incremental increases only once every two months or on a quarterly basis or sometimes even at longer intervals. This is partly because of the difficulties in making bookkeeping changes more often and partly because of the difficulty in policing those changes when made. Well, as the larger firms begin to use computers to calculate their payroll, the argument for such long intervals between increments begins to disappear. It is just as easy to program a computer to add a 5-cent increment every month as it is to add a 15-cent increment every three months.

My latest agreement with Jonathan Logan, the largest apparel firm in the world, is perhaps illustrative of this trend. Most agreements in the apparel trade consist of a few paragraphs. This latest Jonathan Logan agreement has twelve pages of closely packed figures, craft by craft, month by month, and with a change for each year of the agreement. This scares the daylights out of most business agents. They are simply not familiar with this sort of complexity in an agreement. But Jonathan Logan has computerized their payrolls. I get those and feed them into my computer. And this kind of an approach can, in consequence, be enforced.

So the whole pattern of negotiations, at least in my part of the apparel industry, has begun to change. I find, for example, that when in the past I had negotiated piecework increases and had accumulated a total of 10.4444 percent, I could be persuaded that that was a rather difficult bookkeeping calculation and that it should be rounded off to 10.4 or sometimes even 10.0. I can't be persuaded on that any more, however, because 10.4444 can be calculated just as easily by the computer as 10.4 percent can.

So these are some rather elementary illustrations of how the use of the computer for enforcement purposes may well begin to have a feedback effect on the kind of negotiations and the kind of provisions that we will have to deal with. I think we are on the frontiers of a rather exciting period and I am rather pleased that the actuarial tables are on my side.

Elaboration and Discussion

Straus Could I ask one thing about your use of terms? I assume you use "police" and "enforce" in the same way I would use "administer"?

Daniels Yes, you administer and I police.

Straus The ILGWU has a reputation as a union that stabilizes and rationalizes. Do you feel that the use of the computer as an enforcement aid will make it less lucrative for someone to open a small shop and try to beat the contract?

Daniels I don't really think so. I think the forces that make an employer move or that make an employer violate an agreement will still obtain. I don't think any amount of money spent on a computer is going to keep Judy Bond from running away from New York and going down South.

Myers I thought your point about not replacing the individual, at least the business agent, is exactly right; and there is a parallel, I think, with the impact of computers on management.

But as I listened to you describe the problem of auditing the enforcement provisions prior to the introduction of the computer, I wondered whether you might have had the same problem that the insurance companies faced. In order to handle the clerical operations resulting from the greatly increased level of insurance business, it was forecast that it would require the hiring of almost all of the high school female graduates in the country. Fortunately, the computer enabled the insurance industry to meet this very serious labor shortage. In your case, didn't you find that your use of the computer at least limited the need for additional clerical employees?

Daniels It has just begun to. Also, it is providing a solution to a rather strange problem. The ILGWU is a union with a socialist heritage — which means most employees are inadequately paid; so in a way the computer has helped solve our labor shortage.

Straus I wonder about the problem of learning the language of computers. Do you find yourself in a more advantageous position at the bargaining table for having learned about computer languages?

Daniels I sometimes find myself with two sets of negotiations: one with the employer; and then, when that is all done, with my own vice presidents, who turn to me and ask, "What did he say?" I find that I have the additional task of interpreting the data and the material that have passed between us. As a new generation of trade union officers comes onto the scene, hopefully this language barrier is going to diminish; but it does exist now and it is a very substantial problem.

Straus Do you feel that an increased familiarity with computer languages could be useful for mediators and those in the business of trying to produce industrial peace?
  There are some semanticists who claim that through the use of different types of language, the product of thought is actually changed. Now if this is true, those steeped in the new management techniques, having a language of their own, will produce a different way of thinking about problems and of solutions to problems.

Daniels I suspect that this is beginning to be true, but only for very limited purposes and among technicians rather than negotiators.

Ginsburg In some of the examples which you gave, employers are now being requested to furnish payroll information in certain forms. Isn't this forcing a refining of accounting methods where they were rather diverse and complex previously? Aren't you helping to develop systems for accounting which are not only useful to you but also easier for employers?

Daniels This has begun to happen. Such systems have been instituted among the giant firms for payroll purposes. The next step, which is the logical one, is to do the same with health and welfare. The two are related; if we get earnings data, we can then match them with the health and welfare contributions and if they don't check out, there is something wrong.

Anonymous Could you go more into the history of the use of the computer in the ILGWU? When did you begin to use it and how fast did it spread?

Daniels Our first computer was acquired about six or seven years ago and its original purpose was to keep the records of one of our retirement funds and to issue the checks. We used to have regional retirement funds and the first computer was purchased by one of these large regional funds whose headquarters happened to be in the International building. Then when we merged forty-one of our retirement funds into one national fund, the use of the computer blossomed. After this, the computer began to be used by other departments in the International building. It was not planned or thought out; it was like most things that just happen.

Anonymous Who has been pushing the computer into new areas like contract enforcement and runaway shops and so on? Have you been the major force within the union in developing new uses for it?

Daniels I am certainly one, but there are others as well. Our Research Director is quite interested. The head of our health and welfare program and retirement program has been very active. And the people who are involved in compiling the vast amount of material that is required for Government reports, such as those required under the Landrum-Griffin Act and the Pension Fund Disclosure Act, would be lost without the computer.

Meyers What is your judgment on the impact of computers on the quality of collective bargaining — or do you have any judgment at this stage?

Daniels To the extent that facts have always helped to stabilize industrial negotiations, the use of a computer will help — but only to that extent, because the quality of industrial negotiations is a function of a great many things other than just facts. That is why I say that neither you nor I will ever be replaced by a computer.

Myers You stressed the role of the business agent and his importance. To what extent is this business agent aware, first, of the amount and the variety of material which is available within the computer system and, second, of the capability of the system to manipulate these data for studies which might bear on his problems?

Daniels Very candidly, he is not very aware. If anything, the computer is his enemy. At this point he looks upon the computer as that "thing at 1710 Broadway" which checks on him. I think we have a very substantial job ahead of us to educate him on how it can be useful to him. But at this point in time, I would be misleading you if I said we had been able to achieve much of this yet.

Anonymous Are there plans for this type of education?

Daniels Yes, but very frankly, we have so much to learn about its uses ourselves that we must concentrate on that. There are only so many things that even a socialist union can do.

Scheduling and Seniority: The United Air Lines Experience

Charles Mason*

Perhaps a number of you may have seen an article which appeared in the June 1966 issue of *Business Week*[1] dealing with computers and personnel offices. It was prefaced by a cartoon which portrayed a personnel vice president cycling into his office on a reel of magnetic tape while several workmen are in the process of moving out file cabinet after file cabinet, presumably made unnecessary by the conversion to a computerized personnel system. I wonder how many of you found this article being routed to you by your boss with an appropriate comment attached, such as, "When are we going to reach this stage," or "Why aren't we doing this?" I cannot, of course, describe precisely what your experiences may have been in your company. I can only guess that it may not have been too dissimilar from what I have experienced at United Air Lines.

During the first nine months of 1967, the Personnel Administration Office at United purchased some seventy additional file cabinets of various shapes and sizes at a cost of nearly $10,000 for the express purpose of holding "personnel records" of one sort or another. Am I then putting the lie to the potential of computers? Hardly, since if this were true I would not be discussing with you the practical, useful application of electronic data processing to the personnel function. Undoubtedly, many more than seventy file cabinets would have been purchased if it were not for electronic data processing; but more important is the fact that a good deal of information

* We note with sorrow the recent death of Charles Mason. His wisdom and humaneness enriched all of us who knew and worked with him.

[1] "Describing Men to Machines," *Business Week,* No. 1918, June 4, 1966, pp. 113–114.

which is of great value to management would not be readily accessible.

The Need for EDP

At United Air Lines we know that as our company grows larger in size, more efficient ways of maintaining information and retrieving information about each employee must be found. We need to know how many employees we have in the company; how many in a particular classification; how many in a particular organization; how much they are paid as a group and how much they are paid individually; who belongs to the retirement plan and who does not; who belongs to the stock purchase plan and who does not; who used to work for us and why they left; and so on, and so on. Information of this nature, readily available through the use of electronic data processing equipment, is really only the consolidation of raw data. This is not to imply that this information is not valuable and I wonder where we would be without it.

We should also be asking ourselves: what will it cost to grant a specific union proposal; how effectively are we achieving the objectives of any particular program, such as the salary program; has the implementation of a particular policy reduced turnover? For example, and this is timely for the airline industry, in order to have any idea as to what a change in policy regarding the marital status of stewardesses would mean with respect to turnover, it is necessary to know first how many are leaving at the present time because of marriage. Should we spend our advertising money on national advertising or local advertising; what is the relationship between a particular pre-employment test and tenure and so on, and so on. In a company the size of United it would be virtually impossible to evaluate the effect of a particular policy, benefit, or procedure without the aid of EDP.

The use of EDP-generated data in the planning stages for and during the course of union negotiations is also an area which offers a great deal of promise. Unions are now using computers to collect comparative data on a number of issues to determine where one company stands in relationship to others. Many companies are similarly engaged in developing computer uses for personnel administration or collective bargaining. It is to this theme that I now turn my attention.

Present Applications

At United we are currently using computers in the preparation of seniority lists, in the distribution of overtime, in the distribution of flying to each pilot and stewardess domicile, in the pricing out of any number of union and company proposals, in the indexing and reporting of grievances, and in the preparation of stewardess and pilot qualification lists. Some of these systems involve very simple punched card applications requiring the use of card readers and printers only, while others involve some fairly complex and extensive programs requiring the use of third generation computers such as the IBM 360. All of the systems are geared at present to a "batch process" operation, i.e., the input of data, the processing of the data, and the generation of reports are all accomplished at our computer facility in Chicago. While priorities can be and are established, and reports can be and are generated relatively quickly, the restrictions of a "batch type" processing system are as limiting as the opportunities of a real-time, remote-access system are rewarding. A real-time, remote-access system which permits the input and output of data to and from several hundred, or several thousand, locations remote from the central processor offers potential far beyond what we are experiencing today. I will cover first in some detail how we make use of computer capability today and then will close by examining what we believe the future holds for us.

Seniority Lists

The preparation of seniority lists is a simple punched card operation and requires only the keypunching of data into the cards, the sequencing of the cards into seniority order by use of a sorter, and the preparation of the list itself by use of a card reader and printer. For example, the stewardess seniority list is prepared semiannually as required by the contract. When a stewardess graduates from stewardess training and is assigned to the line, the Stewardess Scheduling Department punches an IBM card with the following information:

Name	Company Seniority
Birth Date	Classification Seniority

When a stewardess leaves the classification, the card is removed from the active deck by the Stewardess Scheduling Department.

The seniority lists of employees covered by the various IAM (International Association of Machinists) Agreements are also prepared semiannually, as required by contract. The following information is maintained on punched cards:

Name	Established Point Seniority
Location	Status (furlough, military leave,
Company Seniority	extended illness status, etc.)
Classification Seniority	

Prior to the preparation of new seniority lists, each organization is sent a copy of the current list and is requested to make corrections, additions, or deletions. The IBM deck is then corrected and a new listing is prepared.

Overtime Distribution

The equitable, economical distribution of overtime where large numbers of employees are eligible is a time-consuming, expensive, and error-riddled operation when it is done manually. The number of grievances which result from claims of overtime bypass is excessively high. Each such grievance requires that our management spend time investigating the claim and rendering a decision. More time is spent as the grievance is processed through the various steps of the grievance procedure. If the grievance requires the services of an arbitrator at the System Board of Adjustment, the costs can be substantial. And, of course, if the grievance is sustained, the cost to the company of paying twice for the same work is obvious. Additionally, the dissatisfaction and lowered morale which results from overtime distribution complaints is an intangible cost. In an attempt to reduce our exposure to these kinds of problems, our Line Maintenance organization at O'Hare, which consists of some nine hundred employees covered by the Mechanics Agreement, is experimenting with an overtime eligibility list (Figure 1) prepared by the computer.

Employees are listed in order of eligibility for overtime. Each week the list is amended to reflect transfers, separations, and new employees; and also the employees are put into proper sequence based on the amount of overtime they worked during the week. The listing provides the following information:

DEPARTMENT — refers to Building and Maintenance, Aircraft Maintenance, etc.

TOUR — refers to shift.

WORK GROUP — refers to the particular work group the employee is assigned to.

NAME

TELEPHONE NUMBER — current telephone numbers are required in order to contact employees for overtime.

GENERAL INFORMATION — includes:

1. Classification information, such as inspector, etc.
2. Work Location:
   H — Hangar
   T — Terminal
   L — Line
   C — Check
3. Special Skills, such as taxi and run-up, fiberglass qualifications, etc. are coded with the digits 0 through 9.

RDO GROUP — refers to the day-off group to which the employee is assigned.

PREFERENCE CODE — is the employee's indicated preference for the type of overtime he desires.

   S — Early Start on RDO
   E — Early Start
   L — Regular OT
   D — RDO

For example, SELD would indicate that the employee would accept any type of overtime offer.

OLD BALANCE — is expressed in terms of units with each unit equalling four hours.

OVERTIME UNITS LAST PERIOD — the asterisk indicates the employee's days off and the number reflects the number of units of overtime the employee has worked; again, each unit equals four hours.

NEW BALANCE — reflects the old balance plus what was worked during the last period.

SENIORITY — classification seniority.

RDO PATTERN — indicates the employee's days off for the current period.

CURRENT PERIOD — provides for the notation of employee overtime activity during the current period.

UNITED AIR LINES

OVERTIME REPORT

DATE 3/26/69

CODE: S - EARLY START   E - EARLY START   ON RDO   L - REGULAR O.T.   D - RDO

DEPT PTR	WORK GRP	NAME	TELEPHONE	GENERAL INFO	RDO GP.	PREF CODE SELD	OLD BAL.	OT UNITS LAST PERIOD	NEW BAL	SENIORITY	FILE NUMBER	RDO PAT	TOTAL
1 2	01	C PAPROCKI	-825-5443	LEAD H 6 3	3			**		7-08-55	79386	FSS	17
1 2	01	D L SEADALE	-823-0987	INSP H 567	3			**		11-07-55	57-061	FSS	
1 2	01	R F MUKENSCHNABL	-978-5678	L 1 1	1	D		*		1-06-64	6229	T	
1 2	01	R M PISANKO	-456-7465	H 89	4			**		10-03-66	40330	SSM	
1 2	01	F K JACOBSON	567-7890	H	1		1	*	1	10-17-66	40401	T	8
1 2	01	R F GITTINGS	-8906789	P	7		1	*	1	8-30-63	23519	WT	
1 2	01	G C JONES	-890-4567	L 1 56 93	93	SELD	4	*	4	8-09-65	27008	FSS	12
1 2	01	G E MIKE	-567-5432	L 1234 7 89 2	2			*	5	10-11-65	29282	TF	16
1 2	01	W R FLINN	-986-4523	L 12 6 8 94	94	SELD	1	2 *	6	11-08-65	29413	SSM	
1 2	01	H J GEIBEL	815-838-3614	C 67	1	LD	6	*		9-26-66	24533	T	
1 2	01	F L WOLFE	-546-7890	T 2 4 7 93	93	SELD	12	2 *	18	1-03-66	30144	FSS	

U — indicates the company attempted to contact the employee for overtime but was unable to make contact.

D — indicates that the employee was signed up for overtime, was contacted, but declined the offer.

X — indicates a change in the employee's preference, which occurred after the listing was printed.

One copy of the listing is posted at the hangar, one copy posted at the terminal, and one copy is maintained in the office. The fourth copy is sent to the Data Processing Department with the changes noted and a new listing in four copies is prepared and sent to the station where the process then repeats itself. Since the introduction of this report, the O'Hare Maintenance Department has been able to reduce its clerical staff by five clerks. It is hoped that the number of grievances will decline also.

Flight Crew Scheduling

In the area of flight crew scheduling, prior to the introduction of the computerized systems, various representatives of the stewardess domiciles and headquarters groups would meet for several days in an attempt to distribute the flying to each domicile. The decision, for example, as to whether the New York base or the San Francisco base would be given a particular nonstop New York to San Francisco trip depended to a large extent upon the relative persuasive abilities of the individuals representing the two domiciles. All flight segments were distributed in this relatively haphazard manner; and, in general, domicile representatives fought to obtain the highly desirable flights and to avoid the undesirable ones. Since the smaller bases were not fully represented, it is obvious that they would receive most of the undesirable short-haul flight segments and none of the highly desirable trips. There was, unquestionably, an economic consideration overriding these decisions in that the amount of flying assigned to the various bases could not fluctuate drastically from month to month because of the effect this would have on the number of stewardesses required at each base. Yet there is no doubt that this system was relatively uneconomic and wasteful because the people involved did not have sufficient data available to them to make sound and valid decisions. Without the aid of a computer,

Figure 1   United Air Lines overtime report.

the data could not be made available; and even if data were available, they could not be digested and utilized efficiently.

Since the volume of data was so overwhelming and so interrelated, the errors which resulted were many and highly disruptive. The advent of the computer has enabled the company to do away with the system of allocating flying by committee. What used to take a committee of several persons three days to accomplish poorly is now done in less time and more effectively by one person. It should also be recognized that the committee distributed flying for a system which included a thousand stewardesses, whereas the one person now allocates flying for a system which includes in excess of four thousand stewardesses. The system presently in operation utilizes data stored in the computer for purposes of airplane scheduling. As a by-product, the following information for each flight segment is provided for use in stewardess scheduling:

Trip Frequency	Arrival Station
Equipment Type	Departure Time
Flight Number	Arrival Time
Departure Station	Elapsed Time

These data are provided to the Stewardess Scheduling Department on punched cards; and, through a manual operation, the cards are put together into flight pairings, i.e., combinations of flight segments which meet all contractual legality requirements and stewardess workload requirements. This results in the most economical operation, considering all of these other factors.

The resulting pairings are then compared with data provided via a Matrix Generator program which supplies all the possible combinations. The IBM cards containing the final pairings are then processed through the computer, using a stewardess scheduling program which produces a Domicile Schedule Letter. This report includes, in addition to the data previously listed, the following information:

Group Time	Total Time
Credited Time (Time paid	Meal Allowances
but not flown)	

Also included is the number of stewardesses required to fly each pairing. Additional subroutines have been written which will provide, in this same Domicile Schedule Letter, the name of the hotel to be used on each layover and the type of meals that the stewardesses will have to serve on each flight segment. Yet, even with the aid of the computer, errors occurred in the past which resulted in extra work in the domicile and unrest among the stewardesses involved.

For example, some time ago, a flight pairing was sent to a domicile with an error in the calculation of the duty time; this occurred because of changes in time zones. Some twenty stewardesses were affected by this error and had to have their schedules adjusted because of it. Errors such as this are now virtually impossible because of our conversion to a more powerful computer (an IBM 360) which is programmed to reject any schedules which do not meet specified requirements.

The computer will ultimately have its greatest impact in the domicile, which has the responsibility for preparing the schedules which the stewardesses use to indicate their preferences and for awarding the schedules on the basis of seniority. Errors under our present manual system are frequent and can and do result in serious problems both for the stewardesses and the domicile management.

As an example, at one of our domiciles, monthly lines of flying were prepared and put up for preferencing. The stewardesses expressed their preferences and the schedules were awarded. After this process was completed (at a domicile the size of O'Hare, it takes eleven days to complete this process), an error was discovered which resulted in more days off being shown on the printed schedule than was actually the case. All in all, this error affected some twenty-five stewardesses, some of whom had to have their trips reassigned because the revised number of days off did not satisfy the minimum contractual requirements.

In another case, the total flight time for some thirty-five stewardesses was incorrectly added and was shown as greater than it actually was. The stewardesses involved claimed that the company misled them by the inaccurate total times and that they, the stewardesses, should not have to feel it necessary to check the accuracy of an official company document.

In yet another case, a specific flight involving a round trip to Honolulu from Los Angeles, which at that time was worth about $100, was desired by two stewardesses and should have been assigned to the more senior of the two. As it turned out, the flight was given to the wrong girl and the aggrieved girl claimed that the company should pay her for the trip that she should have been assigned.

All of these situations were protested through the grievance procedure and caused not only discontent among the stewardesses affected, but also cost the company time and money to process the grievances — in one case, up through the System Board. There is no question that computer-assisted handling of these procedures would have virtually eliminated the possibility of these kinds of errors. In the future we will make use of a program which will provide for the preparation of the monthly schedules by the computer.

We are currently in the process of developing computer programs which, after considering a huge number of variables, such as contract requirements, FAA (Federal Aviation Administration) requirements, rest periods, hotel costs, meal expenses, flight time, etc., will generate the optimum stewardess schedules, that is, maximum utilization at minimum cost. These computer-prepared schedules will undoubtedly, for a time to come, have to be modified by humans in order to take into account other factors, such as the number of stewardesses desiring layovers in popular cities such as Los Angeles, New York, San Francisco, and workload conditions, such as heavy load factor trips, rush meal service trips, and short segment trips.

Perhaps some day all of these factors will be subject to computerization and the ultimate program will consider all possible factors, including data that Suzie Smith wants a schedule that allows her to fly into Los Angeles every Saturday to see her boyfriend or that Mary Jones wants a schedule which will permit her to arrive in New York in the morning so that she can attend a Broadway show matinee. I have a sneaking suspicion that the programs required to land a space ship on the moon might not be as complex as those which would have to consider and satisfy the wishes and desires of four thousand stewardesses.

Flight Crew Qualifications

In a business such as ours, where a stewardess cannot be assigned to work a trip unless she is emergency-qualified on that particular aircraft, it is essential that we have pertinent information upon which to base staffing decisions. Not only does the stewardess's home office need to know each stewardess's qualifications, but every crew desk all over the country must have this same information. Airlines, as I am sure all of you are aware, are subject to irregularities due to weather, mechanical problems, substitution of equipment, and so on. Any time an unscheduled crew change is involved it is necessary to know each stewardess's qualifications. For example, if a Boeing 720 is being substituted for a DC-8, it is necessary for the crew scheduler to know if the stewardesses are qualified on the Boeing 720 and, if not, who among those who are available is qualified.

The Stewardess Qualification Report is a list prepared monthly from punched cards and provides the following information:

Name	File Number
Domicile	Equipment Qualifications
Seniority Date	Registered Nurse Qualification

When a new aircraft is scheduled to be flown out of a domicile, it is necessary to know how many stewardesses are qualified on the airplane by virtue of having received the emergency training at another domicile and how many will require qualification training. Since such training must be paid for, the qualification list is helpful in estimating such costs.

Similar data appropriate to pilot personnel are also made available to those who require this information.

Contract Negotiations

During negotiations, by the use of simulation techniques, the effect of union proposals in the areas of flight time and duty time limitations, duty rigs, days-off requirement, meal allowances, or cabin attendant requirements can be evaluated. By altering the variables in the program, the Domicile Schedule Letter can be simulated so as to reflect what would occur if the union's proposals actually were in effect. Each proposal can be priced out individually or in any combination. This simulation technique provides the company with the costs both in dollars and in equivalent stewardesses required.

We have a number of reports which provide us with basic data which can then be used to price out a variety of union proposals. For example, the Union Summary IAM — Mechanics Report indicates by classification (that is, Line Mechanic, Auto Mechanic, Radio-Electric Mechanic, Inspector, etc.) the number of employees in the classification; how many hours were worked at straight time; how many hours were worked on a holiday; how many hours there were of overtime at straight time, time and a half, and double time; how many hours of sick leave and vacation; and so on. It includes a summary number for the total number of hours worked by the employees in this classification. The report also indicates the same basic information as measured in dollars with the additional information of how many dollars were spent on shift differential and late lunches. The computer also calculates the average straight time rate and the average total rate.

By the use of the program which produces this report, we can price out union proposals. If the union proposes an increase in rates of pay, holiday premium pay, shift differential, or late lunch pay, the company's actual payroll can be run on the existing rates and then simulated with the proposed rates. The difference then is the cost of the union's proposal. Similar reports for all classifications are prepared and are similarly used.

The Distribution of Pay Rates Report indicates the total number of employees within each job classification and also the number of employees at each step of the wage scale within the job classification. The weighted average is also calculated in this report. In the event the union proposes a change in the number of step increases within the wage scale, it is again relatively easy, by the technique of simulation, to calculate a new weighted average and thereby price out the cost of the proposal.

The Stewardess Utilization Report provides, on a monthly basis for the system as well as for each domicile, how many hours were actually flown (true utilization) by stewardesses by each type of equipment in the fleet, and how many hours were not flown but credited (adjusted utilization) for each factor, such as vacation, sick leave, junior girling, penalty time, and so on. In addition to the obvious advantage provided by this report of being able to monitor costs and domicile performance, union proposals to increase pay for such things as holding time, call-out, training, or deadheading can easily be estimated both in terms of dollars and additional stewardesses required because of lowered true utilization.

Contract Administration

In a company the size of United, with some seventeen thousand employees covered by various IAM Agreements, there are, of course, a substantial number of grievances each year and an enormous number over a period of years. As you are no doubt aware, the importance of precedence and past practice in the handling of grievances cannot be overemphasized. Our problem in this regard is compounded because grievances are heard and decided at dozens of locations across our vast system, from Honolulu to New York.

JOB 5998----IAM GRIEVANCE INDEX-- 01/31/67

GRIEV NO	STA.	DATE	SUBJ	AGREEMENT	PROVISION	STEP	DECISION
27773	ORD	02-05-60	4D	MECH	4D	2	DEN

FUELING

21144	PIT	07-22-56	4E	MECH	2C	4	WBU
21147	PIT	07-22-56	4E	MECH	2C	3	DEN
24533	IDLMM	05-05-61	4E	MECH	2C	SB	DEN
24534	IDLMM	05-11-61	4E	MECH	2C	SB	DEN
24535	IDLMM	05-15-61	4E	MECH	2C	SB	DEN
30170	ATL	05-22-62	4E	MECH	2C	4	DEN
36074	PHL	11-09-62	4E	MECH	2C	3	WBU
35075	PHL	11-09-62	4E	MECH	2C	3	WBU
39561	IDL	11-26-63	4E	MECH	2C	2	DEN
30170	ATL	08-22-62	4E	MECH	4J	4	DEN

PERSONNEL TRANSPORTATION

12315	LGA	11-06-52	4F	R&S	2	3	DEN
25306	DENDS	08-03-59	4F	R&S	2	2	SUS
25647	IDL	10-27-61	4F	R&S	2C	SB	DEN
33739	IDL	09-31-61	4F	R&S	2C	SB	DEN
55765	IDL	09-31-61	4F	R&S	2C	SB	DEN

MATERIALS TRANSPORTATION

22655	MDWCS	11-11-59	4G	R&S	2	3	DEN
23915	CHICS	06-08-56	4G	R&S	2	3	DEN
24601	DENCS	08-26-58	4G	R&S	2	2	SUS
24606	DENCS	08-03-59	4G	R&S	2	2	SUS
24545	DENCS	08-04-58	4G	R&S	2	4	SIP
31137	BAL	11-12-62	4G	R&S	2	3	WBU
32027	EWR	09-19-62	4G	R&S	2	3	WBU
32031	EWR	09-28-63	4G	R&S	2	3	WBU
38032	EWR	09-26-62	4G	R&S	2	2	WBU
23005	PIT	02-26-57	4G	MECH	2C	2	SIP
26591	IDLJL	03-10-62	4G	R&S	2C	4	WBU

Figure 2   IAM grievance index.

The IAM Grievance Index (Figure 2) is prepared through the use of punched cards. The grievances are classified according to the subject matter involved in the grievance and then listed within subject matter in order of grievance number. The report indicates the station at which the grievance was filed, the date it was filed, a coded reference for subject matter, the Agreement under which the employee is covered, the provision of the Agreement involved, the step at which the grievance was finally settled, and the decision rendered, coded as follows:

WBU — Withdrawn by the Union   SUS — Sustained
DEN — Denied   SIP — Sustained in Part

This report assists those who have the responsibility for investigating and rendering decisions on grievances. If the person hearing the grievance wants to know what the company's practice has been or whether there have been any grievances similar to the one he has heard, he can, by means of the Grievance Index, locate other grievances of a similar nature and determine what the outcome was. If he needs more specific information, he can, by the number assigned to the grievance, locate it and read the file in its entirety. Information such as this can also help when the union makes a claim such as "people are really disturbed about the distribution of overtime." By checking the index we can find out with what frequency the employees are grieving any particular item.

The Promise for the Future

In closing, let me return briefly to the potential offered by real-time, remote-access systems. Computers are providing more and more information to management. The question is, do they need it all?

Let us return for the moment to the Stewardess Qualification List. The crew scheduler does not need to know, for example, that Miss Smith is qualified on DC-8 equipment until he needs a stewardess for a DC-8 and then only if Miss Smith is available at his station. By asking the computer through his remote input/output device, the crew scheduler can obtain information about Miss Smith or any other crew member when and only when he needs such information. He need not maintain qualifications information concerning all ten thousand stewardesses and flight officers employed by United. It will also be possible on a real-time, remote-access system to get needed information not only on Miss Smith's qualifications, but also on what her next regularly scheduled trip is and whether she is "legal" to take the trip, i.e., she will not exceed her legal flight or duty time limitations.

Virtually completely current information about flight crews will be available by the process of "inputting" data into the computer at the completion of each flight segment. Crew schedulers, as a result, will be able to make more accurate assignments based on their knowledge of how many hours a crew member has flown in the past twenty-four hours and in the month so far, how much rest time the crew member has had, how many days off he or she has had during the month, what his or her schedule is for the balance of the month, which one is the most junior and legal to work on a particular trip, and so on. Since the company pays a penalty for disruptions to a crew member's schedule through the application of various Agreement provisions, such costs can be reduced and kept to a minimum when more accurate, current, and complete information is available to the crew scheduler.

There are approximately thirty-eight thousand employees, both union and nonunion, who are eligible to submit transfer requests. When vacancies occur, factors such as seniority and qualifications are considered in determining which employee is to fill the opening. The processing of such requests is accomplished manually at the present time. When a real-time system is operational, the data required for an employee to submit a permanent bid or transfer request will be entered into the computer through remote input/output devices. A manager with a vacancy will query the computer through a similar remote device and receive a listing of the employees who have requested transfers, along with their qualifications. The posting of vacancies will be accomplished by the computer, with hard copies prepared and distributed to appropriate locations, again, through remote devices. Employee bids on these vacancies will be similarly processed.

With forty-seven thousand employees at the present time and projections indicating as many as seventy thousand by 1975, United Air Lines must, through the more efficient use of computers, improve its ability to administer vacation scheduling, grievance handling, layoffs, recalls, and a variety of other activities. Our data processing people tell me that such applications are very much within the realm of possibility and await only the availability of equipment and our ability to justify their purchase from an economic standpoint. When these and many other systems are operational, we may then reach the Utopia depicted in the *Business Week* article cited earlier.

Elaboration and Discussion

Mason The airline industry is certainly interested in — and needs — computers. In fact, I am sure that if the computer had not been invented, someone in the airline industry would have been forced to develop one.

The computer has also been a great help in developing the techniques for making airplanes as well as flying them. As far back as the late fifties and early sixties, they were able to program the riveting of a piece of the skin of an airplane, with one computer displacing sixty-five highly skilled technicians. So we are in an industry where the computer is something we live with and must have or we couldn't be where we are now.

To give you some idea of how this type of thing has an even broader impact than I have indicated in my paper, the present preoccupation of the airline industry is with the two new types of airplanes that are going to come into existence shortly; what we call the next two families of aircraft. One is the airbus, and the other, the Boeing 747. I might add that these airplanes are simply beyond comprehension insofar as their size is concerned. I have been in a mock-up of a 747, and you can put a DC-7 between the nose wheel and the plane's landing gear; this gives you some idea of size. The captain will be sitting $42\frac{1}{2}$ feet above the runway and it takes 3 acres of land to turn the airplane and park it.

Anonymous   Who wants such huge craft?

Mason   The public, because it is the public that wants to go cheaply and quickly to various distant places throughout the world. We certainly are the world shrinkers, if there is such a thing. Of course, in certain segments of the world, man doesn't like the fact that we are bringing him closer together; but we are doing it all the same.

Going beyond these next two types of aircraft, we have the SST (supersonic transport) on the horizon. But let's go to 1985. Lockheed has a movie which they show to airplane manufacturers and to various people who buy airplanes which describes a rocket that will take three hundred passengers from San Francisco to Singapore in forty-two minutes, or from New York to Moscow in twenty-eight minutes. You can't do this sort of thing without having computerized applications on the vehicle.

Anonymous   What about the pilot?

Mason   That is what I am coming to. Everybody knows there is now a Black Box — that is our name for it — that has been developed that allows hands-off flying. When this is completely developed, we may have the displacement of a highly skilled trade. A senior pilot on a major airline can make $45,000 a year flying premium schedules and still have fifteen to sixteen days off at home in the month. This is a part of computerization that isn't here yet; but somewhere out in the seventies, it may have a tremendous effect on the bargaining in our industry. However, that is beyond the scope of this paper.

The applications of computers, insofar as they have affected the labor relations picture in the airlines industry, have been pretty marked. We find their greatest uses, as Bill Caples said earlier, in the administration of the contract. At United Air Lines, we have approximately seventeen hundred separate flights to a hundred separate cities in the United States and Canada every day, and we have that many probabilities of disrupting the flight conditions for our ten thousand flight crews. The problem of designing pilots' schedules so that they will take into consideration the various desires of the individual and still meet the economic needs of a corporation is a tremendously complicated operation.

In my paper I talk about how we are doing stewardess scheduling today with one person where previously it took six to seven — and it is now being done in a shorter amount of time. Also, formerly we only had to schedule for a thousand stewardesses — now we have close to five thousand. We have pilot problems that concern the legal applications which we are required by law to enforce in regards to their rest periods and their qualifications on the various types of aircraft. In all of this, using the computer rather than doing it by hand has given us a big assist.

We signed a new pilot agreement on March 15, 1968, after having been in negotiations on and off for some eighteen months. I am sure that you read in the newspapers about our discussions concerning the crew complement we would have on the new Boeing 747's. What was not publicized was that the negotiations also had a few changes in pilot work rules, although not nearly as many as formerly because we had a planner to take care of all of these proposed changes.

The use of the computer in this type of application has had a positive impact on collective bargaining and in the administration of the contract, and I think that all companies would do well to give such things their particular attention. However, we find that we have to be very careful to sit down periodically with our employees and explain to them why this machine is not overlooking them as individuals and their desires. In other words, there is, and will continue to be, a constantly recurring problem of suspicion concerning what is in the machine. In the example given earlier of the use of a neutral computer, this may work; but even then you have to reassure people that you haven't programmed it slightly differently. All of these things are bound to show up at the bargaining table if you don't keep expounding on these matters.

Siegel May I make a comment? Renault in France had a strike protesting the use of the computer in selecting people for a layoff.

Mason That is interesting because we had two layoffs where we computerized who would go out and there was no problem.

We have twenty thousand people in our management and non-management group who have voluntarily sent in their qualifications indicating that they would like to be considered for any new jobs for which they could qualify. We use this system all the time and we have never had a gripe about it. Of course, I agree with you that a strike could occur that way. Again this comes back to what I was mentioning; you have to have a system whereby somebody whom the people trust is reassuring them that the system hasn't been changed. We have recognized this as a fact and so we have established means of calling in the men and reassuring them. I am advocating this as an operating principle, that's all.

Anonymous Isn't it conceivable that the company could change the program technology? How do the people know you are not going to cheat them?

Mason This would be hari kari. It would be ridiculous for any company to try it. As I say, it would be suicide; you just can't cheat.

Ginsburg I think I see the point of that question. The control of the information which goes into the computer is in United Air Lines's hands; and if I were really suspicious — not that there is any basis for it, of course — but if I were, is there any way of checking so that I can assure myself that my flying time and my other qualifications are recorded accurately? I am sure that you are putting the record in properly; but how can I be certain there haven't been some unwitting errors, something which in some way distorts the records?

Mason Any employee has the opportunity to discuss this at any time. That is my point; you have to have a vehicle for people to question those parts of the system that affect them. As long as you have such a vehicle, you should not have serious problems about the honesty of the system. We have a scheduling committee at every domicile and any change is explained to them. This is what I mean by having a means available for questioning the system.

Ginsburg   Seriously, I think your concept is great.

Mason   I think all this goes through an evolution. All pilot flight plans are now made on a computer and no one questions the flight planning any more. In a trip from Boston to Chicago, for instance, all of the latest weather conditions on wind, bad weather, turbulence, and so on are put into the computer on an instantaneous basis; and the computer gives the captain three schedules, ranked Numbers 1, 2, and 3. He can take any one of the three he wants. Number 1 gives the most economical operation plus passenger comfort. Number 2 gives an alternative and indicates the differences in passenger comfort and cost. Number 3 is still another alternative. The flight plan is very important as to how that trip goes and no one ever questions it any more. This is the sort of acceptance that I hope these other applications will eventually get.

Straus   In other words, are you saying you are dealing with people who had better trust these electronic devices or else they shouldn't be pilots?

Mason   No, I would not quite agree with that. You are dealing with people who understand we have just as much at stake as they do in seeing that this is correct. That is why I don't think the question of cheating comes in to the extent you would think. After all, we have a great interest in seeing that the system operates in the proper way.

Myers   I am interested in how you get these computer applications started; your first point of communication. In part of your paper you discuss a new scheduling program you are developing. Are the potential inputs discussed with the people who will be most affected? Is there any negotiation over what the inputs would be? Are these things discussed with representatives of the stewardesses and the pilots before you firm up the program?

Mason   Yes, they are discussed first with the System Scheduling Committees of the pilots and stewardesses and their recommendations are incorporated where feasible into the program. It is pretty well hashed out at this stage and the programmers don't structure the program at all. All they do is do the mechanical application of putting it on the computer and we have people in our scheduling group who even monitor this.

Penchansky Who decided on the factors that will be included when you talk of a system of multiple factors?

Mason Experience determines what they will be. You see, we did all this as a hand operation for many years, so these factors are pretty well known.

Straus Have you had any grievances over scheduling based on the computer?

Mason No, not as such. We have had grievances over "my schedule should be different," or "I should be entitled to a different schedule"; and I mentioned some cases in my paper where errors were made and noted the consequences of those errors.

But let me put it this way. Flying people aren't going to question the machine to that extent, because our whole life is built around machines. We are machine-oriented and we are change-oriented. The only constant thing we know in our business is that everything will change and we will live with this constantly. We perhaps don't have quite the same situation that other industries have. I don't ever recall — and Vernon Jirikowic can tell me if I am wrong — anybody's objecting to the new technology; complaints only turn on how technology affects working conditions.

Jirikowic That is essentially correct. This is true of most of organized labor. You want to ameliorate any detrimental economic hardship; but as far as opposing new technology, no.

Mason In speaking about new applications, I would like to describe briefly something we used in our recent negotiations.

We had a tremendous problem concerned with the diurnal cycle, which has to do with flying from time zone to time zone; and the pilots wanted some consideration of the problem. By having something that we could run different ideas through, we were able to get answers in very short order, whereas it used to take us a very long time. For example, to get a duty-time provision properly evaluated, the minimum time in which we had ever been able to do it earlier was a week and a half. Now we can do it in as little as two and one-half hours, with an average of four hours; and we did some twenty-five or thirty of them during the negotiations.

We did not discuss these items with the union; we were merely trying out ideas. But it certainly gave management better information and I am sure the union has its own way of doing this sort of thing too. I think where you have complicated working conditions, the computer is a great aid in speeding up the decision process.

Myers   Do you see any possibility of joint queries of computers on questions as they come up on negotiations, questions that are of joint interest to both parties?

Mason   That is a hard one to answer. It overlooks something about the strategy of bargaining. Many times you want to know an answer but you don't want the other party to know you are even interested in the question.

Straus   The question might be raised whether this same thing would apply with an arbitrator coming in and trying to mediate a dispute. Could he have access to this joint data base and, using his own imagination, feed in combinations which might produce a solution?

Cole   Sometimes a mediator doesn't want anybody to know what he is thinking about either.

Mason   We supply mediators with anything they want. We will supply them with answers in any reasonable area.

Cole   But if he asks you then you know what he has in mind.

Mason   That is the whole point on why I am hesitant about joint applications. At United, we are not going to go into too many of these joint efforts because we consider many things that we don't want the other party to know about. We discard more than we adopt; but we have to educate ourselves as to what options or elections we have. There are some ideas I would want to consider that I wouldn't want anybody else to know I even thought about.

Penchansky   The mediator could come in and run a program on your data bank without your knowing. A number of people can use the same data bank and no one person need know that others are doing the same thing.

Mason   In a year and a half, we will have our $55 million computer running. Let the others worry about their side of things.

Ellenbogen   A number of our people at General Electric are thinking of optional benefits. We have had some rather interesting experiences on the needs of younger people and the needs of older people. The young are interested in material benefits while the old are interested in something else. Would you comment on the probability of having various types of optional benefit plans and whether they would create any administrative difficulties in administering them?

Mason   I don't really know the answer to that. I know there are some companies that have tried the so-called cafeteria approach to supplying benefits. You go up to the counter and pick out what you want. General Electric looked at it, but I don't know anybody who has actually formalized it. The tax laws pretty well restrict your freedom of choice.

Caples   Yes, you have real problems with the Internal Revenue Service; the Government is not very cooperative.

Ellenbogen   It certainly looks like an unmanageable thing to us. Let's say you have 300,000 employees and you have a compensation package in which you can allocate among the different forms of compensation ranging from the forms of pay to the forms of bene-fits. The administration of a thing like this is extremely difficult, even with computers.

We talk about hardware, we talk about the computer in terms of machine capability, but one of the most important trends is the shift from the importance of the hardware to the importance of the software. By software, I mean the people and programs needed to make the machine run. So first you have the administrative prob-lem of keeping the books for a benefits program like this. Secondly, within a democratic collective bargaining framework, you have the matter of persuasion to consider. Call it emotion, call it persuasion, call it what you like, but I don't think this type of thing is an easy matter to communicate with employees. How does the employer communicate the terms and conditions of employment to its em-ployees? How does the union communicate to its constituents?

So I think you have two problems right here without going any further. One is mechanical and the other is in the persuasion area. Even if we lick the mechanical and software parts, I am not sure we know enough about the art of persuasion in communicating some-thing as complex as this to assure success.

Mason   I would just like to mention a couple of cases that fit in here. I don't know if they prove anything but they are true cases.

One was a case of a young man who in his twenties and thirties thought that pension plans were a lot of baloney and that a fellow ought to go out and put all his money in the stock market. He never elected to get into our pension plan until he was forty-two years old. He unfortunately developed cancer when he was about fifty-five years old. If in the years that he was running around advocating buying stocks he had been participating in our pension plan, it would have made a difference of about $500 more a month in the benefits his widow received when he died.

There is another case of a man who felt that pension plans should be something that you can use as a sort of savings device. Now United, up until its merger with Capital, would not let a person withdraw his contributions from the pension plan unless he resigned from the company. He could stop his contributions to it but he could not withdraw from it. However, Capital had a provision whereby after a year and a half of contributions to the pension plan, an employee could draw out funds. They used it as a sort of credit bank. In his early years, this particular fellow would save for two years and then draw it out to buy a car or make a payment. Unfortunately, he died from a heart attack recently. I computed that his family lost $300 a month because of this.

What I am saying is that I am not at all sure that we ought to allow too many choices to people. It is true that in your early years, retirement seems a long ways away. But as the stories illustrate, all kinds of things can happen.

Ginsburg It is fascinating to hear this from somebody like you, because I remember when I negotiated my first pension plan in the postwar period, the comment was, "We don't dare write these plans. We shouldn't be telling people what to do. Let's give them the wages and let them buy whatever pension they want."

Caples We were right in that until the Court ruled against us.

Union Representative If you give a fellow the options of savings plans, pensions, employee thrift plans, or even mutual funds, how does the union advise its members as to which of the several options is best for him? Are there not many risks in this process? I think this is important to consider.

Mason This is right. I have had fellows say, "Why didn't somebody tell me that I should have stayed in the plan?" The answer is very simple. We have letters in the file that prove that we did tell him. For instance, there is the case of this fellow who died of cancer. I looked at his record, and we had had five people in the administration talk with him. The last time, I talked with him myself for an hour and a half. He still told me that he could do better in the stock market. Well, he might have if he had done it — but he didn't.

Decasualizing a Labor Market: The Longshore Experience

Vernon H. Jensen

Longshore labor markets have been notoriously casual, but in some ports recent efforts to decasualize the work force have attracted attention. In the port of New York interesting developments have taken place. Although full decasualization has not been achieved, it is noteworthy that a computer has been installed as a central feature in the hiring process.

The earliest contributions to decasualization were made by the Waterfront Commission (a bistate agency created in 1953 to supervise the hiring process) and by the impact of the seniority system (set up ten years ago through collective bargaining). (The Waterfront Commission, however, had found it necessary to write the essentials of the seniority system into its regulations in order to assure compliance throughout all parts of the industry.) Another decasualizing force is inherent in the guarantee of annual income, negotiated by the New York Shipping Association (NYSA) and the International Longshoremen's Association (ILA) in 1965.[1] In exchange for reduction in size of gangs and some flexibilities in assignment of men, the employers gave a guarantee of annual income of 1,600 hours times the straight-time hourly rate of pay, less debits for failure to report or to accept suitable employment, to all dock workers who would qualify. Approximately twenty-one thousand did. The computer was introduced primarily to keep hiring and employment records needed in the administration of the guarantee but was intended, as well, to reduce casualness by facilitating the mechanics of hiring and increasing mobility in deployment of men;

---

[1] New York Shipping Association, "Memorandum of Settlement," April 13, 1965; "Report No. 2345," April 20, 1965.

226

it helped provide a speedy linkage between men anxious for employment and the available jobs.[2]

Assessment of the computer's contribution and its future role cannot be isolated from the problems and vicissitudes of the industry or the state of affairs in the union or the character of the industry's union-management relations. Nor can the Waterfront Commission be left out, for its cooperation in decasualization is necessary.

Complexities of the industry's hiring system created early problems in programming, and new technological developments have recently created new complications and uncertainties. New methods of handling cargo are causing relocation of business which, in turn, has created turmoil in the Union and concern among employers. Additional programming has been checked, at least temporarily.

Decasualization

It is not clear whether the employers in the port of New York, even the major ones, have come to the conclusion that casual labor is costly or whether they have simply been pushed, by circumstances, to grant some of the concessions they have made to the process of decasualization. The Waterfront Commission was forced upon the industry by legislation designed primarily to remove the International Longshoremen's Association from control of the hiring process. The Commission achieves some decasualization by registration of longshoremen and by periodic removal of men from the register when their shape-up and employment records do not meet minimum standards. The seniority system has had a great decasualizing effect, because many men without seniority rating have had difficulty getting regular employment and have not remained in the industry. Inordinate surpluses are a thing of the past. Seniority also helped pave the way for the guarantee of annual income. But, with technical developments that are changing the values of old priorities, rigidities produced by seniority are interfering with the achievement of greater mobility and are causing employers to have

[2] For more details about the immediate background of the development and the experience during the first year, see Vernon H. Jensen, "Computer Hiring of Dock Workers in the Port of New York," *Industrial and Labor Relations Review*, Vol. 20, No. 3, April 1967, pp. 414–432; for the background and details of the hiring system see Vernon H. Jensen, *Hiring of Dock Workers and Employment Practices in the Ports of New York, Liverpool, London, Rotterdam, and Marseilles*, Cambridge, Mass.: Harvard University Press, 1964, pp. 21–117.

not only second thoughts about the guarantee of annual income but some basic worries about the seniority system itself.

Economics

Even so, it does not appear that the employers have come to the conclusion reached by the major employers in the port of London — that casual labor is costly. The story of efforts to achieve decasualization of dock work in England is as long as the one in New York and the path to elimination of casual work on the docks just as tortuous. The historically pervasive fact in both ports is that employers seem to have been unaware of many of the hidden costs of casual employment and may have kept their eyes closed to the obvious ones; for the economies of different employment systems were rarely seriously contemplated, that is, they were never set against the diseconomies of the casual labor market.

The sordid reality is that the convenience of having a ready supply of workers at beck and call saddled the users with costs they did not need to bear, and probably would not have borne, if they had been fully aware of them or were forced to pay for them directly, or if they could not have passed them on to shippers or left them on the backs of the workers, not to mention the costs left to society.

"Buying Out"

The cost of getting out from under a system of casual employment in longshoring is not negligible, of course, because all sorts of practices have long standing in this custom-encrusted industry. Casual dock workers are not without ingenuity in structuring their employment in order to surround themselves with protection and personal or group advantages; and these are prized and defended with vigor whenever threatened.

"Buying out" has been tried and, while it is not easy to make a sale, it appears to be the only way to get out from under uneconomical practices. This is not necessarily unfair, for employers have contributed to the development of such practices. The reason even "buying out" is resisted is because many casual dock workers fear that the advantages they possess might be lost without any convincing, offsetting gain. What appears to be a strange paradox is the fact that some of the casual dock workers like the lack (or looseness) of discipline associated with a casual labor market. Some relish the privileges and preferences they personally enjoy. Hence, for these reasons, considerable resistance to changes in the labor market does exist among them.

In fairness, however, it must be said that the great majority of the men want steady, assured employment. Employers know this, but they have often felt they could not cope with the opposition. It is a sad thing that in New York and in London the unions have not had enough control over themselves or the men to do much seriously in support of constructive efforts for change. Of course, social protest and concern of the community about general economic welfare sometimes comes to bear on the matter, because the social and economic costs to the community are considerable; but such pressures are sporadic and often not sustained for periods long enough to force changes. However, such pressures have been sufficiently strong in both New York and London to help produce some of the changes which have taken place.

England

The National Dock Labour Scheme, in existence in England for nearly thirty years if the wartime scheme is included, provided only for "attendance money," that is, payments for reporting at hiring centers for engagement, and a "fall back" guarantee, minimum weekly earnings if a man received inadequate employment. Hence, it was but a cushion against casualness in employment, not an elimination of it.[3] Nevertheless, there have been serious efforts in the past decade to decasualize dock work. The intersting point is that the major employers in London did not like the fact that they were forced to carry a disproportionate, and substantial, share of the costs of maintaining the supply of workers. The levies to support the "attendance" and "fall back" payments were based on pro rata employment. The result was that the major employers in London were carrying a good part of the cost of maintaining availability of men for the more casual employers, whether these were individual employers in London with sporadic business or those in the smaller ports with irregular demand for men. The major employers came to the conclusion that casual labor is costly and decided that decasualization of both employers and workers was needed to get rid of all the relics of casualness. They became willing to "buy out," with full-time engagement, if restrictive practices could be eliminated. It took some doing, with labor and management negotiating. The government investigated, recommended, and then legislated;

[3] V. H. Jensen, *Hiring of Dock Workers*, pp. 143ff.

and, with the cooperation of management associations and the unions, a program was worked out.[4] The number of employers was drastically reduced by licensing to get rid of all who could not offer reasonably steady work. Many problems are still to be resolved; but, on September 18, 1967, each dock worker in England was placed in full-time employment, with a given employer, in effect, giving him a guarantee of continuous employment or pay.

New York

Employers in New York may come around to a clearer conclusion that casual labor is costly, but it is not likely that they will move to full-time employment. The basic elements of the hiring and employment priorities are so deeply rooted and the parts of the Union so autonomous that a fundamental overhaul could hardly be anticipated. It should be recognized, however, that the existing priorities are a product of casualness in employment and a defense against its impact. The most that might be anticipated is a recognition of portwide seniority for veteran longshoremen before sectional seniority for newcomers to the industry. The issue is a volatile and bitterly contested one. Until it is settled, any further programming of the computer will most likely be held in abeyance.

The Seniority System and the Computer

The programming of the computer had to be structured around the seniority system. Hence, to show how the computer serves in this industry of many employers and complex hiring arrangements, as well as to supply a foundation for discussion of current problems, the basic elements of the seniority hiring need to be presented. The seniority system was built around venerated priorities at the pier, but the seniority districts to be recognized beyond the pier led to dispute. Only a few among the leaders of the Union — and none in the ranks of the employers — wanted portwide seniority. The employers feared it would lead to too many grievances and claims for pay. Most in the Union wanted to preserve employment for the men in immediate localities. The issue was settled by establishing designated sections as the next seniority district, many of which

[4] For the background of the developments, see Ministry of Labour, *Final Report of the Committee of Inquiry under the Rt. Honourable Lord Devlin into Certain Matters Concerning the Port Transport Industry,* London: Her Majesty's Stationery Office, August 1965, Cmnd. 2734.

conformed to the jurisdictions of local unions. Each man was given sectional seniority, but could hold it in only one section. Beyond the section, seniority was portwide, although the concept of borough (or intermediate) seniority had also come into focus and was soon adopted. Longshoremen also carried a seniority classification of A, B, or C based upon the beginning date of their employment in the industry. However, even before the seniority system was completely launched — it was first delayed then established place by place — a demand was made in Port Newark and Brooklyn, as a condition precedent to establishment, that a D category be recognized, and it was. This was demanded, obviously, to give a preference to local newcomers to the industry in these sections. It placed D men in the section ahead of A, B, or C men from other sections. Similarly, borough seniority was insisted upon in Brooklyn and, by supplemental agreement, became a feature of the system. This had the effect of making the exercise of portwide seniority possible only rarely.

Seniority classifications later were increased in number. The ILA feuded with the Waterfront Commission over the control of hiring, perennially seeking the closing of the longshoremen's register. The battle is too long to recount here.[5] Yet an incident in it, although it had other roots, too, was the introduction of medical examinations by the NYSA and the ILA in order, first, to control entrance into the industry and then, later, to exclude newcomers by not granting examinations. But as a prelude to the institution of the guarantee of annual income, and after a long and bitter political struggle, the Waterfront Commission, the NYSA, and the ILA worked out a compromise for closing the register; and the necessary legislation was passed in 1965. Then came a date in August 1966 when the register was reopened and approximately two thousand men were added.[6]

This bit of history is necessary to the explanation of two additional seniority classifications: "medical," those who had been given medical examinations; and "1966," those who were taken into the labor force when the register was reopened. Under sectional and borough seniority, men in these two categories, all newcomers to the industry, were placed ahead of veteran longshoremen from other boroughs or, in some instances, other sections.

[5] V. H. Jensen, "Computer Hiring of Dock Workers," pp. 421–422.
[6] The New York Times, August 12, 1966, p. 50; August 22, 1966, p. 54; August 31, 1966, p. 37.

Computers and the Mechanics of Engagement

The industry's on-line real-time electronic data processing system comprises two IBM System 360 computers, set up in the offices of the NYSA. Fifty-six input and output units, located in the fourteen hiring centers maintained by the Waterfront Commission, are tied in with leased telephone wires for instantaneous retrieval and recording of information needed in the hiring process.[7] In these duplexed computers is a permanent file of all men by gangs, by various dock labor lists, and by their individual seniority classifications.

The system used in hiring longshoremen results in approximately ninety percent of the men being hired and validated for employment the day before they report for work, but it is not the same group each day. The men so hired comprise the regular gangs, additional gangs hired or extended from the previous day, regular list members, and casuals extended from employment the previous day. All such men report directly to the pier without going to a hiring center. Only the men hired as casuals go to the hiring centers.

First Phase — Gang and Dock List Hiring

During the afternoon on a given week day, the first phase of the ordering program goes on at the hiring centers after 2:00 P.M., when the hiring agents appear. They then order their regular men, that is, their gangs and the men from their various dock lists. Each hiring agent has IBM Port-a-Punch cards, one for each gang and one for each dock-list group of twenty-five men or less, e.g., lists for dock laborers, drivers, checkers, carpenters, coopers, or maintenance employees. The cards are prepunched to show the section, the pier, and the type of list. The hiring agents punch out certain columns indicating month, day, and time of reporting. Each card for a gang accounts for all the men in the gang, who are hired as a unit without regard to the seniority classification of the individuals. The cards for the dock lists have a line number representing each man. If the hiring agent does not require certain men, he excludes the ones not desired by punching out the appropriate line numbers; and he may hire without regard to seniority classification but in accordance with custom at the pier. Each hiring agent has a special iden-

7 NYSA, "Report No. 2456," June 6, 1966. See also NYSA, "News Release," December 10, 1965.

tification card which he inserts in the input unit prior to the insertion of his various gang or dock-list cards at time of hiring. Once his identification card and the gang and dock-list cards are inserted, the men are automatically hired and the computer stores this information.

Second Phase — Hiring of Additional Gangs

If gangs in addition to those on the employer's own pier are desired, they may be hired from among those from other piers who are available in the borough after the first phase of the hiring is completed at 3:00 P.M. The computer was programmed to supply lists of available gangs in each borough. Although the computer prints them at the rate of twelve gangs per minute, these lists are far from realistic for the reason that, during the previous hour, the hiring agents, being anxious to secure the services of the particular gangs they desire, have already obtained commitments from the hatch bosses, the leaders of the gangs. The system which had been in operation under the Waterfront Commission regulations permitted hiring agents to consummate gang hirings by personal contact with the hatch boss at the center or, more commonly, by telephone communications with them. The Waterfront Commission did not insist that this form of contracting be stopped when the computer was installed. Hence, the hiring agents do not wait for the lists of extra gangs but use the former system because it saves time and serves their needs. In fact, the hiring of additional gangs is usually finished before the lists from the computer are ready.

When additional gangs are selected, in the informal manner just described, the hiring is consummated by inserting a gang-order card, supplied by the manager of the center, into the computer where it is recorded. If available gangs outside the borough are needed, they may also be hired in a similar fashion once all gangs in the borough have been engaged. Once hired, the additional gangs, unless called back to their own piers, may be continued in employment by simply having the gang-order card inserted into the computer on successive days to record the continuation in employment.

Third Phase — Hiring of Casuals

Unlike the prior-day hiring of additional gangs, additional dock labor in any of the employment categories cannot be hired on the prior day. In the first place, the employer may not know precisely just how many men he will need. He would have to estimate absenteeism and the arrival of cargo. More important, perhaps, is the fact that employers do not want to obligate themselves to pay for more men than necessary in the event of bad weather. It is also contended that information about the availability of men cannot be satisfactorily assembled. However, once the first two phases of hiring have been completed, including the recording of continuation from prior employment, lists of men could be produced by seniority classification and type of work, including suitable types of work for each man. The problem would be to determine availability in the sense of willingness to work or to accept the work offered. There would also be a problem of notification. No doubt hiring by seniority steps would present problems; but with proper attention, it could be programmed.

Until prior-day ordering of extra labor is developed, the practice will continue in which such men will be engaged at the hiring center on the morning of use, although such men, once hired, may be continued in employment on successive days unless called to their own piers by their primary employers. If a hiring agent intends to continue a casual in employment, he may do so, provided the man has not asked for his seniority card, which he probably will do if he knows he will be working for his regular employer the next day or if he does not like the job and believes he can do better the next morning at the hiring center. To continue a casual in employment, the hiring agent inserts the man's seniority card into the input unit and the computer checks to see if he has been ordered back to his own pier in an earlier phase of hiring. It either reports that he is not available for continuation or else records the employment, as the case may be.

The hiring of men as casuals takes place essentially at the morning shape-up in the hiring centers shortly after 8:00 A.M. It is repeated on week days at 1:00 P.M., but this activity is relatively slight. It was intended that in this phase of the hiring the computer, apart from collecting and keeping records of hiring and employment, would make its greatest contribution. The computer was expected to facilitate the process of getting the men to the piers and to increase mobility by matching surplus men in some areas with the need for them in others.

The men who hire out as casuals are men who have no assignment for the day from their regular employers, plus men who have not been established in gangs or on pier lists. The latter are usually men with low seniority who have only recently come to the labor market. But there are a few men with high seniority who do not want to be tied to a gang or pier because they like the freedom to pick and choose. Being good workers they seldom fail to be hired because the hiring agents know them. We have noted that men who are eligible for the guarantee of annual income are required to report daily when not engaged by their own employer or suffer a debit to their guarantee.[8]

As the men arrive at the hiring centers in the morning, they "badge in," as they call it, by inserting their seniority cards into the input unit. The information on the card is transmitted to the computer, which makes an instantaneous check to determine whether or not the man already has been hired in the prior-day hiring and is expected at some pier. If the man is considered available for hiring, the machine types a slip printed in black with his number and an "okay." If, on the other hand, he has been hired on the prior day — perhaps he is trying to evade working with his own gang or on his own pier because he does not like the type of work or he expects to pick up a better job — the computer will send back a slip with his number and a message printed in red, telling him where he should be and making him ineligible, technically, for hiring at that time at the center. Nevertheless, hiring agents, when in need, will hire such men in spite of the prior orders for them to be at work on another pier. Nothing has been done to prevent this so long as the hiring conforms to the seniority steps.

Practice varies somewhat but at each center there is a time when input machines are closed and a man who is late cannot "badge in." Technically, he is not considered available for employment either. But it is not easy to tell a dock worker, who has been in a traffic jam or other transportation difficulty and who is a little late, that he cannot stand for employment. This is particularly so where the hiring has not yet gone beyond his seniority stage. Even if he does not have a slip, the hiring agent knows him, he is there, and he often gets hired.

The hiring of men as casuals proceeds under the control of the manager of the center who is an employee of the Waterfront Commission. He and the hiring agents take their places on a raised platform and the men group themselves by job classifications, that is, deckmen, dockmen, holdmen, drivers, dock labor, and so forth. The

[8] There is also a Waterfront Commission regulation which requires minimal monthly working or reporting in order to justify remaining on the register. This is designed to remove men who are not minimally interested in working in the industry and is the basis for semiannual review by the Waterfront Commission.

steps in the hiring conform to the seniority agreement, starting with pier-level hiring, that is, men from the pier must be taken first. The current order of hiring beyond pier-level is, first, taking men from the section on the basis of their seniority. Basically this means hiring A, B, C, and D men in this order. In Manhattan, "medical" men in the section are taken following D men; while in New Jersey (in the three sections) and in Staten Island, both "medical" and "1966" men in the section are taken after D men.

Checkers and other crafts have their own hiring sequences. The most important group, the checkers, have only portwide seniority; and their hiring takes place only in three centers. Their sequence runs A, B, C, D, E, F, "medical," and "1966," with telephone clearance between the three centers at each step.

When an individual is selected as a casual, the hiring agent hands him a slip, in two parts, which shows the work he has been selected for and the place to report. In turn, the man surrenders his seniority card and the "okay" slip obtained from the output unit. He next passes by the desk in the hiring center where the assignment slip is checked against his waterfront registration card and one-half of it is retained by the Commission agent. He then proceeds to the place of work on foot, by automobile, or by public transportation and, upon arrival, checks in with the timekeeper who collects the other half of the assignment slip.

After the sectional hiring step, the hiring agents insert their own identification cards into the input units and feed in the seniority cards of the men they have hired. This records their employment. The computer stores this knowledge. Then follows borough, or intersectional, hiring. Again, the sequence is A, B, C, and D. In Manhattan, Staten Island, and New Jersey, "medical" workers in the borough follow D men, and "1966" men in the borough follow next. In Brooklyn, after D men in the borough are hired, the order is "medical" in the section, "medical" in the borough, and then "1966" in Brooklyn. Portwide hiring follows borough, or intersectional, hiring. In each area, it runs A, B, C, D, "medical," and "1966." [9]

The computer was programmed to provide lists of men in the various centers who were not employed. These lists were to be com-

[9] V. H. Jensen, "Computer Hiring of Dock Workers," p. 428. This was an agreement worked out by Arbitrator Burton Turkus, signed by the parties and accepted by him on March 28, 1968, as the basis for ending the eleven-day strike which the ILA called against the Waterfront Commission decision to open the longshoremen's register to add men for employment in Port Newark.

piled center-by-center, rather than by borough as was the case with gangs. The computer printed the lists, by seniority classifications, of the men who had badged in but who had not been hired. Apart from the delay in getting them, these lists left something to be desired. The hiring agents were to select men from them, entering the identification numbers of the men desired into the input unit manually. The computer would send this information to the man's home center and the output unit there would print and issue a job ticket, which would be delivered to the man who would then report to the pier indicated and check in with the timekeeper.

Unfortunately, these lists did not serve as intended, due to the fact that men who had no desire to travel to other sections and who did not worry about debits to their guarantee often had left the center. Others who wanted credit for reporting but did not want work elsewhere were on the lists, but actually were not available. On the other hand, some men who knew they would not get employed in their own sections because the volume of employment was going to be slight often "badged in" at their home centers early and hastened to the center where they expected to get employment, rather than wait for the computer to match their availability with jobs. These men were gambling debits against employment. If they got hired, they were credited with working. If not, they would be counted as unavailable for employment in their home centers and suffer a debit to their guarantee. The inducement to take the gamble was the fact that, although technically improper, the hiring agents would usually prefer to hire those physically on hand rather than work through the impersonal lists supplied by the computer.

Hiring agents who did not get enough men, including men from other sections who had come to the center, found it annoying to wait for the lists from the computer and aggravating to use lists when many of the men named were not available. The managers of the centers were prevailed upon to follow the old practice of calling other centers to see what men were available in order to facilitate the hiring. Because the lists so inaccurately reflected the men who were available, it was proposed, a little belatedly, to have a second "badging" for availability. This would have made the lists more realistic; but the ILA, probably fearing additional debiting, would not cooperate, insisting that the men had "badged in" once and that was all that was required. Hence, the informal hiring of men from other centers still continues by telephone.

On March 4, 1968, the rule that men were required to report at their home hiring center was waived, making it possible for a man to badge in at any center of his choice without risking a debit. Why the employers waited so long to make this change is explained primarily by their inertia. They had nothing to lose. The men who were willing to hustle for work resented "badging" at home centers. It delayed getting them to the places where their services were needed. At first the employers undoubtedly thought that without the rule men would evade work and debits by going to centers where work was known to be unavailable. This was an exaggerated fear. They, of course, thought that the computer would facilitate the transfers needed, but in this they were disappointed. (Nevertheless, by the end of March 1968, the Union had made no announcement and the men were being told of the change by the managers of the hiring centers.)

At the completion of hiring, the manager of each center inserts into the input unit information about the level of seniority reached in the hiring for each classification of work. Those men who report but are not hired are credited with reporting unless they have left the center after sectional hiring or have refused the jobs offered. For a long time, all those whose seniority was greater than that of the least senior man engaged in relevant classifications were debited, because they were deemed to have either absented themselves or refused work offered. This has been changed somewhat.

The Union, at the outset, took the position that a man could be debited only if he refused work in the classification he carried on his own pier. Employers, however, took the position that a man had to accept any work he had customarily done anywhere in the industry. The arbitrator upheld the employers, but they were required to tabulate from the assignment cards for the previous year all the jobs each man had performed, in order to determine the types of work required of him.[10] This information about each man was put in the computer. Numerous grievances are now settled when the computer produces the facts about a man who challenges the debits against him.

More recently, there has been a second arbitration related to the debiting problem.[11] The Union contended that the employers could

---

[10] NYSA, "Report No. 2434," March 10, 1966, containing "Kheel Arbitration Award" of February 21, 1966.

[11] NYSA, "Report No. 2565," October 9, 1967, containing "Kheel Arbitration Award" of October 6, 1967.

make debits only to the extent of actual shortages or unfilled jobs. A succession of men might refuse jobs. The employers contended that every man who refused suitable work was to be debited. Much to the consternation of the employers, the Union's position was upheld. To make the decision even worse for the employers, the arbitrator held that the debiting would run upwards from the last man to refuse the work, the least senior man, until the number debited equals the number of men short on the day. No others, even though they had refused work, are debited. It is easy for the employers to argue that the arbitrator contrived this result with false reasoning. Regardless of how it was arrived at, it has the effect of abetting reluctance to work, even malingering.

The computer maintains a weekly activity file on each worker and includes all orders given him, information about his reporting at the centers, and failures, if any, to accept suitable employment. Weekly payroll information, received from employers showing actual hours worked each day, is given to the computer. Each week every worker's record is cumulated. When they occur, each man's vacation, holiday, and unemployment compensation payments are included. The latter information comes from the unemployment insurance agencies of New York and New Jersey. In February 1968, a new service supplied by the computer was put into effect. No longer are longshoremen who claim eligibility for unemployment compensation required to obtain "show up" cards as proof of search for work. Although the old "show up" card system has not been replaced because the Waterfront Commission still insists on "show up" cards for its own purposes, a weekly report from the computer is sent to the unemployment insurance agencies and this is sufficient to establish proof of search for employment.[12]

The cumulated reports are used quarterly to determine whether a worker is entitled to a payment under the guarantee of annual income. It was agreed that if a man's earnings at the end of a quarter were less than three-fourths of the amount of the guarantee at that point, making allowances for debits assigned, he would be entitled to a payment of the difference between his actual earnings and the pro rata amount of the guarantee, with a full settlement, if any, at the end of the fourth quarter. The number of payments during the first year were very few, but with changes going on in the port entailing major shifts in employment, claims against the guarantee are increasing.

[12] *The New York Times,* February 20, 1968, p. 93.

Unsettled Conditions

In past years, movement of shipping operations to different piers and different areas of the port has had little effect on jobs, because space vacated by one employer would be utilized by another. A prevailing rule, sanctified by the years, is that dock workers hold their basic priorities on given piers, regardless of the employer who might be conducting operations there. When all the facilities of the port were being used, even if one pier was superior to another, the opportunities to work on a given pier were about the same regardless of the employer. Hence, the men clung to the piers where they had established priorities and they kept their local work jurisdictions inviolate from intrusion by outsiders.

It has been shown how sectional and borough seniority built protective walls, often conforming to the jurisdiction of local unions. If sectional seniority had something to be said for it at the outset, the addition of seniority classifications to give sectional preferences to newcomers to the industry erased much of it. In a similar fashion, borough seniority undermined the principle behind the avowed purpose of seniority, which was heralded as protection for the veteran longshoremen in the whole port. The employers, the Union, the Waterfront Commission, the Port of New York Authority, and others could have drastically curtailed the severe problems which plagued the port in the Spring of 1968 if the basic principle behind the seniority system had been better preserved and veteran longshoremen had not been placed at a disadvantage vis-à-vis newcomers. With the physical deterioration of certain piers and with technological developments that have caused a shift in employment from less functional to more functional facilities — particularly with respect to the changeover to shipments of cargo in containers — a very serious and volatile situation was created. The wholesale shake-up in job prospects of many veteran ILA members also exacerbated the chronic political stresses in the Union.[13]

When veteran longshoremen who were going hungry in their own areas went looking for work in the newly developing areas to which their work had moved and found themselves standing empty handed while newcomers to the industry exercised "medical" and "1966"

[13] "Seniority Issue Key to Dock Labor Calm," *The Journal of Commerce*, Vol. 294, No. 21,554, November 8, 1967, p. 1.

seniority in the section or borough and took the jobs, they were not happy with the Union, the employers, or the Waterfront Commission. It was a startling thing to many qualified, dedicated, veteran longshoremen, with twenty-five to thirty years' seniority, when they realized that they were caught in a bind of narrow sectional and borough seniority and could not be chosen for employment in another section until all available men in the section or borough were hired, even those with less seniority. Many would have gladly given up the guarantee of annual income and gone back to the old shape-up, under which they would have known they would stand ahead of the newcomers to the industry.[14]

The point is that previously stable employment relationships became unbalanced with the development of the use of containers and with changes in the port. Hiring practices were analyzed and criticized as never before. If the employers were divided and unclear among themselves on certain questions, the ILA, too, and its parts and its members, were upset and divided on the same questions and issues. If some employers, in frustration or desperation, had proposed scrapping the guarantee of annual income or modifying the seniority rules substantially, some leaders in the Union and certain workers would have certainly concurred. At the same time, many men would have been in more serious trouble finding income if it had not been for the guarantee of annual income; all the same it was difficult for some of them to wait for the quarterly payments. It is ironic, perhaps, that still others were able to qualify for their guarantee and yet hold a job outside of the industry.

One of the serious paradoxes was that shortages of men occurred in Port Newark and in adjoining Port Elizabeth while there were idle men in other areas, notably Manhattan and at the old Army Base in Brooklyn. Some employers were insisting that portwide seniority be established as the price for continuing the guarantee of annual income.[15]

Greater mobility was needed, but more than just changing seniority was needed to achieve this. There was a contractual provision which called for travel time when men were called from one borough to another. This was justified by the need to compensate men for the difficulties of traveling when there were emergency conditions.

[14] "Waterfront Commission Public Hearing to Determine Whether Applications for Inclusion in the Longshoremen's Register Should be Accepted," February 21–22, 1968, pp. 189–195.
[15] "Port of Newark Still Plagued by Labor Gap," *The Journal of Commerce*, Vol. 295, No. 21,621, February 14, 1968, p. 25.

This contractual provision came to act as a deterrent to movement under regular need. Employers, naturally, did not want to pay this cost.

Top officials of the NYSA and the ILA held several discussions about imbalances between demand and supply of men in various parts of the port. Both groups publicly advocated portwide seniority, but each looked ahead to the opening of negotiations in 1968. The NYSA recognized the legitimacy of contractual travel time while the ILA was not willing to give it up without getting something in exchange for it. The complexities of the bargaining structure and the diverse interests on both sides made it extremely difficult to open the contract and achieve an agreement. But because these parties made no adjustments, the Waterfront Commission talked of opening the longshoremen's register to relieve the shortages of men in Port Newark and Port Elizabeth. It had great pressure put upon it by the Port of New York Authority, which was unhappy about under-utilization of its facilities and investments, and by local community leaders in New Jersey who wanted jobs for the unemployed in the area. The Waterfront Commission weighed its obligation to see that an adequate labor force was maintained against its responsibility to recognize collective bargaining agreements. Following a public hearing, it decided to open the register and take on 750 men.

The ILA and the NYSA opposed the action. Each went to court to enjoin the Waterfront Commission and achieved a delay. The longshoremen, nevertheless, were so aroused that a portwide strike ensued. No doubt the Waterfront Commission had misread the feelings of the men, because the strike was against the decision of the Waterfront Commission, not against the employers. The strike ran for eleven days before it was settled by an agreement aided by the efforts of Burton Turkus, the port arbitrator. It provided for the formation of gangs to travel to Port Newark, a special procedure for filling out regular lists in order to have men available on the spot, reaffirmation of travel time, alteration of the guarantee of annual income to debit men in the new gangs when they did not appear when called but removed debits for men who reported outside their own section, cancellation of seniority cards for "1966" men who refused to accept employment in the hold, and restatement of the hiring priorities by boroughs and sections.[16] The accord was bitterly as-

[16] *The New York Times*, March 19, 1968, p. 1; March 20, 1968, p. 1; March 21, 1968, p. 93; March 22, 1968, p. 93; March 26, 1968, p. 89; March 28, 1968, pp. 1, 49; March 29, 1968, p. 1.

sailed by those who wanted men added to the register as a contrived result to subvert the statutes and the courts; and a little later, the Appellate Division of the State Supreme Court unanimously confirmed the order of the Waterfront Commission to open the register.[17] Accordingly, the register was opened and 750 men were added. But this is not the end of the matter. Negotiations in 1968 are just ahead. Certainly the future of the computer and its role on the waterfront will have to wait upon these developments.

Conclusion

The computer has done some things well. It has not been able — perhaps not been enabled — to do some of the things desired in a way that is satisfactory. It has not been given some of the things to do that were intended. What it will be given to do, beyond what it now does, will depend upon the solutions to the various problems besetting the industry. Recent developments have accentuated a situation which increases the strife in the ILA and sharpens political challenges. These will add to the normal difficulties at the bargaining table and will interfere with additional intended programming of the computer. The initial promise of additional results from the use of the computer has been checked, at least temporarily.

Elaboration and Discussion

Jensen What I am going to discuss is an illustration of the use of the computer in the administration of contract provisions. I have in mind, specifically, the guarantee of annual employment which was negotiated by the New York Shipping Association with the International Longshoremen's Association in 1964. I think it would be fair to say that the guarantee of annual income in the form that it was negotiated would not have been possible if the parties hadn't anticipated using the computer in its administration. It would be impossible to operate this kind of a guarantee without the computer.

Now the guarantee itself is relatively simple. As I noted in my paper, it guarantees 1,600 hours of employment to all longshoremen or dock workers who qualify. If qualified men work less than 1,600 hours, they get paid the difference between this guaranteed minimum and the hours actually worked, less the debits for times when

[17] *Ibid.,* April 2, 1968, p. 93; April 24, 1968, p. 93.

they did not report when they were supposed to or times when they refused to accept work. The contract requires the dock workers to accept suitable employment. This latter point has caused some problems, which I mention briefly in my paper.

The computer system installed is costly. At first glance, one might think it isn't worth it; but the employers who are closest to the situation tell me that the cost of the computer has been a good investment, for the grievances that they might otherwise have had would have been much more costly than the money spent on the computer.

In my paper, I have also attempted to give a brief background of the situation in New York. I tried to point out that there were three specific contributions to the decasualization of the longshore labor market in the past decade. The first was the development of the Waterfront Commission; its regulations certainly had an important decasualizing effect. The second was the seniority system that was negotiated and arbitrated about ten years ago; this also had a tremendous decasualizing effect on the industry, because a man who did not have a seniority priority did not stay around. As a matter of fact, the seniority system began to create shortages in parts of the port and is still creating problems in this area. But the third development, the guaranteed annual income, also contributed significantly to the decasualizing.

The employers made the choice to accept this guaranteed income because they decided they didn't want a surplus of men around. Before this time, they had been opposed to closing the register of longshoremen which the Waterfront Commission maintained. After the negotiations which produced the guaranteed annual income, they were anxious to have the registry closed, particularly in the eligibility year, because they reasoned that any man who worked 700 hours during the eligibility year would then become eligible for the guarantee of 1,600 hours in the following year. They didn't want a lot of new people coming into the industry and working only 700 hours and then be guaranteed 1,600. So they changed their view on closing the register and joined with the ILA to urge the legislatures of New York and New Jersey to close the register by amending the so-called Bistate Compact under which the Waterfront Commission operates. Before that time, they had always taken the view that the Commission didn't have the right to close the register. (I have also felt that the Commission didn't have the authority to close the register.)

I allude to the development of decasualization in England in my paper for two reasons: partly, to make you aware of what's happening there, but also I think it offers an alternative which has some real interest. In England, the parties followed a very tortuous path toward decasualization. The task took forty to fifty years to complete; but on September 18, 1967, each dock worker in England was assigned to a specific employer. The employers themselves first began the decasualization process; their number in London was cut down to about ten through consolidation and the establishment of consortia. The theory behind this was that no employer should be allowed to hire dock workers in London, or any of the ports in England, who could not reasonably guarantee full-time employment.

All of the men are assigned to one of these employers and are guaranteed annual employment whether there is work or not; but under the present circumstances, I assume that they are all going to be working most of the time, certainly at least in London. Of course this scheme has had a lot of problems, and there has been some opposition. But I mention it because some of the employers in New York sometimes talk about this as a possibility there, because they are a little disenchanted with guaranteed income under the prevailing conditions; they rail especially against the problems created in the administration of seniority provisions.

A current difficulty which I would like to turn to for a moment is something that has nothing to do with the computer, but which is nevertheless having an impact upon the system administered in part by the computer. The problem is a technological one having to do with the development of containerization of cargo and is having an impact on employment priorities never before encountered.

The traditional priorities in New York were a man's priorities on the pier. Employers came and went but the men stayed. A new employer who came to a pier had to take the men who were there. It didn't make much difference to the men which employers were there because the work remained about the same. This was a particularly good arrangement for those men who had priorities on good "earning" piers; they jealously guarded these priorities and they got built into the system.

With the development of containers and the expansion of Port Newark and Port Elizabeth, things have changed. Containerized shipments are not going to flourish on Manhattan. Manhattan has been going down for some time; but the dock workers, and perhaps the employers as well, didn't realize it at the time. The Port Authority, which owns and develops pier facilities around the port, has been developing Port Newark and Port Elizabeth. In order to get the facilities necessary for containerized shipment, it has looked to Port Newark and Port Elizabeth and has encouraged employers to move to these locations. This is now the container area and this is where the future is — there is no doubt about it. Maybe it won't come as fast as some people have anticipated, but it is going to come.

Now the seniority system gives priority to the men in the system. To give a good example, the Grace Line had a substantial operation in the Chelsea area of Manhattan for many years. They suddenly moved to Port Newark and all of the men in this area were out of work. They didn't follow the work to Newark because traditionally they stay on the pier and wait for a new employer to come — but no employer is going to come to this pier. Employers won't hire them as gangs because, for completely other reasons which arose a long time ago, a travel pay requirement was established and employers have to pay two hours' travel time for men they call over from Manhattan. They would rather have men hired in Newark, but the men are not there. And these men can't go over to Newark singly and get employment under terms satisfactory to them because of the existing seniority system. If a man went to Newark, he would have to stand behind all of the young people who had recently entered the industry; and it is very demeaning to a twenty-five year longshoreman from Manhattan to go over and see all of these newcomers in the industry being hired ahead of him. Furthermore, he has to take the leavings. The last jobs handed out are in the hold, and a man with thirty years of experience in longshoring just doesn't work in the hold. He has enough seniority priority that he feels that he is entitled to a much easier job than this. Of course, there are a lot of the longshoremen who are content to accept the guaranteed 1,600 hours a year. They know they won't be employed, as there is no work there. So they badge in and then go to a second job. With the guarantee — and the second job — they do pretty well.

This issue has divided the employers; those who are operating in Newark want the register reopened in order to obtain the men they need. Other employers don't want to open the register and bring in new men who will be located in Newark and then have to pay the guarantees to the men who are left behind. The thrust of the Shipping Association's argument against the opening of the register is that if six hundred men were taken on, there would be another six hundred men, presently underemployed, claiming guarantees under the guarantee of annual income; and if not the whole six hundred, then certainly an increase over the present number. As a matter of fact, even without the opening of the register, the number of men building claims against the guarantee has increased considerably in the last several months.

Ideally, I suppose what you need is a portwide seniority system. The employers are committed to it. The Union is committed to this. However, when I say the Union, I mean Teddy Gleason, who is the president. He can be committed to it because he comes from the checker group and they were consolidated into one local some years back and so have a portwide system. But when you look at the longshoremen and the local power and autonomy that they have, it seems impossible to reach any agreement about a portwide seniority very easily. It may come, but I am not sure how.

Of course the paradox of all this is there was only one person in the whole Union who wanted a portwide system in 1958 and not a single employer who wanted it. Well, I don't know what the future will hold; but the problems growing out of these changes in technology are interfering with the additional programming of the computer and the expansion of the system.

The computer hardware which the New York Shipping Association employs is obviously a great deal more than they need for the purposes which I have described, but they have a lot of other things in mind but haven't gotten around to programming them yet. They have put the payroll records in because this is a direct part of the record keeping for guaranteed annual income.

There is a central record bureau maintained by the Shipping Association where they manually keep continuous records of employment for every dock worker in New York. I was amazed when I first went down and saw how much information they have in this system. They have it all filed away in boxes; and when they want something, they go back and dig out the records. This obviously is a very laborious process. It was anticipated that all this information would be put on the computer, and this should be very simple to do. They just haven't gotten around to it. For a long time they have had a portwide vacation plan and a portwide health and pension plan; but because the employment record system is still administered manually, these vacation and health and welfare plans are also administered manually.

The employers have not done as much with their computer system as one might have hoped, but overall I still think one must be impressed with what they have done. You only have to take a look at the longshore labor market in New York fifteen years ago to see the progress which has been made. Although there are still many problems, I think it is really an achievement what has been accomplished; and the people in the industry need to be commended for what they have done and encouraged to go on and do the things which they still can do. In much of this, I am sure the computer will help them.

The major difficulty ahead is the problem of getting the Union people to agree on a program which they can all support as a unit. This won't be easy because the political power play in the Union is critical. I anticipate that the negotiations this coming summer [1968] will be the most difficult ever simply because the employers will not know — as they have not known in the past — with whom they are going to talk and deal. You can't negotiate with five or six people, all of whom have authority to make decisions. The chief spokesman can be knocked out at any time if he makes the wrong decisions; there is always somebody else sitting there waiting to pick up the negotiations, move in, and then try to do the job better than the last man.

I should make one addendum here. Contrary to all my philosophical feelings, I am a great supporter of collective bargaining; I argue for it whenever I get a chance. It is just that collective bargaining probably can't work under the present circumstances. It isn't really even collective bargaining under the normal definition. It is a rulemaking process, but it isn't collective bargaining.

When Wayne Morse settled the longshore dispute in 1962 — if you recall, much of it was on television — somebody asked him if this wasn't compulsory arbitration. He said, "Of course not; it was mediation. We told them it was this or else." And Gleason was very pleased with this. He had been saying no, no at every step. If you remember, that dispute ran through the Emergency Board, federal mediation, and right up to a presidential commission. At this point there was no place further to go; and it was probably necessary to have someone like Wayne Morse, who could talk with force and knew something about mediation, to force it out. I think that this is the way the next dispute will probably have to be settled too.

I had to laugh earlier when somebody said, "Won't better and more complete information about the bargaining process give you more power?" I am more humble. Considering the long time I have studied the longshore industry, I probably know more about it than anyone else; and I have no power at all. I couldn't settle a single dispute; I am not rough and tough enough. You have to have somebody with broad enough authority to lay the law down and make it stick. The computer doesn't have this kind of authority either. The computer will only work when the parties have already settled their labor problems to a greater extent than they have at present.

Myers Of course, information does not take the place of power; but I would be surprised if you said that information never changes people's perceptions, and surely this is a form of power.

Jensen I wouldn't argue with that.

Brown What has happened on the West Coast? Have they computerized out there?

Jensen They haven't computerized on the West Coast as yet. People ask me why New York hasn't used some of the approaches that the West Coast has, but New York is five times more complicated than the whole West Coast area. The problems are not comparable.

In London, they use the computer to make the assignments of the men to the employers. So they are using the computer, but not on a continuing basis.

Anonymous If the question of portwide seniority is really a key question in New York, is the computer being used to develop the statistics necessary to justify the wisdom for such an approach, perhaps for purposes of explaining it to the whole membership?

Jensen I don't think they need any statistics. They simply need to decide what they are going to do. It would be easy enough to operate on a portwide seniority system. They wouldn't have to program the computer any differently. The information is all there now, and the steps which they go through are the steps which are laid down in the collective agreement.

Of course, the collective agreement would have to be changed if they went to such a seniority system. The employers have been against portwide seniority, particularly when they started guaranteed annual income, because they have felt that a man would run off to a place where he would not be employed and then not work and yet would not be debited against his guarantee. They thought there would be a lot of malingering.

There is a side story to tell about this; I mentioned it briefly in my paper. There have been two arbitrations. One was concerned with debiting. This is a wily union, and they felt that if you are going to debit, you should only debit to the extent of actual shortages. In trying to find a man for a particular job, you might have to go a long way down the seniority list, with one man after another refusing the job because he didn't like it or had something else to do that day, before getting someone to do it. The employers were debiting all of the men who had been asked and who had refused. The Union said that you should only debit to the extent of the shortage. They went to arbitration and the arbitrator upheld the Union and this really affronts the employers. Well, this has caused some malingering.

The other arbitration was to determine what suitable employment really means. The employer said that it means any work that a man had done at any time in the past. The Union said no, the only employment for which a man has to stand and has to accept is the employment under his classification on the pier. The Union was saying that if a man were a driver in the gang on the pier, the only job for which he could be debited would be a refusal to take a job as a driver. Typically, many men who are drivers and who do not want to go to another pier when there is no work in their classification hire out on another job. The employers said these men had to take any job they had previously done or else be debited. The mediator upheld the employers and thus forced them into undertaking a program of determining and recording who had done which jobs in the past. Fortunately, the Waterfront Commission had a system of little assignment cards which were collected and kept. There were a couple of million of them around the port. The employers took these cards and codified the information. They then put it into the computer and now a man can be debited for refusing any kind of work that he has done during the past year.

Penchansky It seems as if there ought to be a different application for the computer. There are changes taking place in the port, changes in the shipping, changes in the cargo. It seems that we ought to go back to what was said earlier and model out what is taking place, the transition in the port, and begin to try to make some long-range predictions for manpower needs.

Jensen I might be able to do that, but what good would it do? The politics of the situation are such that I could have the most rational system worked out, but that doesn't deal with the realities of the situation.

Penchansky It does to this extent. You can accept a system if you can point out what the long-range trends are. You can help the union leader get into a situation where his position is in line with these manpower trends.

Bigelow I was wondering about the possibility of a group, other than labor or management, preparing a model for their own purposes. Such a body might be the Port of New York Authority.

Jensen The Port Authority has a model of the development of the port which the people in the industry on both sides respect; it just doesn't fit their interests. I don't see any fundamental changes while the current people are still living.

There is a real revolution going on in this part of the transportation field. And it reaches into the other elements of the transportation world as well. I think that in another decade, you will see extensive changes in company organizations, in transportation organizations, and in the use of containers for continuous transportation from plant to destination, through trains, trucks, ships, and so on. There are all kinds of plans for this and for the impact that it will have.

But in the process, you have all of the people who are trying to survive and it is not going to be easy for them. This accounts for a lot of the unsettlement on the management side and the difficulty for employers to get together and make any plans at all. People are not in any position to accept plans if they don't know yet how these changes are going to affect them. If they knew they were going to survive, it might be different. By the same token, the men in the Union are uncertain because they don't know what the future is going to be either. They want to preserve their jobs. The stresses and strains in the industry at the present time are almost beyond description.

Straus In this last little dialogue, I think I detect, to use an old hackneyed word, a generation gap. The training that some of us old fossils had was a kind of traditional training. Now some of the younger professors in the room are saying there is a whole new kind of approach to problems, using languages from the New Mathematics and from computers.

I first began to get an inkling of this in attempting to carry on impossible discussions and arguments with my older son, who is kind of a computer buff in the architectural field. I realized that I didn't know what he was saying until I tried to tune in on a different wave length. I still don't know, but at least now I know that these new languages make communications easier.

As I see it, the computer fellows are saying to us old fogies, "Look, we are not talking about new hardware. We are talking about new analytical ways of thinking; and with them, you will come up with different insights, whether or not you use these big machines."

Meyers I was thinking along the same lines, but I asked myself the following question: Are we really not talking of two different sets of variables? One set of variables includes those dealing with persuasion and politics, the making of arrangements within the democratic framework. The other variables are those which are measurable, variables which are used to keep the score but don't really determine an outcome very much. I wonder if we don't have a parallel in the field of labor economics.

There used to be two types of labor economists: the purely industrial type, who was more theoretical than empirical in describing how a labor market operated; and the engineers, who described how economic decisions were actually made, how people developed working rules for doing things. In large measure I think we have solved this problem of getting better integration of the two. The test of a good practitioner is one who is equally comfortable in both areas. What we are facing is a process of accommodation.

Now in looking at negotiations and in considering the role of the computer people, the systems people are like the theorists in labor economics. They can tell you how the integration of two bodies of thought or two sets of variables can take place. We know that economics has benefited from this, and I think that negotiations will benefit from it also. But we have to overcome the gap between the negotiators and the data systems people who, at the extreme, are programmers who talk only to machines. How can they be made to talk to negotiators? I think that this is taking place, but it will

only be successful when systems people recognize that the negotiators have certain aims and any systems that are developed will have
to talk to the negotiators as well as talk to the machines.

Jensen　Maybe we are forgetting what I claim is the fundamental
action of our society, that is, the pursuit of economic self-interest,
the thing that has made this economy go and keeps it going.

The problem with the shipping industry is that it is composed of
many employers all in competition with each other. It is a pretty
rough, cutthroat industry; and this is carried over to the labor side.
The people in it don't theorize or look ahead very much. I criticize
them for this; but frankly, I don't know whether they are really
able to look ahead very far.

In London, they were able to look ahead because the dock labor
scheme they had over there put the cost of casual labor on a pro
rata basis. This meant that the big employers were underwriting the
cost of employees for the casual employers; and they didn't like this
cost, which was running to something like four million pounds a
year. So they decided to get away from the casual system, which
meant getting away from casual employment. There were some of
the left wingers who wanted to go the whole way, and instead of
having ten employers in London have only one. Now if you had
one employer, I think you could do some of this planning you are
talking about; but if you have a multiplicity of employers, you
have this problem of competition which keeps these employers from
dealing with each other openly and honestly. This is the problem
that interferes with the planning. They are not about to do much
of it as long as they pursue their economic self-interests.

Penchansky　You are assuming there is only one path in their pursuit of their economic self-interest; it seems to me there must be
other paths. It seems to me we ought to help them with these
alternatives.

Anonymous　I wonder if you can apply rational solutions to irrational bargaining.

Jensen　I agree with you on this. Collective bargaining is not a
process that proceeds on reason. It is a means whereby the respective parties can get the things that are of interest to them. The
negotiating process is aimed at finding out whether the other fellow
is going to settle. It is not supposed to convince him that something
is reasonable and rational; it is to convince him that if he doesn't

settle, he is going to be hurt. When that happens, an agreement is reached and then it becomes rational.

Straus I am still not convinced that we are communicating. In negotiations, you have a situation where people are operating under a set of constraints. What you are looking for is a plan for some kind of solution that meets the demands of all these people. There must be a series of alternatives, some of which are better than others, which meet these constraints. I think Roy [Penchansky] is suggesting that perhaps there may be a solution which is better than the one that was signed, one that is better in meeting the conflicting interests of all the parties. The computer itself is not going to do it. The computer is a tool; and perhaps in using it, a better solution can be reached, one that better meets the constraints imposed by the political aspects, not one that takes away from these aspects.

Anonymous And certainly the more complex the data, the more advantageous the use of the computer.

Lesieur For most of this conference, we have discussed using the computer in helping in the bargaining and in administering the contract. But we have not talked about the problem of selling the constituency on the agreement that has been signed. How do you get the work force to understand the use of these new tools?

An example of what I am talking about occurred when I visited a plant in the Midwest two years ago. One of the turret operators I know came up and said to me, "Fred, Ralph Anderson, the owner of this company, is a nice guy. He just put us on a fifty-hour week and we don't have any work. He wants to get us more money for Christmas." Later that day I had lunch with Anderson and his executives and I related this conversation to him. Well, he went right up through the ceiling and really got after his executive vice president who runs the place.

What had happened here was that they had gone to complete computerization of scheduling and inventory control. Now for most human beings who work at machines, the only way you know you are busy is if you are up to your armpits in castings, with jobs all over the place. Then you know it is safe to work rather than loaf your way out in order to fill the day. They had put in a very sophisticated way of handling shop orders, with most of the orders and backlog in the paper stage in the computer. This meant you didn't have the stuff all over the floor and things were much more orderly, which I think is fine. But the vast bulk of people on the hourly payroll didn't know what had happened.

I wonder if we ought not to start in the high school system to talk about the wonders that these new tools can perform and the kind of things they can do so you can get people into the work force who are attuned to what is coming. It is difficult to sell. I have been the president of a local union; and, believe me, I have seen it when it has been very difficult to sell a contract to the membership despite the fact that it was a terrific agreement. I wonder if some studies ought not to be done in the area of how to get people to understand the competition they are going to face. Is there anything being done in this area? I hear of a high school getting a company to give them an obsolete computer. This might go a long way toward getting more mature collective bargaining. I would hope that the bargaining committees would take steps in this new era to give the rank and file an opportunity of understanding that this box is not a monster but a useful tool.

Straus I would like to suggest that the old-fashioned mediator was really something like a craft-oriented computer. I recall in the early days of mediation, when I first got into the game, I saw fellows like George Taylor, Will Davis, and Dave Cole at work. The parties would come to old Will Davis and tell him of their problems. His computer mind would then start clicking and he would come up with solutions that they had never thought of and they were back in the game again. I have seen Johnny Dunlop do the same thing many times.

It seems to me that what is being said here is that the disputes of today are not responding to our old-fashioned kind of logic. It may be that the complexities of the problems are so much greater now than before that the old "computers" are breaking down. Maybe it is an old-fashioned model computer that can't handle the input. But some others of us here are saying that these new computers and their logical solutions won't work in this dog-eat-dog world in which we live. Well, I don't think it is any more competitive now than in the days when the mediators were working. Maybe it is more complex, but I don't think the participants are any more avaricious.

I just wonder if fellows like Roy [Penchansky] aren't saying that the old models have broken down. But I wonder if someone like Roy, given the experience of a George Taylor or a Dave Cole,

couldn't then go to work with a computer and come up with much
better solutions than we have now. It isn't a question of trying to
take the human relations out of bargaining or saying that it is any
more or less rational than it was before. It is just that it is more
complex, and therefore the parties seem much more hardened than
in the past.

Penchansky   Please, don't ask me to build the models; Gordon
[Kaufman] is the model builder.

Myers   For my own benefit, and perhaps for some others', I would
like to review the things that have come out of this discussion so
far. The first use we have seen for computers is in information
retrieval. This is what Woody Ginsburg was talking about in his
paper; and, to a certain extent, what Charlie Mason was describing
at United, although his applications went a little further. Here, I
think, the computer and its data bank certainly perform a function
that the industrial relations side of management has long neglected.
The very fact that most of the people who are doing things in this
area are in this room is an indication of how new this simple application of computers is.

The next stage is the using of this data bank. From what I have
heard so far, this information is only used to help management or
labor prepare for its negotiations in computing the alternative costs
of different packages that are to be offered or demanded. We haven't
yet come to the joint costing of alternatives or joint information
retrieval as a preparation for collective bargaining in the sense that
George Taylor was suggesting. I think you don't have to be very
sophisticated to see that this would make a contribution. Although,
as some here have cautioned, if you have too much information or
if it is too structured, this may add to inflexibilities, which is certainly bad for collective bargaining.

The third stage, it seems to me, is in considering the various
alternatives in bargaining. By providing some possible alternative
solutions to complex problems, you would not be substituting for
the human judgment of the negotiators, but would be assisting them
to make better decisions. I think there is a system of analysis that
computer software programming offers to — or imposes on — the
parties.

The final stage is something that Jay Forrester was talking about
earlier. He said that you can develop a model of any system, including a collective bargaining system. He admitted he doesn't know

very much about this area, but by talking to practitioners he said he could develop a model of this system, although it may be somewhat crude at first. This is what designers in the management field do when they attempt to develop a model of a particular system. They talk to knowledgeable people in the field and then they design accordingly.

During lunch, we finally got him to admit that the usefulness of such a model would be in describing that part of the system that is more structured than unstructured. The more problems there are of emotion and feelings in a collective bargaining system, the more difficult I think it is to develop a model that might help the bargainers, either separately or together, or a mediator in trying to understand better how the process works. At least, this is my understanding; but maybe this represents my being on one side of the generation gap that Don Straus referred to earlier.

Most of us older than thirty-five would say that you have to learn about bargaining by long experience and by developing a "feel" for it. But the same thing was claimed for the underwriters in the insurance industry. Many said you have to learn underwriting by a lifetime of experience; but when the systems analysts began an analysis of what an underwriter did, they found that much of it was fairly routine and programmable. Maybe the same thing will occur in bargaining, somewhere way down the road.

Scott Morton When Charlie [Myers] talks of "way down the road," I think a fact that has surprised a number of people in the last few years is how short that road is. It is certainly a long, long way before computers will play a major role or take over decision making; how many years away this is I wouldn't even want to guess. But what surprised us in some research recently was the number of managers in the fifty thousand dollar a year bracket who, although they know nothing about the working of computers, have nevertheless been able to use computer systems to help them understand their jobs right now in 1968. So I think we have to be careful when we say "far down the road"; it may be closer than one realizes.

To re-emphasize a point made earlier, I am not saying that we want the computer to plan out the solutions completely, simply that we can get better answers to guide our strategy through the use of simple or complex models to help us get a better feel for the problem. I think this was a very valid point and it is something that I would categorically state is going to happen sooner rather than later. This projection is based upon experience in a different field than bargaining but certainly one that is similarly unstructured.

Ness   In support of both of those points, it seems to me that it is difficult in many situations to recognize the information processing component of a task. Indeed, in Geoffrey Clarkson's work with trust officers, he found they were performing tasks which proved to be eminently suitable for computerization. The computer was able to go through the process of creating portfolios which to all intents and purposes were identical to those produced by trust officers. The trust officers were quite unwilling to admit that any portion of their job was this mechanical.

I think what this is saying is not that we can sit down and build a perfect model; but, as we begin to recognize inadequacies of our analysis, that we can mold it to a greater congruence with reality. In the long run I can see even those things that are often classed as irrational being incorporated in the model. I suspect it will be a long, time-consuming process, but one that should prove to be profitable to everyone in the long run.

Ellenbogen   I think it is axiomatic in collective bargaining that the best agreement which the parties can reach is one that they have made by themselves and which each can more or less live with. My question is, how much of a better agreement would be reached with the help of the computer, with the help of a third party, or with the help of the various instrumentalities for reaching agreement?

Siegel   You are provided with a different set of eyeglasses.

Jensen   May I give a good definition of a good collective agreement? After all the bargaining process is finished, you get hold of a guy in the plant who is a disgruntled type and ask him what he thinks of the agreement. If he says, "Hell, that is all we could get out of the bastards this year" — that is a good agreement. Here the union got all they could get without striking and the rank and file has accepted it.

Straus   I think I pointed out what I would consider a good agreement. This is one where you can't improve one side without hurting another. An agreement that both sides can live with is not the same as an agreement that both sides can improve upon. You yourself pointed out a situation in longshoring where, with better foresight, both parties could have improved themselves dramatically. I think this is what some of the speakers have been driving at; that by using more sophisticated planning techniques, and this doesn't necessarily mean a computer — just systematizing your thoughts, you might come up with solutions that would improve both sides. These solutions, of course, can be very complicated; and I think it is important not to limit yourself too early or get into fixed positions on certain things.

A Computer-Based Negotiation: Uses and Limitations as a Training Device

John M. Baitsell, Christopher R. Sprague, and David P. Taylor

Introduction

In recent years the curricula of schools of management have been enriched through the use of computer-aided instruction techniques. Many of these techniques take the form of games in which the student is either pitted against a computer or against other students with the computer serving as intermediary. Since some of these teaching methods appear to have achieved some moderate success, at least according to most of the testimony we hear, we were interested in exploring the extent to which a computer-assisted mock negotiation would improve courses in labor relations. Three approaches have been tried.

Simulation of Pay and Vacation Negotiations

The first approach utilizes a labor-management negotiation simulation programmed a few years ago by Brandt R. Allen, then a Research Assistant at the Harvard Business School. This program is devised primarily to demonstrate the ease with which a student can work with a time-sharing computer and only secondarily to indicate what labor negotiations might be like. The only items to be negotiated are rates of pay for three jobs and the number of days of vacation. A student sitting at the computer console first decides whether he wants to play the role of union or management; he then makes either offers or demands relative to the three pay rates and the days of vacation. With each offer or demand the student must indicate his mood on a scale from one to nine: one indicates that he is happy, generous, and ebullient; nine indicates the reverse.

As negotiations progress, the student discovers that, in general,

260

if he remains friendly and makes reasonable offers or demands, the program will move with him to a settlement. If he does not, he finds that the program will be equally stubborn and will negotiate endlessly.

Thus, a player may indicate that his mood is reasonably affable, say a 3, and that he wants $6.00, $5.75, $5.50, and 25 days of vacation. The answer will come back: "The best we can do is $3.94, $3.53, $3.22, with 8 days' vacation, and that is higher than the Teamsters get."

Seventy percent of the time the computer will come up with a counteroffer. Thirty percent of the time it will come up with a statement like: "Why don't you really get down to business, Mr. Jones?" For conveying solutions, the machine is programmed to close up on its counteroffers by splitting differences between its offers and the players' demands according to any specified pattern you may want to introduce in planning the game.

The program also accommodates those who prefer a "spectator" role by letting the student indicate that he wishes to be *neither* management nor labor. In a great display of schizophrenia, the computer will then take both roles and negotiate against itself.

This exercise has proven valuable in familiarizing people with the computer. It has always been preceded by a thirty-minute lecture on what a computer is and can do, as well as the unique advantages of time-sharing. With the lecture and this program, students who have never seen a computer are negotiating enthusiastically in seconds. Occasionally, however, it takes some convincing to persuade a student that there is not a very fast typist somewhere typing back at him.

Negotiations for Airline Crew Scheduling

The second approach to using the computer in negotiations ties into the remarks of Mr. Charles Mason concerning the costing of stewardesses' demands through a computer simulation of the scheduling process. We have obtained from another airline a program which demonstrates how it uses a simulation model to assess how many additional cockpit crews the airlines will have to man if it agrees to certain work-rule changes.

We divide the class into union and management teams for mock negotiations; and, in a move toward the joint use of a computer by union and management teams, we make an IBM 7090 computer available to both sides with a joint program. Each side can make submissions to the computer, changing the work rules for the pilots; and they get, for each set of work-rule changes, a number which purports to show how many regular flight crews and how many reserves would be needed if the company agreed to those work rules for pilots.

Then we tell our students a couple of weeks ahead that the situation is such that the union has to make proposals for work-rule changes before negotiations. The company comes back with counter-proposals before negotiations and we give them an hour and a half to negotiate. In addition, we give them the prior contract and some notion of training costs so they can cost-out training a crew.

In this case, the computer (or, more properly, the simulation model) serves as a testing ground on which both sides can try out proposals on both work rules and wage rates. It is by and large successful, giving a good set of vicarious negotiations. Interestingly enough, we observed some negative reaction on the part of some of our better industrial relations students to the mounds of computer printouts involved. They said, "Here we are in a relatively nonquantitative area, industrial relations, and you insist on invading our domain with a computer." This resentment shortly evaporates.

A More Comprehensive Approach to Negotiations Modeling

The third approach involves a similar use of the computer as an aid to negotiation; but in this case, the teams are able to do a good deal more than in the airline simulation. Specifically, the teams are able to build their own models of the situation, changing not only the numbers (as in the airline model), but also the very structure of the model itself. They are also able to retrieve a great deal of useful information about the work force. We now describe the steps leading to the third approach.

Our feeling is that the computer can be used effectively in two ways to enhance the learning experience in mock negotiations. First, it can be programmed to provide a substantial amount of historical information about industry and area practices to the parties involved in the negotiations. Second, simulation exercises can be programmed for use by the parties to "cost-out" alternative contract provisions or packages where quantitative information is relevant and available. That is, our intention is to increase the reality of the game situation by providing a large volume of information, with analytical tools to process this information quickly.

The Negotiations Game

We began our development of these computer-aided mock negotiations by conducting mock negotiating sessions using a non-computerized case created by the Bureau of National Affairs and embellished by Professor James J. Healy.[1]

A Description of the Game

Let us set the context by describing how the game is administered and then describe the game. This exercise was used in a required survey course in labor relations in the graduate program in the Sloan School of Management at M.I.T. This year there were thirty-four students in the section of the course in which we introduced the game. We divided the students into eight groups on the basis of alphabetical listing. Four of these were designated as representing the union and four as representing management. We assigned a coordinator to each of the teams. The teams got the materials of the case. They met for two one and one-half hour bargaining sessions. At the end of these sessions, if they reached agreement they had to submit to the instructor the terms of the agreement. If the negotiations resulted in a strike at the end of the third hour of negotiations, they had to submit a list of those issues which had been resolved and the remaining points of contention.

Prior to the beginning of the negotiations we were available to give students additional information on the case. Prior to the beginning of negotiations, the students, in turn, had to submit to us minimum union demands and maximum company concessions.

The Burns and Bruce Case

The game situation itself involves a two-plant firm. One of the plants is in Grand Rapids, Michigan, and one is in Fort Hancock, Illinois. The company is in the business of metal fabricating primarily for the auto and agricultural implement industries. The firm was family-owned for a number of years and then went public. It has had a long history of paternalism and stable employment. The negotiations are taking place in January 1959. In 1957 and 1958 there were substantial layoffs which had led to the organization of the firm by an aggressive industrial union. The representation election was won by a narrow margin.

[1] "Burns and Bruce," courtesy of the Bureau of National Affairs and the Case Clearing House, Harvard Business School.

The bargaining is concerned with the Fort Hancock plant, although the other plant is also organized by the same aggressive industrial union. Workers there are in the "Detroit pattern," and their wages are a bit higher than at the Fort Hancock plant. In the local area, many of the other firms pay their workers more than the Fort Hancock plant does. Wages, as opposed to benefits, are noticeably higher in these other local establishments.

There are two additional background factors stressed. The chairman of the board is a virulent anti-union type with particular rancor about the union shop and the payment of Supplemental Unemployment Benefits. The second background factor calls the student's attention to the fact that the company has bid on a Navy contract worth $4.5 million and there are hints that the company will be unsuccessful in this contract if they are in the midst of a labor dispute.

The game also includes a set of ten union demands that are generated by the computer. The game begins with the company teams being required to come up with a set of counteroffers in response to these demands that have been made.

Added realism is created by having a newspaper reporter hound the negotiators as they leave the bargaining table. Copious notes are taken during the negotiations and they provide the basis for a debriefing session with each set of bargainers. This exercise, without the assistance of the computer, has been used with great success for years by Professor Healy.

Some Student Reactions

When we ran this exercise, we found our students asked many questions for which there were no answers. For example, the basic information contained some financial information about the company's immediate past; but this was limited in its depth and coverage. As a result, we were bombarded with questions about the company's forecasts of sales, projected productivity data, and so on, despite the fact that the students had been warned that no additional financial information was available.

Moreover, we got a number of questions asking for more detailed information about the characteristics of the bargaining unit and for more data about comparable plants in the same geographical area or industry. Considerable information had been supplied in the basic game material, but the students were extremely inventive in devising questions and requiring permutations of the statistical data already presented. Basically, the students did their own "costing-out" of the various union proposals and company counterproposals. They were unable, however, to trace through the implications of these cost increases on the future financial status of the firm.

With these considerations in mind, we decided to focus the development of a computer-based collective bargaining game on two elements:

1. A personnel file containing relevant data on each member of the bargaining unit. Information such as the following would be included for each employee: age, length of service, job classification, wage rate, and number of dependents.

2. A model of the firm's economic activity which would, in conjunction with the personnel file, permit prediction of the impact of a variety of substantive contractual changes on profits and industry position. These changes could include modified work rules, pay scales (by classification), vacation plans, health and welfare plans, retirement procedures and pension plans, layoff provisions, and any other issues that might come up in bargaining.

We believed that the data must come in two varieties; the computer should make available different data for management and for the union. Management will receive more accurate and thorough information than will the union, particularly on financial matters; but we hope to permit some compensating disadvantage for management, such as the union teams being able to guess at certain key parameters available to management.

We felt that despite the introduction of computer technology, the strongest and most beneficial aspect of the collective bargaining exercise would continue to be the face-to-face negotiations the students undertake. Hence, we intended to make use of the computer in such a way as to facilitate these exchanges, not to substitute for them. We also hoped that the computer would allow us to make the issues involved somewhat more complicated and thus more suggestive of the true collective bargaining context.

The Development of the Computer Model

After considering what we saw as the available alternatives, we chose to base our simulation on the DATANAL package of programs written by James R. Miller, III, of Stanford University. DATANAL is a data manipulation and display package which operates under the M.I.T. Compatible Time-Sharing Systems. It is a highly interactive system, able to produce "answers" on a tele-type or similar device in very short periods of time.

While DATANAL was first conceived as a system for facilitating statistical analysis, its very flexible data structure and computational ability make it a powerful simulation language.

The DATANAL data structure permits describing data in terms of "cases," "levels," and "properties" in a hierarchical ordering. In our situation, a case on level one is an individual worker whose properties are such things as job category, age, number of depend-ents, years of seniority, and present differential pay rate (relative to the base rate for his job category). Similarly, a case on level two is a job category, one of whose properties is the base rate of pay for this job category. A case on level three is a major labor category like production, maintenance, or clerical.

In such a structure, every case on level one (man) "belongs to" a case on level two (job category) which in turn belongs to a case on level three (major labor category).

Once data have been so structured, DATANAL allows us to get answers to the following kinds of questions:

1. If strict seniority is followed in layoff and rehiring, and if only eighty percent of the work force is currently working, which men are they?

2. If pay rates are raised ten cents across the board, plus five cents extra for production workers, plus three cents extra for job categories two and three within maintenance, what would the additional cost be?

3. How many men have four or more dependents?

4. What would be the cost of giving four weeks of vacation after ten years, if the present policy is to give three weeks after fifteen years? What would be the cost five years from now?

In order to use DATANAL, we first established a personnel file for the Fort Hancock plant which corresponded in every measurable detail to the numbers given in the original case. We then built a model of operations at Fort Hancock using the DATANAL lan-guage.[2]

With the personnel file and the model, the teams were able to cost-out very complicated proposals indeed; but, in achieving this

---

[2] For those interested in further detail concerning this program package, see the DATANAL Manual, Alfred P. Sloan School of Management Working Paper 275–67. The Appendix to this paper is a brief restatement of the model and some run-throughs with the model.

generality, we lost the relative ease of use. That is, we no longer had neat formats and simple input rules such as prevailed in the airline simulation described earlier.

The Results

As we have said, we divided our experimental section this year into eight groups of four negotiating teams. We then decided that we would give two of the negotiating teams access to this package. Of the two groups that would have access to it, one would be able to use it in negotiating sessions; the other one would be able to use it between, but not during, the negotiations.

Nobody used the package. We think the reasons are fairly clear. First, we did not give the teams very much time. We handed out material on a Wednesday and they had to go into negotiations the following Monday. On Monday, they had an hour and a half; and then they had only forty-eight hours before negotiations on Wednesday. Second, the setup time involved in learning to use this particular package is perceived to be quite high (although actually it is not). The question which now can be asked is, what will we do next time to improve the process?

Plans for the Future

First, we will lengthen the time horizon: give the student teams a week between negotiations and two weeks before the beginning of negotiations to familiarize themselves with the package. Second, we can change the case. This particular case turns out to be one in which too many of the basic issues are noneconomic: Mr. Bruce hates the union. The union is young and has just recently won an election by a very slim margin. In fact, of the eight separate student sections we had, the only time we had a strike was when the union and management teams came to the same conclusion: the union decided they needed a union shop and the management decided if they had a strike they could get the union out, because it was so shaky that if the men went out on strike the union would lose the next election. Since they both perceived this, the clear joint conclusion was that there was no real need for earnest negotiations aimed at reaching agreement.

Several other things were suggested by the students in the class. One proposal involved doing away with the pre-set union proposals. Another was to use the computer to change the case into a three-level negotiation by giving the union team a "membership simulator" for strike votes. A third suggestion was that we give the management team a "Mr. Bruce simulator" which would tell them whether they were going to lose their jobs if they acceded to the union demands.

In sum, we consider this first experience with our computer-based game a "qualified failure." The potential for improving such negotiation games in the future, however, is significant; and we believe that a number of useful things came out of this attempt. As every experimenter has said to himself at least once: "Back to the drawing board." A new experiment will be run in Fall 1968 and again in Spring 1969. The greater usefulness of our revised computerization efforts can then be better assessed.

Elaboration and Discussion

Anonymous Industrial Relations Counselors in New York City have a bargaining game they devised a few years ago. It is very interesting because it brings out this matter of trade-offs. There is a set of presentations indicating the alternatives for each point at issue in the contract negotiations and these differences are clearly shown. Also, at any stage of the negotiations, you can tell how well each of the several bargaining teams is doing. Each team's performance is related to the others', so you get a feeling for the pattern of settlements. If one team is either above or below the others, it gets penalized. This adds another dimension to the training.

Straus This is a technical question concerning your bargaining game. On one of these computer printouts, it indicates that the game took only twenty-three seconds of computer time. Certainly it took much longer than this to play the game. How does it work? Every time you type something into the machine, the answer comes right back. Is somebody else also using the machine? How about when you are thinking of your next move?

Sprague The basic idea is to devise a method by which the computer can be slowed down to respond in about the same time span as a human being. A technique called "time sharing" allows the computer to devote attention only to those users who are ready for attention right now. People who are sitting scratching their heads or quietly thinking at the console don't need the computer for the moment and therefore it can be made available to others.

Straus   Does the outcome of the game always end up the same way?

Baitsell   No, these are random settlements.

Straus   Will the individual who is playing against the computer have any effect on the outcome?

Baitsell   Oh, yes. If he changes his mood to nine and starts to move away from a settlement, the computer will get just as angry as he is and will diverge from him.

Sprague   There are really two answers. He can affect the outcome provided it is within the program, but he can't get an outcome not provided for in the program. So the answer is yes and no.

Baitsell   He has to play within the bounds of the game. If a trade unionist gets frustrated and puts in STRIKE, the computer will come back with INPUT DATA INCORRECT — RESUBMIT.

Bigelow   Did you have any negative reaction from your students on the use of the computer? The possibility of a generation gap was mentioned earlier and I wonder if you found that any of the students who were involved in this exercise rejected the idea.

Baitsell   I did get some resentment; because, in my case, there were a lot of Master's students who hadn't previously been involved with the computer. It isn't in the curriculum at Harvard.

David Taylor   We had no resentment in our classes at M.I.T. aside from the usual negative reaction some students have to any experiment.

Penchansky   In any of these simulation models, couldn't a student sit down at a console and, taking an initial bargaining position and specifying different attitudes, run through a number of solutions and construct a matrix of these computer responses? Then, with this matrix, he could apply a minimum-maximum rule and come out with the best settlement.

Sprague   You could certainly do this but you would have to do it many times because of the random elements in the program. This simulation is not quite the same as those models found in classical game theory.

Meyers   As I gather from your paper, the fundamental purpose of the first game — that is, of Brandt Allen's game — is to teach people about computers rather than to teach people about industrial relations. Therefore, I would judge, if I understand what you have done, people do not really learn much about industrial relations.

Baitsell In Brandt's game, no; but in the Horizon Airlines case, yes.

Meyers But if they do get a feel for negotiations in industrial relations from this exercise, it is not because of the computer. That is to say, I suppose you could concoct a set of tables that would give you all the possible outcomes that the computer could give you. So my question is, do you use the computer because you think people ought to get familiar with computers or do you think the computer serves a vital function in teaching people about industrial relations?

Sprague We are trying to teach something about industrial relations as it will be twenty years from now. Maybe I am pursuing the Holy Grail on this, but an example of its usefulness might be for a management that would far rather give away $50,000 in longer vacations than in increased wages.

Any way that we can find to make the trade-offs and the preferences known to both groups and to give each group a chance to evaluate their own proposals against the others' response has to result in what has been loosely called "a better agreement." I think in the long run negotiations simply have to be improved by having better information available to both parties. That is why I am involved in this.

David Taylor Very closely in line with this, I think it is clear from Woody Ginsburg's statements and from Bill Caples's paper that union and management are going to use computers to prepare themselves for bargaining; and these are the kinds of things we are introducing into this game. Furthermore, I think it gives the student exposure to computer personnel systems which is worthwhile in its own right. Also, once we can get this thing worked out, we can make the case more complicated, and thereby make it more realistic and we have provided analytical tools to deal with these complications.

Meyers It seems to me that one of the confusions that runs through a fair part of this discussion is a lack of appreciation of the difference between the desirability of having facts available and the means by which these facts are made available. People built models and had industry studies long before the computer; so having information available doesn't necessarily depend on the computer, although it might be a useful device in compiling the data.

Sprague To be sure, I agree that it doesn't depend on the computer to get agreement on facts; but the usefulness of the facts may very well depend on the computer. To give a hypothetical example, suppose in negotiations the demand is made for the company to provide Blue Shield coverage for the dependents of the workers and the cost is 50 cents a month for each dependent. The company says it can't afford it. I would hope that the union team would be able to sit down at a console and say, "Just a minute, there are only 1,900 dependents and this would cost $950 a month. You can't afford *that?*"

Meyers This illustrates my point precisely because in 1941 I negotiated a Blue Cross-Blue Shield Plan and exactly this question was asked. We figured out what the cost would be and the answer didn't depend on the computer. Of course, it took us a long time to go through the personnel records and count the dependents and then multiply the number by 50 cents, but we didn't have to have the computer to do that. I think this sort of exercise is fine for students to learn about computers and what they can do; but as a means of learning about industrial relations, I don't think it is necessary. In fact, the negotiator sitting in the bargaining room is not going to have a console. He is going to whisper to his staff man to run out and get some item of information; he is not going to say how to get it.

Sprague I claim this is the same thing. The computer in this case serves as a research tool.

Straus I would propose a test. Supposing you took sophisticated trade unionists and management personnel and, with a computer, had them negotiate up to a point where they were deadlocked. At this point, a trained mediator would be brought in and told, "We want to see if you can mediate this dispute. You have access to the computer."

Now it might be that a trained mediator would come up with a solution without the computer, but with all the variables that the computer is capable of considering, you might well come up with solutions that the mediator or the negotiators haven't even thought of.

Sprague If I had one trained mediator with a computer and one without one, I can guarantee that the mediator with the computer can check out more possibilities and offer more alternatives in the same period of time than the man without one.

Anonymous To do what you suggest, Don [Straus], would require an initial program which contained all the components and variables that go into the final package.

Straus I don't think so. As I understand the bargaining game, you can easily change variables.

Anonymous The problem is not really in the total cost of the package. The problem is in the trade-offs between noneconomic and economic variables. For a mediator to solve the dispute in a real-world situation would require the parties to state what their trade-offs are — and this is something they are not about to do.

Straus Of course not, but the mediator can probe out the trade-offs by presenting a number of different solutions. When faced with a very tough case, I have heard experienced mediators say, "As long as I have proposals to throw them, things that they have to study and recheck, I am ahead of the game. The moment I am out of ideas, they will go on strike. If I can keep throwing them ideas, they may soon get tired enough to settle." The mediator has to give the parties things to think about.

Appendix

This appendix includes a sample section of our last computer-based model and a sample session with the model. Figure 1 is a restatement by the computer of the model we created for the Fort Hancock plant. Figure 2 details a sample session with the model.

Thus in Figure 2*a*, we ask the machine to "DISPLAY ALLTOT" where, as we can see from Figure 1*d*, ALLTOT is the total weekly labor bill at Fort Hancock. After a bit of messing about, the machine tells us it is $29,800.

Then we say "DISPLAY AVETOT" and out drops a three-column listing of sixty-six numbers by labor grade (there are twenty-two categories of labor at the Fort Hancock plant): the first column lists average rate of pay by labor grade; the second is the number of men in each labor category; and the third is the total weekly labor bill for each labor grade.

Now all this had been done on the assumption that straight-time employment at Fort Hancock was forty hours per week. We wanted next to see what would happen if we changed the situation to one

```
DESCRIBE ALLTOT VDSC OPDEF COMPLETE

VERBAL DESCRIPTION FOR 22VEC IS -

A VECTOR OF 22 ONES USED TO SUM PROPERTIES FROM LEVEL 2 TO LEVEL 3

OPERATIONAL DEFINITION FOR 22VEC IS -

22VEC = 1 1 1 1 1 1 1 1 1 1 1 1 1 1 1 1 1 1 1 1 1 1


VERBAL DESCRIPTION FOR INCREM IS -

THE DIFFERENCE BETWEEN AN INDIVIDUAL'S RATE OF PAY AND THE LOWEST ALLOWABLE FOR HIS
LABOR CATEGORY

OPERATIONAL DEFINITION FOR INCREM IS -

LEVEL = 1, RECORD = 1, COL. = 13, WIDTH = 4.


VERBAL DESCRIPTION FOR LORATE IS -

THE LOWEST RATE PAYABLE UNDER THE CURRENT CONTRACT TO THIS LABOR CATEGORY

OPERATIONAL DEFINITION FOR LORATE IS -

LEVEL = 2, RECORD = 1, COL. = 9, WIDTH = 4.


VERBAL DESCRIPTION FOR POTRAT IS -

THE POTENTIAL TOTAL RATE PAID, IF MAN IS WORKING

OPERATIONAL DEFINITION FOR POTRAT IS -

POTRAT = LORATE + INCREM

FOR ALL CASES


VERBAL DESCRIPTION FOR SENIOR IS -

THE INDIVIDUAL'S NUMBER OF YEARS OF SENIORITY

OPERATIONAL DEFINITION FOR SENIOR IS -

LEVEL = 1, RECORD = 1, COL. = 25, WIDTH = 4.
```

Figure 1*a*   Computer restatement of the model used in the Burns and
Bruce case.

VERBAL DESCRIPTION FOR PRWSEN IS -

THE INDIVIDUAL'S SENIORITY FRACTILE — 0 IMPLIES LEAST SENIORITY, 1 IMPLIES MOST

OPERATIONAL DEFINITION FOR PRWSEN IS -

RANK DECIMALS ASSIGNED TO SENIOR

VERBAL DESCRIPTION FOR TOTMEN IS -

TOTAL MEN ON SENIORITY LIST
THE TOTAL NUMBER OF MEN ON THE SENIORITY LIST AT B AND B

OPERATIONAL DEFINITION FOR TOTMEN IS -

TOTMEN = 495

VERBAL DESCRIPTION FOR MENWRK IS -

THE NUMBER OF MEN ACTUALLY WORKING AT B AND B

OPERATIONAL DEFINITION FOR MENWRK IS -

MENWRK = 350

VERBAL DESCRIPTION FOR PRWORK IS -

THE PROPORTION OF THE SENIORITY LIST ACTUALLY WORKING AT B AND B

OPERATIONAL DEFINITION FOR PRWORK IS -

PRWORK = MENWRK / TOTMEN

VERBAL DESCRIPTION FOR ACTRAT IS -

THE ACTUAL RATE PAID TO THIS MAN. SAME AS PRTRAT IF HE IS WORKING, ELSE UNDEFINED

OPERATIONAL DEFINITION FOR ACTRAT IS -

ACTRAT = POTRAT

FOR ALL CASES WHERE -

PRWSEN GT 1 - PRWORK

Figure 1*b*   Computer restatement (*continued*).

```
VERBAL DESCRIPTION FOR ACTRT2 IS -

VECTOR OF ACTRAT FOR EACH LABOR CATEGORY, USED FOR SUMMING

OPERATIONAL DEFINITION FOR ACTRT2 IS -

A GROUPED VERSION OF ACTRAT


VERBAL DESCRIPTION FOR NMNWK2 IS -

NUMBER OF MEN ACTUALLY WORKING BY LABOR CATEGORY

OPERATIONAL DEFINITION FOR NMNWK2 IS -

AN ELEMENT COUNT OF ACTRT2


VERBAL DESCRIPTION FOR AVERAT IS -

AVERAGE RATE PAID TO MEN ACTUALLY WORKING BY LABOR CATEGORY

OPERATIONAL DEFINITION FOR 73VEC IS -

73VEC = 1 1 1 1 1 1 1 1 1 1 1 1 1 1 1 1 1 1 1 1 1 1 1 1 1 1 1 1 1 1 1 1 1

        1 1 1 1 1 1 1 1 1 1 1 1 1 1 1 1 1 1 1 1 1 1 1 1 1 1 1 1 1 1 1 1 1


VERBAL DESCRIPTION FOR AVERAT IS -

AVERAGE RATE PAID TO MEN ACTUALLY WORKING BY LABOR CATEGORY

OPERATIONAL DEFINITION FOR AVERAT IS -

AVERAT = ( ACTRT2 * 73VEC ) / NMNWK2

FOR ALL CASES


VERBAL DESCRIPTION FOR CHOURS IS -

THE NUMBER OF HOURS WORKED AT REGULAR TIME -- THE NORMAL WORKWEEK

OPERATIONAL DEFINITION FOR CHOURS IS -

CHOURS = 40
```

Figure 1*c*   Computer restatement (*continued*).

VERBAL DESCRIPTION FOR WHOURS IS —

THE ACTUAL, AS OPPOSED TO CONTRACTUAL, NUMBER OF HOURS WORKED AT B AND B

OPERATIONAL DEFINITION FOR WHOURS IS —

WHOURS = 40

VERBAL DESCRIPTION FOR OHOURS IS —

THE NUMBER OF HOURS IN A NORMAL WORKWEEK WORKED AT OVERTIME BECAUSE OF
CONTRACT PROVISIONS

OPERATIONAL DEFINITION FOR OHOURS IS —

OHOURS = MAX (WHOURS — CHOURS , 0)

VERBAL DESCRIPTION FOR PAYCT2 IS —

TOTAL WEEKLY PAY BY LABOR CATEGORY INCLUDING OVERTIME

OPERATIONAL DEFINITION FOR PAYCT2 IS —

PAYCT2 = NMNWK2 * (WHOURS * AVERAT + OHOURS * .5 * AVERAT)

FOR ALL CASES

VERBAL DESCRIPTION FOR PAYCT3 IS —

VECTOR OF PAY BY LABOR CATEGORY, USED FOR SUMMING INTO ALLTOT

OPERATIONAL DEFINITION FOR PAYCT3 IS —

A GROUPED VERSION OF PAYCT2

VERBAL DESCRIPTION FOR ALLTOT IS —

TOTAL WEEKLY LABOR BILL AT FORT HANCOCK

OPERATIONAL DEFINITION FOR ALLTOT IS —

ALLTOT = PAYCT3 * 22VEC

FOR ALL CASES

OK

Figure 1*d*   Computer restatement (*concluded*).

where the contractual straight-time hourly work week was a thirty-five hour week but where all workers continued to work forty hours and were thus paid at time and a half for five of these hours. At the end of the sequence shown in Figure 2a, we ask for the value of DHOURS (the next contract work week just typed in) and we do indeed find it is now thirty-five. So we then proceed to say: "CHANGE PLABEL CHOURS DHOURS" (Figure 2b). CHOURS was the constraint we had been using for the contract hours. By this last command we say in effect that wherever in this model CHOURS has been used, DHOURS should now be substituted. We then ask for the total weekly labor bill (ALLTOT) under this new state of affairs and find it is $31,662. The additional cost for going to a thirty-five hour week is thus $31,662–$29,800 or $1,862.

We then ask for a display of AVETOT again and once more get our display by labor grade (Figure 2b). The third column numbers are now different from those in the similar display in Figure 2a because the additional overtime costs are reflected in the amount given in Figure 2b.

At this point it occurred to us that from a purely computational point of view the structure of the model was inefficient since we could easily make this computation of additional labor costs for the total labor force. In Figure 2c, we make this shift, eventually saying "DISPLAY SEEALL"; and a bit later we get back three numbers: the average overall labor rate paid at Fort Hancock, the number of men working, and the total cost. These results are obtained by computing with the total labor force rather than by individual labor grade. Thus, in something less than two minutes at the console, we are able to effect a marked structural change in our model.

At the middle of Figure 2c, we proceed to define a new constant, EHOURS, as thirty-seven and a half hours and get a similar estimate for SEEALL. We now find that total labor cost per week is $30,731.

At this point, we lose track of some of the things we had done earlier and decide to refresh our memories on one variable. We ask for a description of PAYCT2, some pay information we couldn't recall. The verbal description follows: "TOTAL WEEKLY PAY BY LABOR CATEGORY INCLUDING OVERTIME."

The remaining pages describe several changes introduced for computing overtime. We changed the number of people who were working. We introduced rules defining who would be hired and who would not be in case of layoffs, and so on.

Further details are not important. What is important is that

```
DISPLAY ALLTOT

ACTRT2 HAS BEEN CREATED.
NMNWK2 HAS BEEN CREATED.
AVERAT HAS BEEN CREATED.
OHOURS HAS BEEN CREATED.
PAYCT2 HAS BEEN CREATED.
PAYCT3 HAS BEEN CREATED.
ALLTOT HAS BEEN CREATED.

IT IS 29800

OK

DISPLAY AVETOT

AVETOT HAS BEEN CREATED.

         1      2.4200      4.0000       387.2000
         2      2.3209     31.0000      2878.0000
         3      2.2794     17.0000      1550.0000
         4      2.2566      3.0000       270.8000
         5      2.1600      2.0000       172.8000
         6      2.0900      1.0000        83.6000
         7      2.1300      1.0000        85.2000
         8      2.1249     47.0000      3994.8000
         9      2.0991     57.0000      4786.0000
        10      2.0431     38.0000      3105.6000
        11      2.1470     24.0000      2061.2000
        12      2.1400      1.0000        85.6000
        13      2.0500      2.0000       164.0000
        14      1.9880      5.0000       397.6000
        15      2.0100      4.0000       321.6000
        16      2.0077      9.0000       722.8000
        17      1.9633     12.0000       942.4000
        18      1.9136     22.0000      1684.0000
        19      1.8583      6.0000       446.0000
        20      1.8162      8.0000       581.2000
        21      1.8121     47.0000      3406.8000
        22      1.7425     24.0000      1672.8000

OK

DISPLAY DHOURS

IT IS 35

OK
```

Figure 2*a*   A sample student session with the computer.

```
CHANGE PLABEL CHOURS DHOURS

OHOURS HAS BEEN DESTROYED.
PAYCT2 HAS BEEN DESTROYED.
PAYCT3 HAS BEEN DESTROYED.
ALLTOT HAS BEEN DESTROYED.
AVETOT HAS BEEN DESTROYED.

CHOURS HAS BEEN CHANGED.

OK

DISPLAY ALLTOT

OHOURS HAS BEEN CREATED.
PAYCT2 HAS BEEN CREATED.
PAYCT3 HAS BEEN CREATED.
ALLTOT HAS BEEN CREATED.

IT IS 31662

OK

DISPLAY AVETOT

AVETOT HAS BEEN CREATED.

        1       2.4200       4.0000      411.4000
        2       2.3209      31.0000     3057.8000
        3       2.2794      17.0000     1646.8000
        4       2.2566       3.0000      287.7200
        5       2.1600       2.0000      183.6000
        6       2.0900       1.0000       88.8250
        7       2.1300       1.0000       90.5250
        8       2.1249      47.0000     4244.4000
        9       2.0991      57.0000     5085.1000
       10       2.0431      38.0000     3299.7000
       11       2.1470      24.0000     2190.0000
       12       2.1400       1.0000       90.9500
       13       2.0500       2.0000      174.2500
       14       1.9880       5.0000      422.4500
       15       2.0100       4.0000      341.7000
       16       2.0077       9.0000      767.9700
       17       1.9633      12.0000     1001.3000
       18       1.9136      22.0000     1789.2000
       19       1.8583       6.0000      473.8700
       20       1.8162       8.0000      617.5200
       21       1.8121      47.0000     3619.7000
       22       1.7425      24.0000     1777.3000
```

Figure 2*b*   Sample session (*continued*).

```
OK

CHAIN
GROUP NMNWK2 NMNWKV
DEFINE TOTALM = NMNWKV * 22VEC

GROUP AVERAT AVERT3
DEFINE OALLAV = ( NMNWKV * AVERT3 ) / TOTALM

DEFINE SEEALL = OALLAV TOTALM ALLTOT

DISPLAY SEEALL

NMNWKV HAS BEEN CREATED.
TOTALM HAS BEEN CREATED.
AVERT3 HAS BEEN CREATED.
OALLAV HAS BEEN CREATED.
SEEALL HAS BEEN CREATED.

IT IS        2.0411      365.0000     31662.0000

OK

DISPLAY OALLAV

IT IS 2.0411

OK

SET?CHAIN
SET EHOURS = 37.5
CHAG?CHANGE PLABEL DHOURS EHOURS
DISL"PLAT"Y SEEALL

EHOURS HAS BEEN CREATED.
OHOURS HAS BEEN CREATED.
PAYCT2 HAS BEEN CREATED.
PAYCT3 HAS BEEN CREATED.
ALLTOT HAS BEEN CREATED.
SEEALL HAS BEEN CREATED.

IT IS        2.0411      365.0000     30731.0000

OK

DESCRIBE PAYCT2 OPDEF VDSC

VERBAL DESCRIPTION FOR PAYCT2 IS -

TOTAL WEEKLY PAY BY LABOR CATEGORY INCLUDING OVERTIME
```

Figure 2c   Sample session (*continued*).

```
OPERATIONAL DEFINITION FOR PAYCT2 IS -

PAYCT2 = NMNWK2 * ( WHOURS * AVARAT + OHOURS + .5 * AVERAT )

FOR ALL CASES

OK

ERASE ? DEFINE PAYCAT = WHOURS * AVERAT


ANY DESCRIPTION (YES OR NO)... YES

NOW TYPE IN A VERBAL DESCRIPTION OF THE PROPERTY PAYCAT.
ENTER A DOUBLE CARRIAGE RETURN AFTER YOUR LAST LINE.

WEEKLY BILL BY LABOR CATEGORY ASSUMING STRAIGHT TIME

PAYCAT HAS BEEN DEFINED.

OK

CHANGE PLABEL PAYCT2 PAYCAT

PAYCT3 HAS BEEN DESTROYED.
ALLTOT HAS BEEN DESTROYED.
SEEALL HAS BEEN DESTROYED.

PAYCT2 HAS BEEN CHANGED.

OK

ERASE ALLTOT

ALLTOT HAS BEEN ERASED.
SEEALL HAS BEEN ERASED.

OK

DEFINE ALLTOT = NMNWK ? DEFINE ALLTOT = TOTALM * WHOURS * OALLAV

ANY DESCRIPTION (YES OR NO)... YES

NOW TYPE IN A VERBAL DESCRIPTION OF THE PROPERTY ALLTOT.
ENTER A DOUBLE CARRIAGE RETURN AFTER YOUR LAST LINE.

WEEKLY BILL FOR FORT HANCOCK ASSUMING STRAIGHT TIME

ALLTOT HAS BEEN DEFINED.

OK
```

Figure 2d   Sample session (*continued*).

```
DEFINE OTIMEB = ALLTOT + TOTALM * OHOURS * OALLAV * .5

ANY DESCRIPTION (YES OR NO)... YES

NOW TYPE IN A VERBAL DESCRIPTION OF THE PROPERTY OTIMEB.
ENTER A DOUBLE CARRIAGE RETURN AFTER YOUR LAST LINE.

EXCESS DUE TO OVERTIME CONSIDERATIONS

OTIMEB HAS BEEN DEFINED.

OK


DEFINE SEEALL = OALLAV TOTALM ALLTOT OTIMEB


ANY DESCRIPTION (YES OR NO)...


SEEALL HAS BEEN DEFINED.

OK

DISPLAY SEEALL

ALLTOT HAS BEEN CREATED.
OTIMEB HAS BEEN CREATED.
SEEALL HAS BEEN CREATED.

IT IS     2.0411     365.0000     29800.0000     30731.0000

OK

CHANGE PLABEL EHOURS CHOURS

OHOURS HAS BEEN DESTROYED.
PAYCT2 HAS BEEN DESTROYED.
OTIMEB HAS BEEN DESTROYED.
SEEALL HAS BEEN DESTROYED.

EHOURS HAS BEEN CHANGED.

OK

DISPLAY SEEALL

OHOURS HAS BEEN CREATED.
OTIMEB HAS BEEN CREATED.
SEEALL HAS BEEN CREATED.

IT IS     2.0411     365.0000     29800.0000     29800.0000

OK
```

Figure 2*e*   Sample session (*continued*).

```
DESCRIBE MENWRK

STATUS INFORMATION FOR MENWRK IS -

ORIGIN IS SET COMMAND
PTYPE IS SCALAR
NROWS IS 1
NCOLS IS 1
LEVEL IS 0
DFMODE IS TEMPORARY
CRMODE IS TEMPORARY
BLOCKN IS 1
BLOCKA IS 3017

VERBAL DESCRIPTION FOR MENWRK IS -

THE NUMBER OS MEN ACTUALLY WORKING AT B AND B

OPERATIONAL DEFINITION FOR MENWRK IS -

MENWRK = 350

OK

CHAIN
SET MENWKG = 325
CHANGE PLABEL WE""'MENWRK MENWKG
DISPLAY SEEALL

MENWKG HAS BEEN CREATED.
PRWORK HAS BEEN CREATED.
ACTRAT HAS BEEN CREATED.
ACTRT2 HAS BEEN CREATED.
NMNWK2 HAS BEEN CREATED.
NMNWKV HAS BEEN CREATED.
TOTALM HAS BEEN CREATED.
AVERAT HAS BEEN CREATED.
AVERT3 HAS BEEN CREATED.
OALLAV HAS BEEN CREATED.
ALLTOT HAS BEEN CREATED.
OTIMEB HAS BEEN CREATED.
SEEALL HAS BEEN CREATED.

IT IS        2.0421     342.0000     27936.0000     27936.0000

OK
```

Figure 2*f*   Sample session (*continued*).

```
Q?ERASE MENWRK

MENWRK HAS BEEN DESTROYED.
MENWRK HAS BEEN ERASED.

OK

SET MENWRK = 342


ANY DESCRIPTION (YES OR NO)...

MENWRK HAS BEEN SET.

OK

CHN?CHANGE PLABEL WEN?CHANGE PLABEL MENWKG MENWRK

PRWORK HAS BEEN DESTROYED.
NMNWK2 HAS BEEN DESTROYED.
NMNWKV HAS BEEN DESTROYED.
TOTALM HAS BEEN DESTROYED.
AVERAT HAS BEEN DESTROYED.
AVERT3 HAS BEEN DESTROYED.
OALLAV HAS BEEN DESTROYED.
ALLTOT HAS BEEN DESTROYED.
OTIMEB HAS BEEN DESTROYED.
SEEALL HAS BEEN DESTROYED.
ACTRAT HAS BEEN DESTROYED.
ACTRT2 HAS BEEN DESTROYED.

MENWKG HAS BEEN CHANGED.

OK

DISPLAY SEEALL

MENWRK HAS BEEN CREATED.
PRWORK HAS BEEN CREATED.
ACTRAT HAS BEEN CREATED.
ACTRT2 HAS BEEN CREATED.
NMNWK2 HAS BEEN CREATED.
NMNWKV HAS BEEN CREATED.
TOTALM HAS BEEN CREATED.
AVERAT HAS BEEN CREATED.
AVERT3 HAS BEEN CREATED.
OALLAV HAS BEEN CREATED.
ALLTOT HAS BEEN CREATED.
OTIMEB HAS BEEN CREATED.
SEEALL HAS BEEN CREATED.

IT IS        2.0421   342.0000  27936.0000    27936.0000

OK
```

Figure 2*g*   Sample session (*continued*).

```
QUIT
R 184.883+63.750

R DATANAL
W 1120.4

OK

CLOSE ZLABOR

ZLABOR HAS BEEN CLOSED.

OK

OPEN ZLABOR

ZLABOR HAS BEEN OPENED.

OK

CLOSE MLABOR

MLABOR HAS BEEN CLOSED.

OK

OPEN ZLABOR

THERE IS NO P-STRING CALLED 'ZLABOR'.

TYPE THE NAME OF THE DATA BASE TO BE OPENED... ∂INT. 0

OK
```

Figure 2*h*   Sample session (*concluded*).

this is a fairly powerful general purpose package for modeling and for getting the consequences of changes in rules, changes in numbers, and so on quite quickly and "on line." We pay a price for this kind of generality; we no longer have things laid out in neat format. But in return for not having elegant *looking* output we can get precisely the output we want to designate as we go through and define all the names of the variables, change parameters, and ask our questions.

Comments on the Conference Discussion

Douglass V. Brown

While these remarks are billed as a summary of the conference, they should more properly be taken as a summary of my own tentative conclusions. No brief summary could possibly do justice to the wide range of issues and opinions that have been set forth during these past two days.

One's opinions, of course, are colored by one's own experience, or lack of experience. Biases, conscious or unconscious, are developed. In the areas we have been discussing, I know that I have at least two such biases. The first has to do with computers; the second, with industrial relations in general and with collective bargaining in particular.

I was born and brought up in the noncomputer era. I hate the damned things. I don't trust anything that comes out of them. And every now and then something happens that keeps my distrust alive.

Item: At M.I.T., every person with the rank of instructor is expected to proctor so many examinations per year. The assignment lists are spewed out by the computer. A few years ago, the computer turned out such a list for the Sloan School. The list of names proved to be precisely that of our Fellows in Africa.

In the area of industrial relations, my experience persuades me, rightly or wrongly, that "art" or "judgment" or "hunch" will continue indefinitely to play a major role. There will continue to be, or so I am persuaded, many important factors that cannot be reduced to computerized or computer-type processes.

In spite of these biases, I am convinced that in a whole spectrum of industrial relations activities the computer will increasingly be used, and will have to be used, by firms and by unions. But I do not see, as some of the discussions may have suggested, that there is a dichotomy between art and judgment, on the one hand, and the

286

computer, on the other. I see them rather as complementary, in a sense reinforcing each other.

It is perfectly clear, I think, that the computer is increasingly going to be used as an instrument for the storage and retrieval of information in a host of personnel functions, including the administration and policing of the agreement.

It also seems very clear that the computer is going to be used increasingly as a tool in preparations for negotiation. After all, like Mount Everest, the information and the computer are there. As we have seen, large firms and large unions are using the computer; and its services are being made available to smaller unions. It may be only a question of time before similar services are available to smaller employers. With the spread of collective bargaining in the public sector, new and inviting territory for the use of computers is opening up.

With respect to the stage of actual negotiations, I am inclined to feel that our discussions may have underestimated the usefulness of the computer, even in its simplest role as a storehouse of information. To be sure, "facts" will not settle many collective bargaining issues. But similarly, a lack of data, or inaccurate data, can create problems. Particularly in smaller situations, the availability of computerized information might help to ease impasses based on misconceptions.

Apart from its capacity as a storehouse, the computer seems destined for increased use during negotiations. We have been told of its use for "costing-out" proposals and counterproposals at United Air Lines and in other situations. We have had examples of demands and of contract provisions that would not have been possible in the absence of the computer. It seems quite safe to predict extended use of the computer for the generation and evaluation of potential new arrangements.

Several of the participants in the conference have expressed concern over what they perceive as a decrease in the effectiveness of the mediator's role in recent years. Growing intransigence of the parties or complexity of the issues may explain the phenomenon. But there is another possible explanation. It may be that, with the increased sophistication of the parties, two of the traditional tools of the mediator — the provision of new information and the suggestion of new solutions — have been blunted. Perhaps only the mediator, and not the parties, should be permitted to have access to the computer.

Concern has also been expressed that the computer will have the effect of bringing about a degree of uniformity in the outcomes of collective bargaining that would have undesirable effects. This result would presumably stem from the greater centralization made possible by the computer. Here it seems to me important to recognize that the issue of uniformity or nonconformity is one for determination on policy grounds. The computer itself is neutral; it can be used to further either policy.

This summary would obviously be inadequate without reference to the use of computers in model building and simulation. There are many kinds of models. They need not be mathematical models, and it is not always necessary to put them on the computer. On the other hand, Gordon Kaufman convinced me that, even if you strip the computer of all of its arithmetic properties, you could still do a lot of things with the computer that you couldn't do in any other way. The computer can be a powerful tool in simulating alternatives and evaluating their consequences. I suspect that we have seen only the beginning of these uses of the computer in the industrial relations area.

With all these concessions to my computer-loving friends, my biases have taken quite a beating. Perhaps it is time for a bit of resuscitation. Just because the computer can be used for a particular purpose, it does not necessarily follow that it should be used for that purpose. There are costs associated with the use of the computer, costs that may be strategic as well as monetary. My plea here is a twofold one. First, let's not use the computer simply for the sake of using the computer. Second, let's not let our fascination with the computer cause us to neglect the thousand and one other things that must be done to complement or even validate the output of the computer.

This last caveat leads me to my final point. I have indicated my belief that the computer is going to be used more, and perhaps enormously more, in the industrial relations area than it has been used in the past. This means, or so at least it seems to me, that computer people must learn enough about the other aspects of industrial relations and collective bargaining, and industrial relations people must learn enough about the potentialities and limitations of the computer, to be able to work together in a fruitful fashion. This, to me, is an intriguing and not unattainable goal.

Index

Agreements. *See* Bargaining; Collective agreements; Contract
Allen, Brandt R., 260
American Arbitration Association, 23
American Standard, Inc., 42
Arbitration. *See* Dispute settlements
Armour case, 184
Austin, Barrie, 70 n. 2

Baitsell, John M., 6
  on the collective bargaining game, 269
Bargaining, coordinated, 10–11, 22–23, 35–45 *passim*, 57, 63–64
  George Taylor on the three steps of, 64–65
  role of computer in, 98–99. *See also* Contract negotiations; Data base; Model building
    Brown on, 287–288
    Caples on, 21, 85–92 *passim*, 93–94, 96, 104
    Caples' questionnaires on, 81–85 *passim*, 109–120 *passim*
    Cole on, 18, 181, 187
    Daniels on, 97–98 *passim*, 101, 189, 201
    Dunlop on, 188
    Forrester on, 256–257
    Ginsburg on, 53–54, 58–59, 181–182
    Jensen on, 248–249, 253–254
    Kaufman on, 164
    Mason on, 219–220, 223
    Meyers on, 185–186, 252–253
    Mills on, 166–167
    Myers on, 96, 104, 257
    Ness on, 258
    Penchansky on, 164
    Scott Morton on, 257–258
    Simon on, 88–89, 96
    Sprague on, 270
    Taylor on, 178–179 *passim*

Bargaining game, of Industrial Relations Counselors, 268. *See also* Negotiation, mock, computer assisted
Benefit plans, available data on, 78, 167. *See also* Union health and welfare funds
  "cafeteria approach" to, 24, 223–225
  enforcement of contributions to, 194–195
  growth of, 26–27, 122
  models of, 62
Bigelow, Robert P., 95, 101, 251, 269 on issue of privacy, 182, 183
Boeing 747, 218, 219
Brown, Douglass V., 6–7, 24–25, 249
  comments on conference, 286–288
Bueschel, Richard T., 70
Building trades. *See* Union health and welfare funds
Bureau of National Affairs, 263
Burns and Bruce Case, 263–264, 273–276
Business Week, cartoon in, 203

Caples, William G., 4, 20–21, 94–95, 99–100, 225
  on contract-negotiation preparation, 93, 99
  on government data banks, 101–102
  on role of computer in bargaining, 21, 85–92 *passim*, 93–94, 96, 104
Clarkson, Geoffrey, 258
Cole, David, 4, 5, 17, 66, 99, 223
  on dissemination of information, 18, 183–184 *passim*
  on muscle society, 179–181
  on role of computer in bargaining, 18, 181, 187
  on teachers and strikes, 186

289

Collective agreement, definition of a good, Jensen and Straus on, 258–259. *See also* Contract negotiations

Communications Workers of America, 19, 50, 109

Computer, business agents and, 202
  challenge of data, 62–63, 219–222 *passim*
  hiring, 232–239
  joint use of. *See* Data base, joint use of
  layoffs, 220
  need for understanding, of, 254–255
  "neutral," 14, 94
  problems encountered in using (Caples' questionnaire), 105–106
  resentment of, 269
  sample student session with, 278–285

Conciliation. *See* Dispute settlements

Conglomerates and multiplant companies, 36–37. *See also* Bargaining, coordinated

Contract administration, 12–14, 93, 214–216, 243–244. *See also* International Ladies' Garment Workers' Union (ILGWU), use of computer in contract enforcement

Contract analysis, 23, 29–30, 45–51 *passim. See also* Industrial Union Department, data banks for contract analysis

Contract negotiations, emphasis on uniformity, 57–58 *passim*, 64, 177–178
  frequency of (Caples' questionnaire), 75–76
  future of. *See* Bargaining, role of computer in
  increased complexities in, 26–28, 53–55 *passim*, 198
  preparation and study groups for, 10–12, 14–15, 28–29, 58–59, 64–67 *passim*, 78–80, 93, 99
  present use of computer during, 12, 81–82, 106–107, 213–214

Contracts, acceptance of, after negotiations, 66–67, 254–255 not programmed in full text, 95–96

Corporate economic profiles. *See* Industrial Union Department, data banks

Cramer, Harold, 172 n. 12

Daniels, Wilbur, 5–6, 13, 16, 182

Daniels, Wilbur (*continued*)
  on administrative costs in apparel trade, 157
  on business agent and computer, 202
  on history of computer at ILGWU, 201
  role of computer in bargaining, 97–98 *passim*, 101, 189, 201

Data, challenge of, 62–63, 219–222 *passim*
  lack of, 65
  value of, in building trades, 167
Data banks, and centralization of labor movement, 187. *See also* Industrial Union Department, data banks
  centralizing of, and individual rights, 182–183 *passim*
  cost of collecting and maintaining, 95, 99
  in field of public employment, 18, 86
  government, 101–102, 167, 183
  in support of lobbying activities, 9
  Taylor on, 178
Data base, as a collective bargaining tool, 17–18, 58–59, 100, 178–179 *passim*, 181, 182, 256, 271
  available for bargaining (Caples' questionnaire) 76–78
  joint use of, 14–15, 18, 100–102 *passim*, 181, 184, 223, 256
Data Centers, at McGill University, 10 n. *See also* Industrial Union Department
DATANAL package of programs, 265–266
Davis, Will, 255
Dispute settlements and American Arbitration Association, 23
  decrease of role of mediator in, 179–181 *passim*, 255–256, 287
Dubinsky, David, 189
Dunlop, John T., 5, 18, 183, 184–185
  on the Armour agreement, 184
  on data banks, 187–188
  on role of computer in bargaining, 188

Eisenhart, C. and Swed, F. C., 175 n. 16
Ellenbogen, Jack, 24, 258
  on optional benefits, 223
  trend to software, 224
England, dock workers, decasualization of, 228, 229–230, 245, 249, 253
Ex-Cello Plant, 61

Fano, Robert, quoted, 1–2
Food Machinery and Chemical Corpo-
    ration (FMC), 37–42
Forrester, Jay W., on model for collec-
    tive bargaining, 256–257 *passim*
  on modeling and uncertainties, 102–
    105 *passim*

General Electric Company, 24, 42–45,
    52–53, 223–224
Ginsburg, Woodrow L., 4, 17–18, 95–96,
    225
  on data base and role of computer in
    bargaining, 53–54, 58–59, 181–
    182
  on errors in computer input, 220
  on refinement of accounting methods,
    200
Gleason, Teddy, 247, 248
Government data banks, 101–102, 167,
    183
Grievances, analysis of (Caples on), 99–
    100
  and the IAM Grievance Index, 12–
    13, 214–216
  over contract interpretation, 24

Hardware versus software, 224
Health and welfare funds. *See* Union
    health and welfare funds
Healy, James J., 263, 264

Industrial Relations Counselors, bar-
    gaining game of, 268
Industrial Union Department, data
    banks for contract analyses, 29–
    30, 50
  corporate economic profiles, 10–11,
    50, 52–53, 61–62. *See also* Bar-
    gaining, coordinated
  national contract survey, 10, 30–35
    passim, 54–57 *passim*
  and text entries, 34–35
  of NLRB election histories, 8, 38–39,
    42–45, 46, 59–60
  of NLRB unfair labor practice
    charges, 8–9, 51, 60–61
International Association of Machinists
    (IAM), and contract analysis, 23,
    45–49
  Grievance Index, 214–216
  profile of a union, 52, 68
International Brotherhood of Electrical
    Workers (IBEW), 50, 62–63, 75
International Harvester, 48

International Ladies' Garment Work-
    ers' Union (ILGWU), use of com-
    puters in contract enforcement
  current uses and nature of the in-
    dustry, 190–192 *passim*, 197–199,
    200, 201
  present and future areas for appli-
    cation, 192–197
International Longshoreman's Associ-
    ation. *See* New York longshore
    labor market

Jensen, Vernon H., 6, 16, 227 n
  on arbitration cases, 250
  definition of a good collective agree-
    ment, 258
  on role of computer in bargaining,
    248–249, 253–254
  on stresses and strains in longshore
    industry, 251
Jirikowic, Vernon E., 222
  on use of computers at IAM, 65, 67–
    68
Joint use of computer. *See* Data base,
    joint use of
Jonathan Logan, agreement with, 198

Kaiser Steel Company, 18, 164–165
Kaufman, Gordon M., 4–5, 15–16
  on objectives of study and on simu-
    lation, 159–165 *passim*, 167
Kellogg, Frazier, 3
Kheel, Ted, 180, 238 n

Lanham, Elizabeth, 70 n. 2, 71
Layoffs, computerized, 220
Lehmann, E. L., 175 n. 15
Lesieur, Frederick G.
  on change in role of research depart-
    ment, 67
  on selling the agreement, 254–255
  use of a model, 164–165
Ling-Temco-Vought (LTV), develop-
    ment of, 36–37
Link-Belt, 37
Lobbying activities, and data banks, 9
Longshore labor market, on west coast,
    249. *See also* England, dock work-
    ers; New York longshore labor
    market

McGill University, Industrial Relations
    Centre, data center, 10 n

McLean, Ephraim R., 3rd, 158
  on centralization of labor movement, 187
  on joint use of government data, 101
Management, current use of computers, 19–20
  Bueschel and Lanham studies on, 70–71
Management Preparation for Collective Bargaining, M. S. Ryder and others, 28–29
Marshall, Byron, 121
Mason, Charles M., 6, 12–14 *passim*
  on black box and pilots, 218–219
  on data base and role of computer in bargaining, 219–220, 223
  on new types of aircraft, 218
  on optional benefits, 224–225 *passim*
  on suspicion of computer input, 219–222 *passim*
Mechanicsville, New York, volunteer fire department, 176–177
Mediation. *See* Dispute settlements
Meyers, Frederic
  on fundamental purpose of the bargaining game, 269–271 *passim*
  on role of computer in bargaining, 185–186, 252–253
Miller, James R., III, 265
Mills, Quinn, 161, 162
  on a model for collective bargaining, 166–167
Model, and benefit plans, 62. *See also* Union health and welfare funds, and management policies in building trades
  getting trustees to use, 164–165
  of Port Authority, 251
  used at United Air Lines, 213–214
Model building, 11–12, 15–16, 94, 102–105
  for collective bargaining. *See* Bargaining, role of computer in; Negotiation, mock, computer-assisted
Morse, Wayne, 248–249
Multiplant companies and conglomerates, 36–37. *See also* Bargaining, coordinated
Murray, Philip, 180–181
Myers, Charles A., 3, 164, 249
  on computer and clerical employees, 199
  on data and a data base, 63, 182, 184, 187, 256

Myers, Charles A. (*continued*)
  review of the discussions, 256–257
  role of computer in bargaining, 96, 104, 257
  "Some Implications of Computer for Management," 69–70

National Labor Relations Board
  election histories of, 8, 38–39, 42–45, 59–60
  and unfair labor practice charges, 8–9, 51, 60–61
Negotiation, mock, computer-assisted, three approaches to
  more comprehensive approach to negotiations modeling (Burns and Bruce Case) 262–271 *passim*
  sample section of model, 272–277
  sample student session with model, 278–285
  negotiations for airline crew scheduling, 261–262
  simulation of pay and vacation negotiations, 260–261
Negotiations, of contracts. *See* Contract negotiations
Ness, David N., 258
New York longshore labor market
  arbitration cases and strike settlement of, 238–239, 242–243, 250
  and containerization of shipments, 245–246
  decasualization of, early contributions to, and difficulties in "buying out," 226–228 *passim*, 228–229
  and guarantee of annual income, 226–229 *passim*, 235, 239, 241
  possible model of, 251
  and seniority system, 226–232, 240–244 *passim*, 246–247, 249–250
New York Shipping Association, 226, 231, 232, 238 n, 242–243
  central record bureau of, 247–248
New York Times, quoted, 1, 2 n. 3

Penchansky, Roy, 4–5, 15–16, 63, 161, 163, 223, 250–251, 253
  on computer and uncertainty of individual decisions, 97–98 *passim*
  on funds, fund management and consultants, 155–159 *passim,* 165–166
  on mock negotiation game, 269
  on model and collective bargaining, 164

Personnel administration, major company use of computer for, 8, 70–71

Profile of union membership, 52, 68, 192

Programmers and programming, problems with, 80, 197–198

Public employment, data banks in field of, 18, 186

Renault experience, 220

Rezler, Julius, 70 n. 2

Rosenthal, Morris, 53

"Runaway shop," 9, 196–197

Sawing and logging saw mills, 62

Scott Morton, Michael S., 257–258

Segal, Martin, 163

Siegel, Abraham J., 99, 102, 104
  on Renault, 220

Simon, Herbert A., 88–89, 96

Simulation. *See* Model; Model building

Sprague, Christopher R., 6, 268, 269, 270
  on computer as a research tool, 271

Straus, Donald, 183, 184, 199, 221, 251–252, 271–272
  on a good collective agreement, 258–259
  on computer language, 200
  on computer and data base as a tool, 18, 62, 65, 100, 223, 254, 271
  on decrease in effectiveness of mediators, 255–256
  on mock negotiation game, 268–269 *passim*

Study groups. *See* Contract negotiations, preparation and study groups for; Data base, as a tool

Swed, F. C., and Eisenhart, C., 175 n. 16

Taylor, David P., 6, 269, 270

Taylor, George, 5
  on data base and computer in bargaining, 178–179 *passim*
  on Kaiser negotiations, 183
  on maximizing of objectives and uniformity, 64, 176–178
  on three steps of collective bargaining, 64–65

Textile Workers' Union of America (TWUA), 50, 56

Turkus, Burton, 236 n, 242

Unfair labor practices, 8–9, 51, 60–61

Uniformity, contract negotiations and emphasis on, 57–58 *passim*, 64, 177–178
  in outcome of bargaining, 288
  and piece work settlement, 194

Union, election histories, 8, 38–39, 42–45, 46, 59–60
  profile of a union, 52, 68, 192

Union health and welfare funds simulation study of fund financial behavior as a tool for measuring quantitatively changes in
  elaboration and discussion of, 155–167 *passim*
  experimental design, 147–154
  goals and objectives of study with background on the industry, 121–129 *passim*
  mathematical recapitulation of assumptions, model and simulation strategy (Appendix A), 167–174
  model building, 135–140
  output, 142–145
  parameter estimation, 141–142
  summary, 154
  test of independence of employee (Appendix B), 174–175
  validation, 145–147
  work patterns, 129–134

Unions, expanded role of research departments, 26–28 *passim*, 54–55, 63
  number of, involved in negotiations (Caples' study), 73–75

United Air Lines, computer needs, 203–204, 217–218
  current use of computer, 205–216, 219
  future use of the computer, 216–217, 218–219

United States Rubber, enforcement of discipline in, 181–182

United Steel Workers' union, 49

University of California (Los Angeles), Institute of Industrial Relations, 70 n. 2

Waterfront Commission, 226, 227, 231, 242–243, 244
  computers maintained by, 232
  regulations of, 233, 235 n, 239

Wilson and Company, 36–37

Women's apparel industry. *See also* International Ladies' Garment Workers' Union

Women's apparel industry (*continued*)
    administrative costs in, 157
    nature of, 190–191
Woodworkers union, 61–62

Zack, Arnold M., 18
    on a data bank in field of public
        employment, 186